HOW CAN I DISCIPLINE MY CHILD WITHOUT INFLICTING INJURY OR INCURRING HATE?

WHAT DO I DO WHEN JOHNNY OR JANE JUST SAYS "NO"?

CAN I REALLY HAVE ANY CONTROL OVER MY TEENAGER?

HOW DO I KNOW IF MY CHILD IS MANIPULATING ME?

WHAT DO I DO ABOUT FIGHTING? LYING? SLOPPINESS? DRUGS? HOMOSEXUALITY? HOSTILITY?

All too often parents realize too late the mistakes they made in bringing up their children. Now this highly creative, thoughtful, and understanding guide makes it possible to offer the proper discipline at the moment and in the manner it is needed—both to make childhood the rich period of development and experience it should be, and parenting the joy it can be.

HOW TO DISCIPLINE—WITH LOVE
(from crib to college)

DR. FITZHUGH DODSON is an internationally renowned psychologist whose previous million-copy best sellers, *How to Parent* and *How to Father*, have been translated into eight languages, and received acclaim from educators and parents all over the world.

The father of a girl and two boys, Dr. Dodson draws from his parental experience as well as from his more than twenty years of professional work, both as a psychologist and an educator. He has appeared on numerous TV and radio shows, and is in great demand throughout the country as a lecturer.

A member of Phi Beta Kappa, Dr. Dodson is an honors graduate of Johns Hopkins and Yale universities, and received his Ph.D. from the University of Southern California.

Ø

SIGNET Books You'll Want to Read

HOW TO DISCIPLINE— WITH LOVE

from crib to college

by
Dr. Fitzhugh Dodson

A SIGNET BOOK

NEW AMERICAN LIBRARY

This is an authorized reprint of a hardcover edition published by Rawson, Wade Publishers, Inc. The hardcover edition was published simultaneously in Canada by McClelland and Stewart, Ltd.

SIGNET, SIGNET CLASSIC, MENTOR, PLUME, MERIDIAN AND NAL BOOKS *are published by New American Library,*
1633 Broadway, New York, New York 10019

FIRST SIGNET PRINTING, SEPTEMBER, 1978

8   9   10   11   12   13   14   15   16

PRINTED IN THE UNITED STATES OF AMERICA

To Elise with love

CONTENTS

HOW TO DISCIPLINE—WITH LOVE

from crib to college

1

INTRODUCTION

According to my latest unscientific count, there are approximately 1,823 books and pamphlets on the subject of child discipline. Typically, books on discipline are built around a *single* system, such as "active listening" or "behavior modification" or "the use of spanking to establish the authority of the parent" or some other approach that says, "This is *the* way to discipline your child."

However, once you understand the true nature of discipline, you quickly see the inadequacies of a single system. For what is discipline? *Discipline is teaching.*

When we discipline children we are teaching them two things: to use desirable behavior, and to avoid undesirable behavior. Very few people see this clearly.

I recall a nineteen-year-old patient of mine on whom I was taking notes regarding his life history and family background. As I approached the subject of discipline I asked: "How did your mother discipline you?" He answered, "Actually, she didn't discipline me at all; we got along pretty well!"

This young man, like many people, thought of discipline as "something negative" that parents do to children to make them behave. He did not realize that discipline is *a process of teaching that goes on all the time*. When he stated that he and his mother got along well, he did not think of that as *continuous positive discipline*.

If discipline is teaching, it then becomes very clear what is wrong with only one approach to the subject. Let me use the analogy of a fifth-grade teacher. Suppose we oversimplify her

1

class and say she has twenty-six "average" children (even though there is no such thing as an "average" child), two slow learners who are considerably behind the others, two gifted children who are light-years ahead of the others, and two little hellions whose chief interest is in raising Cain. Can the teacher use *one* approach to successfully teach history or math or science or English or any other subject to all thirty-two of those children? Obviously not. She needs an individualized approach, tailor-made for each child.

It is the same with discipline. There is no one approach that will work at all times with all children. The approach must be tailor-made to fit the uniqueness of the child.

In discussing discipline it is important to take the age of the child into account. It is amazing that age is not even mentioned in many theories of discipline. Yet it is obvious that you do not teach desirable behavior to a two-and-a-half-year-old in the same way you teach desirable behavior to an eight-year-old or a fifteen-year-old.

Many theories of discipline also do not make allowances for differences in parents. They simply state: "This is how you should handle such and such a situation." They don't raise the question: "Is the parent going to feel comfortable handling the problem that way? Will his own feelings cause him to be incapable of following the suggestions in the book?"

Some parents feel much more comfortable with one approach to discipline than another. Psychological research may indicate that a particular approach works best when dealing with a specific situation. This is fine for Parent Smith. But Parent Jones, because of his own personality or the way his parents raised him, cannot operate with that approach. It goes against the grain and he is doomed to failure from the start. He cannot really put his heart into it, and his children will sense this. For him, this "sure-fire" approach will not work.

For these reasons, I believe a new approach to discipline is needed. And this book will provide it in the following ways.

First, I am not going to teach you *one* approach to discipline. Instead, I will describe many different *strategies of teaching,* strategies by which you can teach your child desirable behavior and teach him to avoid undesirable behavior.

The motto of this book is: "There is more than one way to skin a cat." From the many different teaching strategies you may select the ones that best suit your child. Remember that your child is truly unique, born with a combination of genes and a biological temperament different from those of any other child in your family, or indeed any child anywhere.

The fact that some children are easier or harder to raise than others is simply due to their innate biological temperament. The discipline techniques that will work smoothly with an easy-to-raise child may fail miserably with a hard-to-raise child. You need to find the right combination of teaching strategies by which your unique youngster can be taught desirable behavior.

Second, this book takes a *developmental approach* to discipline, beginning when your child is born and taking him up to age twenty-one. Whether you are aware of it or not, every day of your life you are teaching your child either desirable behavior or undesirable behavior, or a combination of both. So the use of discipline is not something that goes on only on those occasions when your child "acts up." Discipline is something that goes on *all the time*.

After I discuss a number of strategies of discipline, I will trace the development of a hypothetical youngster from birth to age twenty-one, showing which strategies are most appropriate at each stage of development. Then, once you have become familiar with the contents of the book, when your child presents a problem you are not sure how to handle, you can look it up in the index and refresh your memory on the suggested strategy to cope with that particular situation at that particular age.

Third, you need to find the teaching methods that suit you and with which you can feel comfortable. Please at least *try* a new method of discipline until you understand it (the feedback technique, for example). Remember that any new teaching method is bound to feel strange at first. If you find, after sincere effort, that some recommended method feels "foreign" and is just "not you," drop it and use another method.

Now let's look at the major teaching strategies, the ones most likely to enable you to teach your child to be a self-disciplined person by the time he is twenty-one. First you need an overall view of these strategies. Then we will start at birth and see how these strategies can be used at each stage of your child's development from infancy to adulthood.

2

RAPPORT: THE EMOTIONAL FOUNDATION OF ALL DISCIPLINE

Parents are lucky when it comes to the subject of discipline (although few realize it). As I have pointed out, discipline is really teaching. And we have learned from many thousands of experiments how to teach anybody almost anything. Not only can we teach babies, children, teenagers, and adults, but we can also teach cats, dogs, pigeons, hamsters, dolphins, monkeys—almost any kind of animal you can name.

In many ways, teaching animals is remarkably similar to teaching humans. Humans, however, are more "human." The point is that we know, from repeated experimentation, which teaching methods work and which do not. So the teaching of discipline has a firm scientific foundation. Parents are lucky because this information is available when we ask ourselves the question: How shall we go about teaching our children desirable behavior? ("Desirable" and "undesirable" behavior would probably be defined differently by different parents. But by desirable behavior I mean such things as obeying the reasonable request of a parent, playing cooperatively with other children, or doing required schoolwork; and by undesirable behavior I mean such things as persistently refusing to

4

obey a parent, hitting other children, stealing, or disrupting a school class.)

Consider a fourth-grade teacher instructing her class at the beginning of the school year. What does she need to do first in order to do a good job of teaching her pupils? Her first responsibility is to lay an *emotional foundation* for all the teaching she will do that year. She must establish *good rapport* with the students. By *rapport* I mean a mutual liking and respect, good "vibes" between the teacher and her class.

She can do this in many ways. There is no one correct method. But she must get across to her students that she likes them, that she will enjoy teaching them, and that they will have a mutually profitable time during the year they will spend together. If a teacher does not take the trouble to get to know her students and establish a solid rapport with them as individuals, she will not be able to teach them much of anything.

For example, when I taught at the high school or college level, it was my practice not to spend the first class lecturing on psychology, but rather to concentrate on building rapport. I encouraged the students to tell a little about themselves, why they were taking the class (even if it was only that it was required), and what they hoped to get out of it. This gave the students the feeling I was genuinely interested in them as persons and what they had to say. And it demonstrated that the class would be taught in the form of a dialogue rather than as a series of one-way "canned" lectures. During that first class I was not teaching them facts about psychology, but I was building rapport. Without good rapport, they were not going to want to learn about psychology.

When doing therapy with children it is also important to establish rapport before beginning psychological testing or therapy. When a new patient is a child, I do not immediately plunge into psychological testing or asking questions. Instead, when a child comes to see me for the first time, I greet the child in the waiting room and ask: "Do you like doughnuts?" (In twenty years of practice I have yet to get a negative answer!) Then I say, "Fine! Let's go get some doughnuts," and we walk over to a shop near my office.

During the time we walk to the shop, eat our doughnuts, and return to the office, we usually talk about a variety of subjects. Such as: what pets the child has, what his favorite TV shows are, does he have brothers or sisters, and are they pests (almost invariably they answer "Yes!"), what sports he likes to play or watch, is his teacher at school nice or mean, what he likes best about school, what he hates about school, and so forth. In this way I establish rapport with the youngster, letting him know that this grownup is interested in him and the things he likes and doesn't like. By the time we return to my office, instead of being stiff and frightened, the child is relaxed and usually enters enthusiastically into his first psychological test.

No matter whether you are a schoolteacher or a child psychologist, to teach a child you first need to establish good rapport.

The same holds true for a parent attempting to teach positive discipline patterns to a child. Good rapport is the foundation.

Unfortunately, many parents ignore this basic psychological premise. They often issue commands or make requests of a child without ever bothering to establish rapport. Many parents believe their children should obey requests and commands simply because they feel children should obey parents. This is akin to a teacher assuming the class will want to work on a history lesson simply because the teacher tells them to. Not so. The child has to feel good about the teacher in order to do what the teacher wants him to do. And it is the same whether we are talking about a schoolteacher or a parent-teacher.

What does this mean in practical terms? For one thing, it is fortunate for parents that their children take approximately a year to outgrow the infant stage and start to crawl or walk. Problems of discipline do not ordinarily arise until the youngster is a toddler. That gives parents a solid year to establish rapport while the child is still a baby. All the times you fed your child, cuddled your child, played with your child, sang to your child, and bathed your child have made you a much-loved person in your child's eyes. Your child wants to please you. As your child becomes a toddler and you begin to teach that child to behave in certain ways and not behave in other ways, you have a huge deposit of rapport to draw upon.

From toddlerhood on, many parents make a critical error. They neglect the task of continuing to build rapport with their children to do this or not to do that. But to limit the things on their minds. And so they limit themselves to telling their children to do this or not to do that. But limit the parental role to that of a "command-giver" totally ignores the importance of reestablishing rapport at each step in the child's development.

It is crucial for parents to spend part of the time with their children simply enjoying being together. And nothing more! Nothing is being required of the children. No commands, requests, lectures, or moral messages are being issued. Parent and child are merely taking a walk together, playing a game, eating a snack, or enjoying a movie or TV. From toddlerhood on, you need to keep reestablishing rapport by spending some time each day or each week with your youngster, just having fun together. The kinds of things you do will, of course, vary with the age and stage of your child's development, and with both of your tastes.

Incidentally, one reason there is such a "generation gap" between parents and adolescents is that parents have not usually taken the time or trouble to find rapport-establishing activities for them and their teenagers. These should generally be of a one-to-one nature. I have had several female patients tell me how thrilled they were as teenagers when their fathers brought them flowers and took them out to lunch or dinner. The mother of a teenage girl can usually find many opportunities to enjoy being alone with her daughter, whether it's going out somewhere together or just sharing information. Taking an adolescent shopping or to a movie or sports activity—depending on the tastes of your teenager—is almost sure to make a hit.

When you are playing checkers with your child, going for a walk, or taking her out for an ice cream cone, you happen to be teaching desirable things about personal relationships. But you are also building the rapport that makes you a warmly loved person. And that is the emotional foundation of all you are going to teach her about desirable behavior. The importance of rapport underlying *anything* you want to teach your child might be summed up in the words of the poet John Masefield: "The days that make us happy, make us wise."

3

ESTABLISHING A POSITIVE REWARD SYSTEM

I have pointed out that establishing rapport needs to go on continually between you and your child, for rapport is the foundation of the house of discipline. Now we come to discipline itself. What are the discipline strategies for teaching your child desirable behavior? In my opinion, the most effective method is a *positive reward system*. Although it is the most powerful teaching strategy, unfortunately it is also the one parents use least.

Here is an example, from animal behavior, of a positive reward system. Near Los Angeles, there used to be a family amusement park called Japanese Deer Village. At the time it was open, a staff member, animal psychologist Dr. Leon Smith, taught wild bears from Hokkaido, Japan, to play basketball. When the bears arrived from Japan they were in a wild state and obviously did not know too much about basketball. Yet Dr. Smith taught them without resorting to any of the things parents often do. He did not yell at the bears. He did not lecture. He did not scold or moralize. He did not spank the bears.

What did he do? His entire teaching strategy was based on a positive reward system. *And nothing else.* The bear was in one corner of the enclosure near the basketball backboard, and over in another corner was the basketball. If the bear merely moved around in his corner, nothing happened. But if he headed even the slightest bit in the direction of the basketball, he was rewarded with a small piece of meat. Dr. Smith followed this procedure consistently, in small steps, until he managed to get the bear near the basketball. Next he rewarded the bear for picking it up and then for carrying it to the basket and shooting.

Obviously all of these things did not happen in one training session. But once the training was complete, whenever Dr. Smith throws a basketball into the enclosure the bear would run over, pick it up, take it near the basket, and shoot.

Although this illustration is simple, it has profound implications for all parents. Let's see what Dr. Smith did:

First, he defined in his own mind exactly what behavior was desirable and what behavior was undesirable. Getting the basketball and shooting at the basket was desirable, and *no other behavior was desirable.*

Second, Dr. Smith set up a payoff for desirable behavior (in this case a piece of meat), but no payoff for undesirable behavior.

Third, the payoff did not come in one huge amount at the final outcome of the desired behavior (shooting at the basket). Instead, the payoff came in small steps. It was these small steps that enabled Dr. Smith to get the bear over to the basketball in the first place, and finally to shoot for the basket.

The essence of a positive reward system is that there is always a payoff for desirable behavior, but there is no payoff for undesirable behavior. *When an action is followed by a reward or payoff, that action is likely to be repeated.*

Although few parents use this positive reward system, many unwittingly use the *exact opposite.* They unknowingly give payoffs to their children for *undesirable* behavior, and therefore teach their children the exact opposite of what they intended. Millions of parents are unwittingly teaching their children undesirable behavior!

When a child is behaving as his parents would like—playing cooperatively and amicably with a playmate, sharing his toys in a friendly manner, not whining or being petulant, obeying his parents' requests—what happens? Is he rewarded? Is there a positive payoff? Is he given a hug or a word of praise or appreciation? No. He is ignored. His parents take this desirable behavior for granted and say nothing. They are totally unaware that by giving no payoffs for desirable behavior they are teaching their child to stop behaving in desirable ways.

But notice what happens when the situation reverses. Instead of behaving well, the child acts up. He hits his friend, throws his soup on the floor, torments his younger sister, steals money from his mother's purse, becomes defiant and refuses to obey. In short, he exhibits any one of a thousand kinds of undesirable behavior. What consequences result from this? When he was behaving well, his parents ignored him. But as soon as he behaves badly the child gets immediate attention. His parents scold, lecture, spank him, or in some way give him immediate negative attention.

When parents act this way, they violate what I call *The Law of the Soggy Potato Chip.*

A child obviously prefers a fresh potato chip to a soggy one. But if his choice is between a soggy potato chip and no potato chip at all, he will settle for the soggy one. In the same way, a child prefers his parents' positive attention to their negative attention. But if the choice is between negative parental attention and no attention at all, he will usually choose the negative attention. To a child, even negative attention is better than being ignored.

A parent intends negative attention to be a punishment. But, strangely enough, to a child it may act as a reward! In this case, the parent is unwittingly teaching the child to tease his sister, fight with a playmate, steal money from mother's purse, or other types of misbehavior.

The result is that so many parents are teaching their youngsters the exact opposite of what they really want to teach them. They are busy eliminating desirable behavior from the child's life by not rewarding it. At the same time, they are busy training the child in undesirable behavior by rewarding it with their negative attention.

What can you do to avoid these mistakes that other parents are making? You can set up a positive reward system, beginning when your child is a toddler and continuing through adolescence. Some of you reading this may be thinking: "But my child is already eight years old—what do I do now?" Don't worry. You can set up a positive reward system for your child at any age, although the earlier you start the easier it will be. Once your child reaches adolescence it is more difficult to begin, for an adolescent is in a natural state of rebellion against his parents, as part of his stage of development.

This chapter presents a general overview of how to set up a positive reward system. Later chapters will show how various strategies of discipline can be used at each stage of development—from toddlerhood through late adolescence—and exactly how to apply them.

Meanwhile, to make it specific, imagine you have an eight-year-old boy and that this is an entirely new procedure for you. How do you go about setting up a positive system of discipline for him?

First you need to make a clear-cut distinction between his feelings and his actions. More detail on this will appear in chapter 9, but I need to touch briefly now on this important point. By *feelings* I mean internal states of emotion, such as love, joy, excitement, anger, sadness, or fear. This world of feelings is your child's private world, and there is nothing a parent can do to influence or change it. Your child cannot help feeling excited or sad or fearful or angry. He is not responsible for his feelings; they come into his mind unbidden.

A child's actions are quite different. These are outward, observable events that are subject to control. A child cannot help feeling angry, but he can stop himself from throwing sand at another child, hitting his brother, or stealing a toy. Although parents can do little to influence a child's feelings, they can do a great deal to influence a child's actions.

When we are talking about designing a positive reward system for a child, we are talking about his *actions*, not his feelings.

Next, it is important that you deal only with actions that are *observable*. If you can't see and count the action, it is not subject to parental influence and control. For example, when dealing with parents in my clinical practice I will ask them, "What are the things your child is doing that bother you? What actions do you want to see changed?" Often they will say things such as, "He doesn't take responsibility." Then I explain that they have to be able to see and count the action, which is impossible with something vague like "aggressive" or "responsibility." So we may end up changing "He's too aggressive" to "He hits his brother." That is something definite and clear that we can work on. Or we change "He won't take responsibility" to "Instead of hanging up his clothes in the closet, he leaves them all over his room."

You now have two valuable rules to help set up your positive reward system. First, design the system for a child's actions but not for his feelings. Second, a reward system cannot deal with actions that are vague and ill defined. You must be able to see and count the action.

These are general principles. To make this vivid and concrete, let's create some positive and negative personality characteristics for your imaginary eight-year-old. In designing a positive system, the first step is to take some time to make three separate lists:

A. A list of actions you approve of and want him to continue
B. A list of actions you want him to do less of
C. A list of actions you want him to do more of

The three lists might contain items such as these:

A. Actions you want him to keep on doing:
1. He asks interesting questions; he's very inquisitive. You know that this trait will help him to be a success in school and in later life.
2. He's cooperative when asked to do things around the house (but not all the time!).
3. He's affectionate at times and gives you spontaneous hugs.
4. He can play for relatively long periods of time with his friend Jonathan without getting into arguments or fights.
5. He hangs up his clothes in the closet (sometimes!).

B. Actions you want him to do less of:
1. Verbally teasing and bickering with his six-year-old brother.
2. Hitting his brother.
3. Screaming when he doesn't get his way.
4. Refusing to obey you at times (when your requests are reasonable ones).

C. Actions you want him to do more of:
1. Hanging his clothes in the closet.
2. Doing his homework regularly.
3. Playing with his brother in a more friendly and constructive manner.
4. Making his bed.

The first list describes the desirable actions your child is already performing. All you have to do is to arrange a payoff for these actions. He doesn't have to do the action all the time. Even if the action is occasional, that is enough. For example, he doesn't *always* have to hang his clothes in the closet. Even if he does this only a few times a week, you can strengthen this action with positive payoffs. For here we come to the basic rule of the whole positive reward system: *When an action is followed by a positive payoff, it will be strengthened and be repeated.* The positive reward system is based upon *actions and consequences.* Positive consequences strengthen actions and build them into strong and lasting behavioral habits.

Basically there are two kinds of payoffs. "Love" payoffs in the form of praise, kisses, hugs, or other verbal or physical demonstrations of affection. And "thing" payoffs, such as a trip to the ice cream store, some candy, the opportunity to stay up a half hour later at night, the chance to watch a special TV show, the opportunity to spend an hour with you doing whatever he wants, being awarded points on a chart, which will enable him to earn something he particularly wants. If you start with your child when he is very young, "love" payoffs will do most of the job, and you will only need to use "thing" payoffs for special situations.

Here are examples of how to use positive payoffs when your eight-year-old is using desirable actions. When he asks an interesting question and shows curiosity, compliment him on it. Say something like, "That was a good question, George. You're really smart to think of that."

If he's cooperative when you ask him to do things around the house, give him more of the same kind of praise and affection. Or if he has been especially cooperative for several days, you could say, "George, you've been doing things so well around the house lately, I'm going to take you out for an ice cream cone" (or a doughnut or some other special treat he likes).

When he and his friend have been playing cooperatively for a relatively long period of time, you could interrupt them with the surprise announcement: "George and Jonathan, you've been playing so nicely together, I think I'll take you to the ice cream store for a special treat."

The rewards or payoffs you give your child are of two kinds: payoffs that come every time the child has performed the desired action, and payoffs that are spaced out at random, so that your child cannot know exactly when he will get the reward.

When your child is first learning to behave in a new and desirable fashion, it is important that he receive a payoff every time he acts in the new and desired way. But as he learns new behavior and begins to perform reasonably regularly, you can space out the payoffs and reward him in an intermittent or random fashion. You don't need to reward him every single time. For example, when he and his playmate are playing cooperatively, you do not need to take them for a special treat every time. Just do it unexpectedly and occasionally. If he should complain: "Jonathan and I are playing nicely, Mother—how about a special treat?" simply tell him: "Special treats are for special times." It is important not to give a special treat or payoff when a child asks for it. If you do, you will soon find that you are teaching him to beg. *The parent must be the one who controls when the special treat comes, not the child.*

You will be surprised how easily your child will adjust to receiving only occasional payoffs. What happens then is that he will continue the good behavior because he has become used to it and because he knows it pleases you, and that pleases *him*. Eventually the good behavior itself will be satisfying to him. This is a lot different from behaving in order to get a tangible "thing" payoff, even though he enjoys that when he gets it.

When you reward your child for behavior you approve of, it not only keeps him doing these things, but it has a positive effect on you as well. You will cultivate the habit of looking for actions you can reward. By praising your child for good things, *you are unconsciously training yourself to concentrate on positive things.* Unfortunately, many parents do the reverse. They are on the lookout for the wrong things their child does and are ready to pounce on him. Such parents are on the lookout to catch the child in the act of being bad. You are going to do the opposite. You are going to try to "catch your child in the very act of being good"—and reward him

The motto of our positive reward system is "You can catch more flies with honey than you can with vinegar." By contrast, parents who focus on the negative behavior of their youngsters seem to be saying: "We think we can catch more flies with vinegar than we can with honey."

For example, take a father who consulted me about the behavior of his four-year-old. The boy was a disruptive child, with the reputation of being the leader of the Junior Mafia at his nursery school. He grabbed the toys of other children, bossed them around, and hit them if they didn't do as he commanded. Still, he was not 100 percent bad! I tried to get the father to see his son's positive features. The father needed to build on these rather than to relate to his son only by scolding and berating him for his negative behavior.

I asked the father, "What does your son do now that you approve of, that you want him to continue doing?" Do you know, that father was unable to name a single good thing about his four-year-old! So I suggested a few things, just to make him realize that the actions of his youngster were not all bad. I pointed out things like, "He comes to nursery school without a fuss and likes it. He has a lot of energy. He doesn't let other children boss him around and use him for a doormat." Finally the father began to understand that some of his son's actions were desirable. We could then begin our positive reward program by training the father to praise these actions. When the boy heard words of praise from his father for the first time in his life, he became more responsive. Once that was accomplished, we moved on to planning rewards for the learning of new and positive actions.

Which brings us back to our hypothetical eight-year-old. We have talked about actions the child is already doing that are desirable. Now we come to the actions we want the child to do more of or less of. In other words, we want the child to learn new behavior patterns. And we need to design rewards or payoffs for these new action patterns.

First you need to make a relatively complete list of all of the people, places, things, and activities that constitute positive rewards or payoffs for your child. Following is a list I have parents fill out. It is reproduced with the permission of Dr. Paul Clement, who designed it.

REWARDS OR PAYOFFS FOR MY CHILD

A Survey Sheet for Parents

One of the best ways to help us understand the personality of a child is to know the people, places, things, and activities to which the child is attracted and which please the child. Such people, places, things, and activities can be called rewards or payoffs. Actions that are followed by a reward or payoff will probably occur more frequently in the future. If we want to strengthen existing actions, or if we want to teach a child new actions, then we should follow these actions with a reward or payoff. This survey is designed to help parents identify the most affective rewards or pay offs for their children.

1. PEOPLE

List the ten people with whom your child spends the most time each week. Put the person with whom the child spends the most time after "1," the person the child spends the second most time after "2," and so on. In making your list, consider brothers, sisters, parents, playmates, relatives, etc.

1.   6.
2.   7.
3.   8.
4.   9.
5.   10.

There may be other people, children or adults, with whom you think your child might like to spend more time each week, but doesn't get to, at present. For instance, you may feel the child would like to spend more time with you, his parents, on a one-to-one basis than he does at present. List below any people you feel your child would like to spend more time with than he presently gets to.

1.   4.
2.   5.
3.   6.

2. PLACES

List, in order, the ten places where your child spends the most time each week. Consider such places as his room, the family room, backyard, kitchen, classroom, the park.

1.   6.
2.   7.
3.   8.
4.   9.
5.   10.

There may be other places he would like to spend more time, but doesn't get to. List these places in order.

1.   4.
2.   5.
3.   6.

3. THINGS

List the ten things in order that your child spends the most time with each week. Consider such things as specific toys, TV, pets, books, bicycle, skateboard, dolls.

1.   6.
2.   7.
3.   8.
4.   9.
5.   10.

List other things your child does not own, or to which he does not have ready access, that he would like to have.

1.   4.
2.   6.
3.   5.

List your child's ten best-liked foods and drinks. Include candy, desserts, and other treats. Include items you may not allow your child to have very often, but which rate high on his list of preferences.

1.   6.
2.   7.
3.   8.
4.   9.
5.   10.

4. ACTIVITIES

List the ten activities on which your child spends the most time. By activities we mean such things as watching TV, reading, playing sports (be specific), going to the movies, playing a musical instrument, swimming, riding a bike, using a skateboard.

1.   6.
2.   7.
3.   8.
4.   9.
5.   10.

List activities in which you think your child would like to engage more frequently than he does now.

1.   4.
2.   5.
3.   6.

When parents take the time to fill out such a list of rewards it often helps them understand their children much better. Most parents don't consciously spend time thinking about their children in these terms. When they do, they get a much clearer understanding of what people, places, things, and activities *actually* motivate their children and hence are *already* serving as rewards or payoffs.

One of the prime reasons for filling out the list of rewards is to help parents see the specialness of each of their children. There is no universal set of rewards that applies to all children. One child's reward is another child's aversion. Each child is unique, with its own specific set of people, places, things, and activities that motivate *him* or *her*.

You now have a list of many possible things that can be used as rewards.

Now let's turn to the list of actions you want your eight-year-old to do less of. Pick one action to work on at a time. This is important, for it is difficult to work on changing several action patterns at once. Let's say, arbitrarily, that you choose physically fighting with a brother or sister as an action you want to change.

Tht first thing to do is to analyze What Follows What. What consequences follow such a fight? Let's say that after analyzing the situation you determine that what follows fighting between the brothers and sisters is that you give one or both of the children a scolding, a lecture, or spanking. Now you realize you are unwittingly bre... Law of the Soggy Potato Chip. Your negative attention... warding and strengthening the habit of fighting, and that is the last thing you want to happen.

So, your first step is to stop rewarding the fighting by your negative attention. Instead, design the other side of the program, which will reinforce friendly behavior between your children.

Let's say you decide to reinforce the two children at times when they are getting along reasonably well and that this will be done on a random schedule, during three separate times of the day.

1. In the morning, before the children go off to school, one payoff.
2. In the evening from the time when the children are called in for dinner until bedtime, two payoffs at different times.

A payoff is most powerful when it can be given *immediately* after the action you want to reinforce. After some discussion, you may decide that the best payoff for immediate reinforcement is candy. Your task is to find one time in the morning and two different times in the evening when the children are getting along reasonably well and not fighting. As I mentioned previously, your job is to catch the two children "in the very act of being good!" At these times, give them both candy, at the same time saying: "I'm glad to see you two getting along well without fighting; here are some sweets for you." If you feel up to it, you might dish out some praise as well as candy, but only if you feel this sincerely.

We now have established a reward program in which there is a positive payoff for *not* fighting, and no payoff for fighting. You may be wondering at this point: "But how do I stop them when they *are* fighting?" That will be dealt with by the Time Out, which I will describe in a later chapter.

Basically, what you do with negative behavior is to ignore it, unless the negative behavior falls into one of these three categories:

1. It is harmful to the child or someone else.
2. It is destructive of property
3. It just plain "gets on your nerves."

There are things you can do about negative behavior in

each of these categories, depending on the age of the child. These will be dealt with at length in later chapters. Don't jump to the conclusion that Dr. Dodson believes you should let the child do what he pleases, no matter how obnoxious the child is, that if the child wants to scribble on your walls with crayons or carve his initials in the grand piano you should ignore this negative behavior and concentrate on the positive side. I am not saying any such thing. These kinds of negative behaviors should be stopped promptly, but not by the mistaken methods most parents use.

What I want to emphasize in this chapter is that designing payoffs and rewards for positive behavior will take you a long, long way in your discipline program, particularly if you begin when your child is young.

Frequently during lectures to parent groups on the subject of positive payoffs, someone rises in the question period and asks: "But isn't this bribing the child?" No, it is not! A bribe is money or a gift given in order to get someone else to do something illegal or immoral. The activities we are talking about here are not illegal or immoral or undesirable activities. They are all desirable, such as not hitting, cleaning up one's room, and doing homework.

When a father or mother works for a company, the company pays them wages on the basis of work performed. When we use a positive reward system, we do the same thing on a child's level. Learning not to hit a sister or brother, to clean one's room, to do one's homework, and many other things are actions that are part of our "work" as a child. The positive payoffs are our "wages." We should no more label these positive payoffs "bribes" than we should so label the wages of a father or mother.

Remember, too, that as we gradually switch from a system of rewarding each and every time to a system of spaced-out rewards, we are teaching the child to develop self-satisfaction, which becomes its own payoff for doing certain worthwhile things. Our ultimate goal is to enable our child to grow up to be an adult who is self-disciplined, who has learned to *reward herself* or *himself* for desirable behavior.

The more you use positive payoffs with your child, the more you have a well-functioning reward system working, the less you are going to need the other strategies of discipline. Why? Because there will be less negative behavior to cope with.

4

CONTRACTING

Most American parents are unfamiliar with the term *contracting* as applied to parent-child relationships.

Of course we are familiar with contracts in the world of business, when we buy an automobile or a stereo system or a house. In business contracting, two persons make an agreement: Party A promises to do something (deliver a new automobile) and Party B promises to do something in return (pay a certain amount of money in specified ways).

As a discipline method in the home, contracting is based on exactly the same concept. The contract is an agreement between parents and a child (or children). The child promises to do a particular thing, and the parent promises to do something in return. (You do X and I'll do Y.) Or to put it another way, if the child changes his behavior in a certain way, the parent will, in turn, change his behavior in a certain way.

The contracting system is actually an offshoot of the positive reward system. The positive reward system works more or less unilaterally. The parent decides what good behavior he wants to reward in his children and nudges them in that direction with payoffs. There is usually no element of negotiation involved. But contracting is based on negotiation and cannot exist without it.

Here is an example of contracting between a parent and his son Harry, age ten.

PARENT: Harry, I wonder if we could work out a contract for you to wash the dishes three nights a week.

21

HARRY: Maybe.

PARENT: How about me treating you to a trip to get an ice cream cone for those nights?

HARRY: Naw, that's no big deal.

PARENT: Well, suppose you could stay up an hour later those three nights?

HARRY: Well, I kind of like that idea, but I think I've got a better one. How about paying me a dollar each night I do the dishes?

PARENT: No, that's too much money. But wait a minute. How about this one? What about a trip to the ice cream store those nights, and you can buy *anything* you want in the store?

HARRY: You really mean that? Anything?

PARENT: Anything.

HARRY: Even a double banana split?

PARENT: Yep.

HARRY: You're on, Dad!

PARENT: Okay, we'll write it down and sign it just like people do in business.

He gets a piece of paper and writes:

I, Harry Falconer, promise to do the dishes on Monday, Tuesday, and Thursday nights. In return for Harry's doing the dishes on those nights, I, Roger Falconer, promise to treat him to anything he wants at the ice cream store.

Signed ————————————

Harry Falconer

————————————

Roger Falconer

Let's analyze this example of the contracting process and discuss how to make the contract work well for both sides.

First, this contract is a mutual agreement between father and son, resulting from a negotiation process between them. Let's contrast this with something that is *not* a contract. A parent may say: "I won't let you go to the movies Saturday if you haven't done your homework." This is not a contract, since there has been no negotiating. It is simply a unilateral statement coming from the parent.

Second, the negotiation process results in a commitment on both sides. Harry commits himself to do the dishes three nights a week. Roger commits himself to take his son to the ice cream store on those nights and buy him anything he wants.

Third, the commitment is written down. Although a contract can be purely verbal, there are several very good reasons why contracts are usually written down. An agreement in written form prevents misunderstanding and arguments about it later. There is a copy for each person, and everybody can see exactly what it does say and what it does *not* say. Make an original and a carbon so that each party can have a copy. Second, with children between the ages of six and twelve it is psychologically more impressive and effective to have the contract written down. All of this seems more businesslike and worldly to a child of this age, and helps to insure his being highly motivated to fulfill his end of the contract.

Fourth, the contract should be concrete and specific. All the actions specified in the contract should be observable and countable. Avoid vague, unclear items such as: "Jack promises to be nicer to his sister" (Can you observe that? Can you count it?) or: "Nancy promises to be more cooperative around the house." You can't observe or count things like that. Write down specific ways in which Jack agrees to treat his sister, or specific ways in which Nancy agrees to cooperate.

Fifth, the contract should be positive in nature. The child should agree to *do* something, rather than agree *not* to do something. It is much easier to get cooperation and motivation if the contract is stated so that the child has something positive to do to earn a payoff.

Many times parents state objectives to a child in a very negative way, such as: "If you don't do your homework tonight, no TV for you, young man!" Exactly the same idea could be stated in a positive way: "As soon as you have done your homework, you can watch TV." Contracts work the same way. With a little bit of thought you should be able to state almost any idea in a positive rather than a negative form so that you can base a contract on it.

Sixth, the contract must be fair. Both parent and child must end up feeling they have made a good deal. If the child believes he is doing too much for what he is getting, he will somehow manage to sabotage the contract. And if the parent feels he is "paying" too much for what the child is doing, he will feel he is being cheated, and somehow arrange to take it out on the child.

In general, it is up to the parent, because he is older and wiser, to gauge the fairness of the contract. The parent has the ability to look into the future better than the child. He should make sure that as a parent he does not agree to put out more than he feels the child's contribution is worth. And he must also gauge from the silent language of the child's behavior whether the child is genuinely satisfied with the "wages" for his changed behavior. For instance, if a child, in answer to a proposition from his parent in the negotiation process, says rather weakly, "Yeah, I guess I would do it for that," the parent can inquire further and say, "You don't sound very positive about our contract. Are you sure you think that's a fair deal for you?"

Seventh, the contract should be designed to be successful. This means that parents should not expect a mature or perfect performance from the child in the beginning, but only a rough approximation. The child's performance will improve as he receives his payoffs and feels more and more positive about the contract. If the parents are perfectionistic about what they expect in the beginning, the child will be doomed to fail rather than succeed. And if either parent or child does not fulfill his obligation—whatever the reason—then something must have gone wrong psychologically during the negotiation process.

Eighth, the ability to negotiate is not something either parent or child is born with. Both have to *learn* how to negotiate. The parents have the power. They have to learn to give up some of this power and develop the art of compromise. The child has even less idea of negotiation and compromise, but he can learn it quickly. Almost all negotiation involves compromise by both parent and child.

It is important to pick a good time to negotiate. Never try to do it in the heat of a battle or conflict. Contracts should be made rationally, not emotionally.

When working out a contract, the first step is for each person to try to state the problem or difficulty without "putting down" the other party. If a parent says "Our problem seems to be that Jerry acts like an obnoxious brat to his sister," this is stating the problem in a putdown manner. But if the parent says: "The problem we want to work on is that Jerry hits his sister," this is reasonably objective and not a putdown.

What are the rewards the parents can offer the child in the contract? Consult the Parents' Survey Sheet of Payoffs, which

I describe in the last chapter. This will give you a comprehensive list of payoffs that may genuinely interest your child.

Please do not get the impression that the only things you can offer are money, a new toy, or a food treat. You can offer him the right to stay up an extra half hour or hour reading in his bed every night. (Which also helps to increase his reading ability!) Or you can offer him a special hour or half hour of time alone with you, without any brothers or sisters around. With younger children, for instance from ages two to five, you can offer silly things, such as seeing you make funny faces or dance a jig or stand on your head (if you can do it). You would be surprised how psychologically powerful such humorous parental behavior is to a very young child. The young child also loves to be able to *control* the behavior of the parent, so any contract involving this is usually a sure-fire hit with a small child. For example, the parent's part of the contract could be to do whatever the child tells him for ten minutes.

Here are some further rules about payoffs, and how to use them in making contracts.

First, a payoff should always come *after* children have performed what they promised, never beforehand. If you give them what you promised and then they don't do what they promised, you're stuck. (That also means that something has gone wrong during the negotiation process.)

Second, the payoff should be as immediate as possible. This is based on the psychological fact that the faster the payoff, the more powerful it is in strengthening the good behavior for which you have contracted. When a young child has done what he promised to do (such as putting away toys), you should *immediately* stand on your head or dance a jig as you have promised.

With an older child, if the payoff is a movie on Saturday for cleaning up his room every day, you cannot, of course, deliver the Saturday movie on a Tuesday. Instead, post a chart or checklist in the child's room or in the kitchen, and give him a check mark or gold star each day as soon as the child has cleaned up the room. This furnishes a certain amount of immediate payoff and is a tangible assurance that the Saturday movie will be forthcoming.

Third, when you make contracts with your child, you should model your contracting after a teaching machine or a programmed book (which is a teaching machine in book form). A teaching machine or programmed book is based on the idea that the student begins with very easy questions and slowly works his way up to the hard ones. This way, the student develops a feeling of self-confidence and mastery as he finds he can cope with the first questions with ease. As he proceeds through the book or machine, he finds he can handle harder and harder questions. Your contracting should work the same way. In the beginning, negotiate contracts that are very easy for your child to perform. Accept promises only for what you are sure he can handle and is willing to do. Then you can gradually work your way up to more difficult contracts.

Fourth, it's important that your child have the freedom to grumble and gripe, as long as he does what the contract specifies. When a child is grumbling or griping, he is expressing his feelings, which is perfectly all right. After all, the contract merely specifies that he take out the trash or clean up his room. It doesn't specify that he has to *like* to do it. Remember the all-important distinction we have made between a child's *feelings* and a child's *actions*.

Fifth, avoid the type of contract or checklist in which the child is given points for good behavior and loses points for bad behavior. This is almost always self-defeating. As the child loses points for bad behavior (particularly if the child loses a lot), he soon becomes resentful and adopts a "What's the use?" attitude. The checklist should only have points for good behavior. Because then the child is always heading toward his goal even if he earns only a few points at first. Taking away points for bad behavior will almost always cause a child to become discouraged and resentful. He will soon want to give up or to sabotage the contract.

Here is an example of another contract. An eleven-year-old boy, Jerry, and his parents were in family therapy with me. Jerry initiated the need for a contract because he wanted to go out and play with his friends on school nights, which his parents objected to. Finally, after much back and forth negotiation, they worked out a contract. Jerry promised to do the following things:

1. Be home at mealtimes.
2. Do his homework for that night, if he has any. (The parents decided to accept Jerry's word as to whether he did in fact have homework and did in fact complete it.)

3. No skateboarding at night, because it is dangerous.
4. Be with a friend or friends and not by himself at night.
5. Be home by 9:00 P.M.

Mother and father, on their part, promised that if Jerry fulfilled these five aspects of the contract, he would be allowed to be outside any night of the week until 9:00 P.M.

As an addition to the contract, if the school reported that Jerry had not done an important homework assignment or report, he would lose one week's privilege of staying out at night. Since the parents were rather wary and skeptical about his contract, it was further agreed that this first contract would have a one-week trial run to see if it would work.

Another reason for writing down the contract is that there is a great temptation for one or both parties to smuggle in or take out things that are not in the original contract. In his case the parents smuggled something in. Jerry got a bad interim report from school, and the parents would not let him go out that week, telling him he had violated his contract. Jerry protested that there was nothing in the contract about bad interim reports, and he was right. During my next therapy session with the three of them, I pointed out to the parents that while it may have been unfortunate for Jerry to get a bad interim report, there was nothing about interim reports in the contract, only about undone homework. Since he had fulfilled his side of the commitment, they were obliged to fulfill their side.

We also see in this story an example of typical parent behavior. When the child does something bad, the parents often renege on the contract, even though the particular bit of bad behavior was not in the contract. This is why it is so important to write down the contract and make it very specific.

In this contract, both Jerry and his parents had something to gain. The parents had been having trouble getting Jerry to do his homework. Every night he had a list of excuses as long as your arm why he couldn't start on his homework "right now." But the contract gave Jerry a powerful incentive to do his homework and not fool around, because as soon as he had completed his assignments he could go out and play with his friends. Because his parents were concerned about Jerry's safety, they included the items that specified no skateboarding and that he must be with his friends, not alone.

As mentioned earlier, many contracts involve a checklist or

chart. For example: Suppose you have contracted with your eight-year-old that if she feeds the dog every day during the week she will get to go to the movies Saturday afternoon. You introduce the idea of a checklist or chart because you want to provide some immediate reinforcement each day she feeds the dog. You won't get any immediate reinforcement if nothing happens until Saturday.

But if your child makes a checklist and gives herself a check mark every day after she feeds the dog, then putting the check on the chart is reinforcing to your daughter. It reminds her that she is that much closer to going to the movies on Saturday. Some children find gold stars more impressive; if so, use them instead of checks. Whatever is reinforcing to your child, use it, so that every day the child has *something* that reinforces the accomplishments that day.

When the promised payoff is far in the future, you will need a more tangible reinforcement every day, instead of just a check on a chart. For example, suppose your ten-year-old is working toward a new bike which costs $125.00. The child's part of the contract is to hang up her clothes, make her bed, and clean her room every day for four months. If you left the contract in this form, you would quickly find that the prospect of a new bike in October is much too far away to be powerfully motivating to your youngster now. (We call this kind of unrealistically long-range payoff a pie-in-the-sky motivation.)

But you can work out a contract that has a strong daily reinforcer and at the same time the powerful long-range reinforcer of the new bike. You negotiate a contract in which the child is to hang up her clothes, make her bed, and clean her room each day. Every day that the child fulfills her part of the contract, she gets a dollar bill, which is kept in a special place. The dollar bills gradually accumulate toward the magic figure of $125.00, at which point the child will get the new bike. Now you have not one but two things that powerfully motivate the child to keep her part of the contract: the new bike, which she looks forward to getting in the future, and the growing bundle of dollar bills, which is tangible evidence that the bike is forthcoming.

In this example, the basic payoff was the new bike. Here are some other examples of what can be earned with check marks on a chart: special time spent alone with one parent; reading an extra story to the child at night; staying up later at night, usually coupled with reading in bed; a fishing trip, a camping trip, or a certain number of pennies or a nickel or dime for each mark on the checklist.

It is also good for the parent to think ahead to a new payoff while the present payoff is being earned. Ask your child what she would like to work for after she has earned the payoff on her current contract. Swimming lessons? Being taken to a baseball, football, or basketball game? A special movie?

In addition to teaching your children good behavior through the use of contracting, you are also giving them training in the art of negotiation. This will be of immense help to them later in the adult world. After your children become accustomed to contracting, you may find them beginning to take the initiative in suggesting contracts to you for things they really want. Then, of course, you are in a very favorable position to work out a contract of value to both sides. When your children really get the hang of contracting, you may overhear them saying to one another or to a friend: "Hey, I'll work out a contract with you!"

With respect to the time span of a contract, for younger children (five and under) the contract should extend no longer than the day you work it out. With children six to twelve, it can extend as long as a week (or longer, with a long-range payoff combined with a daily payoff, such as the bike and the dollar bills). With teenagers the length of the contract can follow the breaks in the school year: the fall semester, the spring semester, the summer vacation.

Once your preteen youngster is familiar and comfortable with contracts, you have an invaluable technique to use in the adolescent years. Where other discipline strategies will often not work with teenagers, contracts will. Why? Because the adolescent values the adult nature of the contract and the fact that he and his parents are approaching the contract as equals.

When the behavior with which you are concerned is under control, you no longer need a formal contract. You can gradually fade out the contract in the same way you gradually space out payoffs in the positive reward system. For example, when your youngster is reading eagerly and consistently, you do not need payoffs for reading. The contract did its work and is no longer needed.

5

HANDLING
UNDESIRABLE BEHAVIOR

So far we have talked about teaching your child desirable behavior through the positive reward system. I am sure you are wondering at this point: "That's fine for building up good behavior, but how do I handle bad behavior? What do I do if right now my fourteen-month-old is biting another child or my seven-year-old is beating up his brother or my eleven-year-old is stealing from stores?"

Before I teach you how to deal with undesirable behavior I want to tell you how *not* to. Most parents try to deal with undesirable behavior by the use of *punishment power*. It is important, therefore, to make sure you know why punishment power is a very poor and inefficient method, and often ends up making the undesirable behavior worse rather than better.

When parents use punishment, they scold, they yell, they lecture, they take away privileges, they threaten, or they spank.

What is wrong with these kinds of punishment?

First, they violate The Law of the Soggy Potato Chip. The parent intends the punishment to make things sufficiently unpleasant for the child so that he will change his behavior for the better. Unfortunately, the punishment (negative attention) is better than no attention at all and often acts as a payoff for the child, strengthening the very undesirable behavior the parent wants to get rid of!

Second, a person who punishes is teaching other people to avoid him. How can you be an important and positive influence in your child's life when he wants to avoid you because you are a scolder, moralizer, yeller, or spanker?

Third, punishment is merely an attempt to curb undesirable behavior. Punishment, in itself, does not teach or motivate a child toward more desirable behavior. Punishment tells a child what *not* to do; it doesn't tell him what *to* do. Consider our jails and prisons. If punishment worked as a system for teaching people better behavior, then when criminals are released from jail after three or eight or eleven years, they would go straight from then on. Do they? The evidence is otherwise. A fantastically high percentage are back in prison in a relatively short time.

Fourth, punishment power loses its effectiveness as children grow older. Punishment power may be temporarily effective (as far as outward behavior is concerned, if we ignore the feelings deep inside the child) with a young child of five or seven, but when a child gets to be eleven or twelve or into his teens, the old devices of taking away privileges or scolding or spanking have lost their effectiveness.

Because most parents have never been exposed to any other method of handling misbehavior, they take it for granted, as they would the law of gravity, that punishment is the only way to curb it. For that reason I want to analyze some of the types of punishment used with children, but analyze them as if they were being used on adults.

1. *Scolding.* You lost fifty dollars in a poker game last Saturday night and your wife scolds you. "Herbert, how many times do I have to tell you you're a lousy poker player? You're out of your league with those so-called friends of yours. Unless you can magically find some way to learn to play a decent game of poker, I suggest you give up playing for money. Or maybe you could find some high school kids who play on your level. But I'm sick and tired of you losing money that we need."

Analyze this kind of scolding. It's similar to the things that parents say to children. Would you like to be on the receiving end of such criticism? Does it motivate you to change your behavior in the future? Of course not!

2. *Lecturing.* You backed your car out of the garage and into your husband's new car. He lectures you. "Now, dear,

how many times have I told you how to back up a car? You turn around and look behind you. You don't look forward and try to back up by looking in the front mirror. Sometimes I don't know what to do with you. I think I'll have to treat you like a ten-month-old child because you act like one. How in the world could you possibly do something like back into my new car? I don't understand you at all."

How do you like the lecture? Does it motivate you to be more careful next time? Hardly. It probably makes you feel like *deliberately* backing into his blankety-blank new car! And once again, many children are unwilling listeners to such lectures from their parents.

3. *Taking away privileges.* You have overspent the money budgeted for food and household expenses this month. It is the eighteenth of the month and you have no money left to buy food. Your husband says he is sorry but he will have to take away your department store charge account for six months. How does that make you feel? Does it motivate you to do better with the food budget next month? Absolutely not. It probably makes you seethe with fury at your husband and feel like lousing up next month's food budget also!

4. *Sending you to your room.* Carrying home your wife's best dress from the cleaners, you slip on the wet pavement and accidentally rip the dress down the back. For punishment she sends you to your room all day Saturday, *with the kids,* and tells you not to come out until dinner. How does that motivate you?

5. *Spanking.* You have not kept a running balance on your checkbook and consequently you find you are three hundred dollars overdrawn. Checks are bouncing right and left. Your husband grabs you, marches you into the bedroom, and paddles you with a sturdy paddle. Does this make you feel like being extra careful with your checkbook? Or does it merely make you furious at your husband and determined to get back at him in some way?

We can see at once the absurdity of trying to compel adults to more desirable behavior by inflicting punishment. But somehow we have difficulty seeing that it is just as absurd to expect punishment to teach desirable behavior to children.

What punishment power does produce in children, teenagers, *and* adults is hostility, resentment, and the desire for retaliation. And you simply cannot teach children and teenagers desirable behavior by arousing these negative feelings.

All right, then. If punishment is a poor and inefficient way of dealing with undesirable behavior, what can we use in its place? That is the subject of our next chapter: alternatives to punishment in dealing with misbehavior.

6

NEW WAYS OF DEALING WITH MISBEHAVIOR

If we eliminate punishment from our repertoire for dealing with the undesirable behavior of a child, what can we use in its place?

First, we can eliminate payoffs for undesirable behavior. This method may be used for behavior that does not harm the child or others, does not destroy property, or does not get on your nerves.

Let me explain what I mean by eliminating payoffs. For almost any kind of undesirable behavior, your child is somewhere, somehow, getting some payoffs. It is your job to find and eliminate them.

Let me start with an example from the animal world. Suppose you have a guinea pig in a cage with a lever in it. The guinea pig has been trained to press the lever to get a food pellet, and it always works. Suppose you want him to stop pressing the lever. How would you go about it? You could try "punishing" him by giving an electric shock every time he presses the lever. And this would "work" for a while. But sooner or later, the effects of the punishment would wear off and he would resume pressing the lever to get the food.

So how do you get him to stop? Easy. You eliminate the payoff of food. At first he will press the lever more often. It's as if he's saying to himself: "Hey, how come I don't get food anymore when I press this lever? Maybe if I press it harder or more often it will work again!" But sooner or later, when pressing the lever yields no more payoffs, he will finally stop for good. No more payoffs, no more lever pressing.

Now let me give you an example from the world of children. Some years ago a mother consulted me about the behavior of her nine-year-old son. There were four children in the family, but according to her, Wayne was the "black sheep." She told me all the things he did that bugged her and concluded by saying: "He doesn't even eat his cake the same way the other children do. And he knows it just infuriates me!" I inquired what there was about the way he ate his cake that bothered her, and this is what she told me.

Whenever they had a piece of cake for dessert, Wayne would peel off the icing, roll it into a ball, and then eat only the icing, leaving the rest of the cake on his plate. For some reason this absolutely infuriated his mother. I suggested a way to handle the situation, and after some discussion she reluctantly agreed.

The next time they had dinner, there was chocolate cake for dessert. Sure enough, Wayne proceeded to peel off the icing. His mother said nothing. She just sat there, gripping the table hard and bleeding internally. Puzzled by her silence, Wayne looked up and said, "Hey, Mom, I'm peeling off my icing!" "I know," she said. "Aren't you going to say anything?" he asked. "No," she replied. Wayne was much mystified by his mother's new and strange behavior, but he continued his usual procedure of rolling the icing into a ball, eating it, and leaving the rest of the cake on his plate. He did the same thing for six or seven more nights, with his mother keeping silent. On the eighth night, to his mother's amazement, he ate his cake the same way the other children in the family did.

When his mother came in for her next appointment, she was absolutely dumbfounded by what had happened. She asked me: "How come he finally changed the way he eats his cake?" I replied: "He was getting payoffs each time he ate his cake the old way because he knew it bothered and upset you. When there were no more payoffs he ate his cake the way the other children did."

Here's another classic situation in which the elimination of payoffs works beautifully. Typically, four-year-old children will begin to bring home four-letter words, which they will try out on you. If they get a shocked and horrified response, this constitutes a payoff and will immediately strengthen the use of the four-letter words. But if you ignore your child's use of these words, then there are no payoffs, and they will gradually fade away.

I had one interesting variation of this from my practice. This mother made no response to the four-letter words her four-year-old brought home, and so they gradually dropped out of his vocabulary. But he had a little friend from whom he learned the word "tushie." For some obscure reason this particular word bothered the mother. As soon as the youngster discovered this, he dropped all the other words and concentrated on "tushie." For a couple of weeks everything was "tushie!" "Mother, can I have a tushie sandwich? Mother, how about ice cream and tushie pie? Can I play tushie in my sandbox?" Finally I was able to get the mother to stop giving payoffs to him for "tushie" and his use of the word faded away.

Removing payoffs works fine for all behavior except those actions that fall into the three categories I mentioned before:

1. Actions that will hurt or endanger the child or someone else (it is obviously not wise to ignore his behavior if he is about to hit his little brother with a toy truck).
2. Actions that will destroy property (scribbling on walls, banging a metal car against your grand piano).
3. Actions that are dangerous neither to people nor property but that just plain get on your nerves. (For example, your three-year-old may be sitting in the back of the car as you drive along, singing over and over, "Donka, dinka, banner," and after a half hour or so of this most parents would feel highly exasperated.)

So what can you do in these undesirable situations? By far the most effective discipline method you can use is the Time Out. Here is how it works.

First, the Time Out is *not* a punishment and should not be confused with anything similar that *is* used as a punishment. If your child is hitting his younger brother, you say, "Stanley, I cannot have you hitting Jimmy, so I think you need a Time Out. For a Time Out you go to your room and stay there for five minutes. I will let you know when the five minutes are up." (If he does not have a room of his own, send him to the bathroom or some similar place where he can be alone.)

Notice the advantages of a Time Out. You have geographically disrupted the undesirable behavior. He cannot be hitting

his brother when he is in his room and his brother is elsewhere. This means that each time your child uses undesirable
behavior, you can geographically disrupt it by means of a
Time Out.

Second, since a Time Out is not a punishment, it does not
violate The Law of the Soggy Potato Chip and thus unwittingly strengthen the undesirable behavior you are trying to
eliminate. The Time Out is merely a bland, relatively boring
five minutes in which nothing exciting happens.

Incidentally, after I had taught some parents how to use a
Time Out, I found that they had made it into a punishment
and completely negated the effect the Time Out is supposed
to create. If a mother screams at her child: "All right for
you! I've told you a thousand times to leave your sister alone
and you don't do it, so now you're going to have a Time Out,
young man, and see how you like it!" When parents add
punitive comments of this kind to a Time Out, they make it
into a punishment, with all the disadvantages previously mentioned.

A Time Out should be administered in as cool, calm, collected, and prompt a manner as possible. That means you do
not tell a child to stop doing something twelve times and then
give him a Time Out. No one remains very cool, calm, and
collected that way.

Once you get the child in his room, it matters not in the
slightest what he does there. The purpose of the Time Out is
to disrupt the undesirable behavior, and simply being in his
room does that. If you try to police what he does in his
room, you will be reinforcing undesirable behavior by your
negative attention. When the five minutes are up, tell him
that and nothing more. Do not say things such as: "You can
come out of your room now," or, "You can come out and
play now," or give any type of directions as to what he can
do. Merely announce that the five minutes are up.

Third, a Time Out is valuable because it is such a versatile
discipline technique. It can also be used with two children,
putting each in a separate room. Or three. In fact, if you
have enough rooms or places to put the children, it can be
used with any number of children! It is particularly helpful
for bickering and fighting between siblings. Let us examine
what typically happens when fighting breaks out between siblings. Both of them rush to mother and begin to complain
bitterly: "Julian started it!" "No I didn't either—Ethel was

teasing me!" Poor mother. No matter what face she may present to the children, she feels like this inside: "Holy Hannah, here we go again! I've got to play Courtroom, be both prosecutor and judge, find out who started it, and punish the child who did. I get so sick of doing this."

With the use of the Time Out, no parent need ever play the game of Courtroom again. When the siblings are bickering or fighting, simply say: "I see you two kids [or three or four] are not able to get along very well right now. You need a Time Out. Julian, you go to your room, and Ethel, you go to your room, and I'll tell you when the five minutes are up." "But, Mother, he started it," says Ethel. "I'm not interested in who started it," says mother. "You both need a Time Out."

Fourth, one of the best effects of the Time Out is not on the children but on the parents. Parents feel much more comfortable and self-confident in dealing with their children's misbehavior. They know no matter what crops up, and no matter how many children it involves, they now have a discipline technique that will work.

You can begin using this discipline method at about age three and it will work up to about age twelve. The earlier you start using the technique the better. After using it for a while, you may begin to hear your children say, in a resigned tone of voice. "I know, we need a Time Out!"

Some parents with young children encounter a special difficulty in using the Time Out. These parents find that their youngster refuses to go to his room when they tell him. (This is often part of a larger problem where the parent has lost authority in the home because she is afraid to say "No," but we will speak about that later, in chapter 9.) If a child defies a request to go to his room, the parent should escort the child physically to the room, even if the child is kicking and screaming, get the child inside, and close the door. The parent should stand outside the door, in silence, and hold the knob firmly to keep the door closed for the required five minutes. Depending on how stubborn the child is, it may take several days or weeks for the child to realize that there is no sense in fighting the Time Out. For once a Time Out has been called, the child is going to go to the room and stay there for five minutes.

I am sure some of you are wondering "All this may work fine in the home, but what about outside the home? In a store or driving a car, for example?" Obviously the Time Out does work best in the home. But it can also be adapted to other places. For instance, if you are driving to a picnic or a lake or beach or movie, and there is no particular hurry, you can stop the car and apportion a child or children to a particular spot in the car. Or if that won't do it, you can stop the car and have the children get out and station themselves in separate places in a field or parking lot for five minutes. If the children are anxious to get to the picnic or beach or wherever, this usually needs to be done only once!

Although the Time Out works beautifully with children three years or older, it is not suitable for very young children (those eighteen months to two years) and is particularly ill-suited to children whose language development is very limited. So this next discipline technique is for mothers of very young children. I call it the Reverse Time Out, but it is also irreverently known among parents as Mother's Vacation in the Bathroom. Instead of isolating the child, as in the Time Out, it is the mother who is isolated.

Here's how it works. When your very young child is driving you up the wall with her demands, and will not leave you alone, do not try to send her to her room. Instead, put yourself in a room where she can't get to you. Take a good book or magazine, retreat to the bathroom, and lock the door. Once you are in the bathroom, do not respond to the child in any way. Her cries, entreaties, or banging on the door are all to no avail.

Be especially careful not to relent and come out if the child has been banging on the door for twenty minutes or so. If you do, you are giving her a very powerful payoff to keep banging for an almost unlimited period the next time you retreat to the bathroom.

Wait for the child to give up and for the atmosphere to be calm and peaceful outside. This is the desired behavior you want to promote. Att his time, and *only* at this time, you give a payoff by opening the door and coming out of the bathroom. If your child starts to act up again with demands, screams, or tantrums, go back into the bathroom and lock the door. Never use Reverse Time Out as a threat. Do not say, "All right now—mother's going to go into the bathroom." If a Reverse Time Out is needed, simply do it. But don't hold it over your child's head as a threat.

Another method of dealing with undesirable behavior is through physical restraint of the child. This pertains mainly to emergency situations, where the Time Out is not fast enough. For example, if your four-year-old is about to stab a playmate in the eye with a sharp stick, you run over and grab the stick out of his hands. Hold his arms firmly in both of your hands and say to him loudly and forcefully: "Sticks are for playing in the sand or digging in the dirt; they are not for stabbing or hitting people."

Or a four-year-old may be flailing away with his fists and feet at his younger sister. His temper is too far out of control for a Time Out to be very effective, and so you rush over, sweep him up in your arms, and immobilize him until his temper subsides. Meanwhile you are saying to him: "You're so angry I have to hold you tight until you feel better."

What I am really saying is that you need to use common sense. If swift emergency action is called for, use a discipline technique that embodies swift emergency action rather than one that is leisurely.

7

OTHER WAYS
OF DEALING WITH
MISBEHAVIOR

The next strategy for dealing with undesirable behavior is *environmental control*. Many parents do not use this method, and thereby create totally unnecessary problems for themselves.

Watch preschoolers at play on a well-designed playground. Do you see any negative behavior—apart from occasional sand throwing? Generally you do not. The children play happily and pleasantly together because the environment is adapted to their age level. They do not have to adapt to an adult environment, which is unsuitable.

On the other hand, observe houses in which there are toddlers between the ages of one and two years. Often the house is exactly as it was before the couple had a child. Fragile and expensive vases and knick-knacks abound, and the mother rushes frantically around the house yelling "no-no" to the child and slapping his hand. The environment is not adapted to the age of the child. The child is expected to behave like an adult (which he cannot, since he is only a toddler).

What a needless frustration for both mother and child! If the home environment is controlled so that it is safe for the toddler to explore (and the fragile adult things are put away), then the child will feel as comfortable as he does on the playground, and the mother will feel at ease.

41

The principle is very simple: You must control your child's environment so that there is little he can do in the way of undesirable behavior. If his environment is filled with things that tempt him into misbehavior, trouble will follow.

A very familiar illustration of the importance of environmental control is the long car trip. Over the past twenty years many families with preschoolers have told me stories such as this: "We drove back to visit my folks in Nebraska last month, and you wouldn't believe what went on in the car! I was almost driven out of my skull—never again!"

As I inquired about the details of the trip, something like this emerged: The mother and father often drove for five hours at a time without a stop. Parents rarely admit to themselves what kind of behavior they expect of their youngsters. If they did, it would be something like this: The children are to sit quietly in the car and look contentedly out the windows as the scenery rolls by. Obviously such behavior is completely unrealistic for preschoolers.

Such an environment is an invitation to disaster. The parents should provide interesting games and toys to keep the youngsters occupied. When it becomes obvious that the children are nearing the end of their frustration tolerance, the family should pause for a snack or stop at a park or playground where the children can work off their bottled-up energy for twenty minutes or so. Furthermore, special toys or games can be hidden around the car to be brought out when the situation begins to deteriorate.

By planning the environment of the trip, parents can provide outlets for the normal high-energy output of their preschoolers. This is much easier than trying to control the child's energy level (which really can't be done) or ignore it (which can't be done either).

This tactic applies to school-age youngsters as well. I know a family with a nine-year-old son. On long car trips they stop every couple of hours at some place with restrooms and drinking water or soda pop facilities. They tell their son "Run!" and he races happily back and forth around the place, working off his excess energy. After eight or ten minutes they all pile back into the car and go on their way, much more content than when they stopped.

Here's another familiar situation. A family has two boys, ages eight and six. The whole family is planning to go on a weekend camping trip. If the parents are wise and, remembering their children's past behavior, anticipate what will probably happen during the weekend, they can expect considerable bickering between the boys. What can they do to prevent this? One of the simplest ways is to exercise environmental control. Let each boy invite a friend. Chances are that much of the energy that would have gone into making his brother's life miserable will go instead into playing with his pal. Once again, an ounce of environmental control prevents a pound of hassling.

One final example. Over the years, parents have told me about young children stealing money from their mother's purse, father's wallet, or from a drawer where cash is kept. The child doesn't steal anything outside the home. There are several things that can be done about this behavior, such as design a positive reward system for not stealing, or apply countermeasures if money is stolen. However, by far the simplest thing is to get a good lock for one of the drawers and keep any loose money in it. By using environmental control the parents will eliminate the problem of stealing.

The moral of environmental control is this: When confronted with misbehavior on the part of your child ask yourself this question: Is there anything I can change in my child's environment that will eliminate the problem? If there is, change it. In this sense, environmental control is *preventive* discipline.

Next we come to the principle of *natural consequences,* wherein a parent allows unpleasant but natural consequences to happen when a child does not act in a desirable manner. An example may make this clearer.

A mother and father consulted me because they were greatly disturbed by the behavior of their thirteen-year-old boy and eleven-year-old girl. Particularly in the morning. After the parents had pushed, cajoled, wheedled, and done everything but dance the fandango to get their two children off to school on time, they were emotionally exhausted. They were at the end of their rope and didn't know what they could do to improve the situation.

As a simple corrective procedure, I suggested that the parents do only two things each morning. They were to wake the children up, but only once—if the children went back to sleep it was their problem! Then the mother was to tell the children when breakfast was ready, but only once. That was *all* the parents were to do.

The children were told that if they were not ready when the car-pool driver came, it would be their responsibility to get to school as best they could. But they would not be allowed to ride their bikes. (That would be too much fun!) They would have to walk to school, and that was a long, long walk. These things were simply and matter-of-factly explained to the children. In other words, the responsibility of getting to school in the mornings shifted from the shoulders of the parents to the shoulders of the children. The natural consequences of not getting dressed and ready on time would be that the children would have to walk.

What happened? For four or five days nothing happened—the children were dressed and ready when the car-pool driver tooted. And then one Friday the children were not ready on time, and the car-pool driver, who understood the new arrangements, drove off. Well, a storm broke loose at home. "Dad, we've missed the car pool; you've got to drive us!" The father and mother refused to do anything about it and went about their business. One day the next week the girl was on time and drove off with the car pool, but the boy missed it. And that was the last time the parents had trouble with either one.

Another situation made to order for the principle of natural consequences is that of getting to meals on time. The mother acts as if it is her responsibility, rather than the child's, to get him to meals on time. Younger children can be called—once. Older children, who may be farther away from home, can be provided with an inexpensive wristwatch. Dinner is set for a certain hour, and those who are there on time enjoy the pleasant natural consequences of a hot meal. Those who are not there on time get the unpleasant consequences of a cold meal or missing the meal altogether if the rest of the family has eaten it all. (The mother must resist the temptation to warm over the meal if the child is late, for this only teaches him to be late.)

I remember a patient of mine who used natural consequences to good advantage on a camping trip. He had told his boys, ages ten and twelve, about the importance of putting a foam-rubber pad between their sleeping bags and the ground cloth or tent cloth. He noticed that Harry had forgotten to do this and left his foam-rubber cushion inside the camper. However, he said nothing about this to Harry, even though his wife whispered, "Tell Harry he's forgotten to take his foam-rubber pad to the tent." The next morning, Harry complained of being terribly cold in the night. The father asked the boys what Harry could have done to make himself warmer, and they came up with answers such as "zipped up his sleeping bag tighter," or "burrowed deeper in his sleeping bag." Finally he pointed out that Harry had not put his foam-rubber cushion between his sleeping bag and the ground cover of the tent. Harry had suffered the natural consequences of neglecting good advice. But from then on he never forgot to use his foam-rubber pad. However, if his father had reminded him, Harry would have learned nothing.

The basic principle of natural consequences is to let your child learn from experience, wherever possible, when it cannot possibly result in serious injury. If the natural consequences are pleasant, the child will continue to act that way. If the natural consequences are unpleasant, the child will be motivated to change his actions.

The temptation is often great to protect your child from unpleasant natural consequences. But if you protect him, he will not be motivated to change. You will be stuck with having to take care of him instead of his learning to take care of himself. So giving him the chance to learn through natural consequences ultimately boosts his self-confidence and self-esteem.

8

THE PROS AND CONS
OF SPANKING

Spanking is a form of punishment so widely used it deserves a chapter in itself.

Some psychologists and psychiatrists have stated explicitly that no parent should ever spank a child. I think this is non-sense. Picture a well-meaning but naïve mother who has read one of the "non-spanking" books on child-raising. Oh, how she longs to whack her misbehaving child on the bottom! But the book says she will be a terrible mother if she does. And she believes the book. So she holds on by grim willpower and doesn't spank. But the tension between her and the child is so thick you could cut it with a knife. I think this is a com-pletely wrong and unrealistic approach. Far better for her to give her child a few quick swats and clear the air. Then the two of them can start over.

I want to emphasize that spanking is a very poor and inef-fective method of teaching. If parents were 100 percent per-fect, there would be no need for spanking at all. But they are not. They are fallible human beings who become impatient, lose their tempers, and often demonstrate just how "human" they are. So I make allowance for the occasional use of spanking because of the fallibility of parents, and not because it is a valuable discipline strategy for teaching good behavior to children. My position is far different from that of those parents to whom spanking is the only discipline tool they know to keep their children in line.

46

In fact, let me give you a little bit of an inside story to show how little I have used spanking with my own children. I did not spank my daughter at all, because she was such an easy child to raise and there was no occasion when I was tempted to spank her. I spanked my oldest boy about twelve or thirteen times from the time he was approximately two until he was eight or nine. I spanked my youngest boy about three or four times during approximately those same ages. As you can see, spanking did not figure very large in my repertoire of discipline strategies. By spanking, I mean a few good swats with your hand on the child's bottom.

If you use the good discipline strategies outlined in this book, there will be very few times when you are so frustrated that you will have the emotional need to spank. And you want to spank as seldom as possible. Since spanking is a punishment, it suffers from all the psychological drawbacks that go with any form of punishment (it violates The Law of the Soggy Potato Chip, etc.).

Whenever we spank a child we are teaching him to hate us, fear us, and avoid us. How can we be a good teacher to our child if we have taught him to hate us, fear us, and avoid us? Furthermore, some kinds of spanking arouse a deep desire for revenge and retaliation. I can still vividly recall the four or five times my father whipped me with his leather shaving strap. I will never forget how I hated him at those times and vowed that when I grew up I would get even.

Spanking, like other forms of punishment, is useless as the child gets older, say eleven or twelve. Who is going to be able to spank a teenager unless he is a professional wrestler? (And even a professional wrestler cannot prevent his teenager from running away from home after the spanking!)

The real tragedy is that so many parents simply accept spanking as their main means of discipline. That is truly sad. These parents do not see how ineffective and harmful a constant diet of spanking is to parent-child relationships. They do not realize what a vastly different youngster they would have and how enormously more satisfying their relationships with him would be if they used such creative and humanistic discipline techniques as the positive reward system, the Time Out technique, and others advocated in this book.

A final word about one particular kind of spanking—the kind that results from something other than the child's misbehavior. You spanked your child, but afterward you realize he didn't deserve it. Perhaps you were having a fight with your husband and you took it out on your child. When you realize this, go to the child and say something like this: "I know mommy lost her temper and spanked you this morning. But I realize now it wasn't really your fault. I was having a fight with Daddy and I took it out on you, and I'm sorry." When a parent is able to say something like that, it does wonderful things for the child.

Our national obsession with spanking is apparent to me whenever I appear on TV or radio talk shows. Every time I am asked about discipline, the interviewer almost inevitably brings up a question about spanking, as if this were the most important part of discipline for a psychologist to comment on.

Let me sum up my position: I do not believe that spanking is an efficient and valuable tool in child discipline. I do not agree that if only more parents spanked their children, our children would be better behaved. But neither do I believe that it is a terrible sin against the cosmos for a parent to spank a child occasionally.

Although spanking ranks low in the effective techniques of discipline, it would certainly be an absolute saint of a parent who could raise his children without giving them a few good wallops now and then.

9

ESTABLISHING THE AUTHORITY OF THE PARENT (or, Who's Running the Show?)

Numerous books and magazine articles lament the decline of firm parental discipline and the rise of permissiveness. Permissiveness is blamed for the rising crime rate, drug abuse, immorality, vandalism, violence, acne, and Little League elbow. And poor Dr. Spock catches the blame for much of this. He is accused of misguiding a generation of parents by teaching them to be more permissive in raising their children.

Facts do not get in the way of those who lead the attack on permissiveness. For one thing, many of the parents whose children are in trouble with the schools or the law, or both, have never read Dr. Spock. Indeed, many of those parents have never heard of him! How, then, could Dr. Spock be a "bad" and "permissive" influence on a parent who has never heard of him or read him?

There are other facts that do not support the idea that permissiveness is ruining our country. For example, it was quite clear from their public statements that the thirty-eight people who were indicted or jailed in the Watergate affair did not approve of permissiveness. Still their antipermissiveness stance did not deter them from breaking the law of the land.

And the Vice-President who verbally attacked both Dr. Spock and permissiveness saw fit to resign rather than face criminal charges.

Just what is meant by the term *permissiveness* anyway? (You will notice that many of its opponents do not even bother to define it!) By permissiveness I mean that the parent is afraid to say no or set limits for the child, and, in general, has abdicated his authority as a parent and turned it over to the child. When you define permissiveness in this way, I think the great majority of American parents are *not* permissive. They *are* running their families; they have not abdicated their authority. And that's why *most* children do not get into trouble with the law, do not cause problems in the schools, do not become drug abusers.

This chapter, then, is not addressed to the majority of parents, who have retained their family authority, but to that minority who are desperately trying to keep control over their children, but are not succeeding. Of course we are talking about obedience to reasonable parental authority. If you have a child who refuses to obey *reasonable* parental authority, then you have a real problem. None of the discipline techniques I have mentioned previously in this book will work without the child's basic willingness to obey parental authority.

Several examples that will illustrate what I mean involve the experiences of two of my patients. (Incidentally, I have changed the circumstances, as I always do with clinical examples, to disguise the identities and protect the anonymity of my patients.) Both patients are mothers of only children. I see them on the same day. One is my 8:00 A.M. patient, the other my 9:00 A.M. patient. Since they come in one right after the other, I was struck by a similarity between the two that did not appear on the surface.

My 8:00 A.M. patient is a twenty-seven-year-old divorced woman with a three-year-old girl. The mother came for help because, as she put it: "I feel like my daughter is running the family instead of me." Her little girl is enormously determined and stubborn. When asked to do something she doesn't want to do, the child goes into a screaming temper tantrum. The mother reported that she had screamed once for forty-five minutes without stopping. The mother had been giving in to the child to prevent these tantrums, until finally, in desperation, she came to me for help.

My 9:00 A.M. patient is a thirty-six-year-old married

women with a four-year-old boy. Whereas the three-year-old girl controls her mother overtly and crudely, the little boy controls his parents more subtly. He will eat only certain things—fish sticks, carrots, peanut butter sandwiches, and milk. He absolutely refuses to eat anything else. The child's pediatrician assures the mother that although the boy is not getting a balanced diet, it is nevertheless adequate. But this does not reassure her. She worries terribly about her son's nutrition and she constantly hovers over him, coaxing and cajoling him to eat other things. The child simply refuses, saying that he hates it and will not eat it.

These children, although quite different in many respects, are alike in one thing: They are running the family instead of the parents. The parents are pleading with them to do something or to stop doing something. The children have the power the parents should have. Who's running the show? The children!

Whether your child is a three-year-old, a nine-year-old, or a teenager, if he knows that he really has the power in the family, you have lost as a parent. You are like a boss whose employees pay no attention whatsoever to what he says.

Another example is a patient with a three-year-old boy. One day the boy was systematically kicking out the screen door on the back porch. The father told him to stop. The mother interrupted with, "Don't say that to him, remember what Dr. Spock says." To which the father replied, "The hell with Dr. Spock!" The mother said, "You may as well resign yourself to the fact that the screen door will be broken." The father replied that he would not allow this to happen. He picked up the child and told him again, very firmly, not to kick the screen door. The child immediately kicked the father. Both parents panicked and rushed about trying to find something to pacify the child. By doing this, of course, they didn't have to resolve the problem of the screen door, or that the child had kicked the father, or face the fact that the child had taken the parental authority into his own hands.

What has brought about this wishy-washiness among a minority of parents in America today? I think there are two basic causes.

First, many parents feel quite uncertain and apprehensive about how to bring up children. In the old prechild-psychology days, parents were not aware that the way they raised their children could determine how they turned out. They simply did not know if their children grew up to be drug addicts, or criminals, or alcoholics, it would be because of the way they raised them.

When I was a child there was a word I frequently heard that is seldom used today. The word is *disposition*. A child might have a "mean disposition" or a "good disposition" or a "sunny disposition." *Disposition* meant the innate temperament and personality of the child, which would emerge in later childhood and in adult life. Nothing could be done about it. The way parents brought up the child had nothing to do with it and could not change the outcome. This belief may have been scientifically incorrect, but was it very comforting to parents! It enabled them to raise their children without worrying too much about what kind of job they were doing.

Those were parents' beliefs in 1900. Then a minister could preach in his sermon about a son who became a drunkard and disgraced his loving mother and father, holding him up as an example of how terrible it was to do such a thing to loving parents. Today a sophisticated congregation would laugh at such naïveté and say: "What did the parents do when they were raising their son that caused him to become an alcoholic when he grew up?"

One important effect of this new sophistication has been to make many parents unsure of themselves. They are terribly afraid of making mistakes in raising their children. In certain situations where our grandparents or great-grandparents would have taken firm and decisive action, based on common sense, many parents today hesitate, for they are secretly thinking: "What if the way I'm handling the situation is wrong?"

What can be done about this? Obviously we can't turn the clock back to 1900, with its naïveté about psychology and child-raising. So how can we help parents get over their fear of making mistakes?

Let me use an analogy. I know absolutely nothing about repairing or taking care of an automobile. I can tell the difference between the carburetor and the engine, and that's about all. If I were suddenly called upon to do the job of an auto mechanic, obviously I would have a fear of making mistakes, which would cause me to perform in an unsure manner. But if somebody taught me first, carefully and painstakingly, how to do the work of an auto mechanic, my fear of making mistakes would decline amazingly. When you are on familiar ground, you don't harbor the same fear of making errors as when you are in strange territory.

The job of raising a child from birth to age twenty-one is obviously more complex than that of being an auto mechanic. You need information such as the ages and stages of child development, and the typical characteristics of each stage. You need to know how to teach or discipline your child at each stage. Every parent, in short, needs training in child psychology and teaching, because every parent, whether aware of it or not, *is* a child psychologist and a teacher.

Unfortunately, very few parents receive this kind of training. Since so few parents are trained for the job of raising children, is it surprising that so many feel unsure of themselves and worry that they may make mistakes?

Although the answer seems obvious, it will probably take years to take care of the obvious. A start is being made, however. A few high schools in the United States have begun to teach students the principles of parenthood. In addition to classroom instruction teenagers are exposed to nursery school children, where they get experience with real, live, wiggling, squirming youngsters. I foresee the day when we will be wise enough to expand this to *all* high schools in the United States.

But high school is not the total answer. For many high school students, parenthood seems far away, and teaching about it will not "take." Most mothers and fathers feel their first real need for training in parenthood when their first child is born. There the baby is, twenty-four hours a day, and he won't go away! That's the time for adult education classes all across the country, so that both mother and father can be trained in the principles of parenthood.

If you are worried about making mistakes in raising your children, I suggest you find a good course in parenting. The Red Cross has excellent courses throughout the country called Parenting from Birth to Five. Adult education centers and colleges also have such courses.

Now we come to the second (and major) cause of parental permissiveness. The type of parent who is constantly appeasing a child, giving in to the child's whims and demands, and letting the child push her around is doing this for a basic psychological reason. Deep down she is operating on this unconscious motto: *If I don't do what my child wants, he won't love me.* A brief anecdote will illustrate what I am talking about. The anecdote sounds so strange and far-out you will have to take my word for it that it is the truth.

A few months ago, I went into a toy store near my office. As I entered, I could not help noticing that the counter was piled three feet high with wrapped gifts, and the sales clerk was busy wrapping more. Since I knew the clerk quite well I inquired: "Emily, what's the big deal going on here?" She pointed to the end of one of the aisles and whispered: "It's the birthday of Mrs. Benson's five-year-old." I must admit that I was too curious to keep silent. When Mrs. Benson brought five or six more presents to the counter to be wrapped, I said, "Pardon me, but I'm curious. Who are all the presents for?" [There must have been twenty presents.] Mrs. Benson answered: "They're for my daughter, Harriet. It's her fifth birthday this Saturday." I said: "Wow! How come so many presents?" Mrs. Benson replied, "My daughter's not going to grow up and say her mother didn't love her. And I'm going to take Polaroid pictures of all the presents to prove it!"

Obviously Mrs. Benson was terribly afraid her daughter would not love her. And obviously there are many mothers and fathers who are also afraid that their sons and daughters will not love them. They are afraid that if they are firm, if they are decisive, if they say no and mean it—in other words, if they use their parental authority—they will lose the love of their child. Merely recommending to a parent with a psychological hang-up like this that she use firm discipline will not work. She has to overcome her fear that if she is firm she will lose her child's love. She needs to use the technique of negative thinking (see chap. 15) to overcome her need to appease. Enrolling in a class in assertiveness training in a college or psychological institute may also be helpful.

If none of these things works, then such a parent needs help through individual or group therapy with a competent professional person: a psychologist, psychiatrist or a psychiatric social worker.

You see, the mother who is afraid her child will not love her if she is firm in her parental authority needs more than information about discipline techniques. She needs more than well-meaning advice to "be firm." If she could, she would. What she needs is professional help in changing her feelings, in ridding herself of her fears that her child will not love her, so that she can dare to be firm as a parent.

As a footnote to this chapter, I want to reiterate that the great majority of parents in this country, in my opinion, are not permissive. However, many parents who are not permissive when their children are under twelve may change, and the virus of permissiveness invades their parenting when their children become teenagers. Why is this? Very simple. These are the parents who, without any knowledge of the kinds of discipline found in this book, rely solely on punishment power. This may keep a child "in line" up to about age twelve. Then things change drastically. As one mother put it, "My boy's too big to spank at fourteen, and even if I could do it physically I'm sure it wouldn't do any good. What do I do now?" At this point a number of parents who up till now have not been permissive find that their old punishment devices don't work anymore, and they don't have anything else to use. A number of these parents end up by being permissive and letting their teenagers walk all over them simply because they don't know what to do. We will talk about this situation and how to handle teenagers in chapter 11, The Mutual Problem-solving Technique, and again in the chapters on early adolescence and late adolescence.

10

THE FEEDBACK TECHNIQUE

So far I have dealt with discipline techniques for handling your child's actions. Now I am going to discuss how to deal with your child's feelings. Earlier I described the difference between feelings and actions. Feelings are internal states within your child's mind, such as fear, love, joy, excitement, sadness, and anger. He cannot control his feelings. They come into his mind unbidden. He cannot will them away. But actions are quite different. Your child can control his actions (or, if he is very young, a year old perhaps, be in the process of *learning* to control his actions). Your child cannot help feeling angry at his brother, but he can keep himself from hitting or punching him. Because of the enormous differences between feelings and actions, parents need to handle the two differently.

Sometimes, when lecturing around the country, I am asked for what amounts to a "list" of actions a parent can allow a child. Such a list is an impossibility, because certain actions that Parent A would be comfortable with would be unacceptable to Parent B. This is quite all right. Whatever list of actions is acceptable to a parent, that he can defend logically and reasonably to his children, makes sense. There is no *one* "correct" list of acceptable or unacceptable actions that will fit everyone.

However, when we come to the area of feelings, I can be more specific and definite. I believe that parents should allow their children to express *all* their feelings—positive and nega-

56

tive—through the medium of words. Unfortunately very few parents do allow their children to express their feelings in words. Particularly their negative feelings. The reason is that *they* were not allowed to express their feelings when they were children. I can recall vividly having my mouth washed out with soap for expressing a few negative feelings toward my mother.

Nevertheless; children do have positive and negative feelings, and parents must find ways to allow their children to handle these feelings. What are our choices?

1. We can teach our children to keep all their feelings bottled up and express none of them. This will result in a very "mechanical" type of child, one who is more like a windup doll than a spontaneous, outgoing person.

2. We can allow our children to express all their positive feelings but none of their negative feelings. The child is allowed to say things such as: "I love you, Mommy," but not: "I'm mad at you, Mommy." This teaches the child to repress all negative feelings, with bad consequences for her mental health.

3. We can permit our children to express all their positive feelings and some of their negative feelings, provided they can do so in a "nice" way. Whenever a mother and father seriously propose this solution, I ask them if they have ever had a quarrel in a "nice" way! (Or have their quarrels involved heated negative emotions, like those of all other husbands and wives?)

4. We can encourage our children to express all of their feelings, negative and positive alike. This is the position I advocate (although it was certainly not the way I was raised) and I will tell you why.

First, when children are allowed to express their feelings, particularly their negative feelings, it offers them a safety valve, like the safety valve on a boiler, which prevents it from exploding. Allowing the child to release his feelings prevents him from exploding also. I think of the San Diego high school student planning to enter the ministry who shot and killed both his parents. The neighbors were shocked, not only because of the tragic nature of what had happened but because he was known as such a "good boy" and a "model child." I did not know the young man or his family personally, but I strongly suspect that he was brought up not to express any negative feelings. He had no safety valve for his angry feelings, and they finally erupted in the tragic murder of his parents.

Second, if a child is systematically taught to keep negative feelings bottled up, he cannot get them out of his system periodically and make room for positive feelings to come in.

Third, a child, particularly a young one, cannot discriminate and hold back *only* negative feelings without pushing down positive feelings as well. This reminds me of an experience with an eight-year-old child in the playroom of my office. The walls of the playroom are of Celotex covered with vinyl so they can be washed easily. In order to encourage shy and withdrawn children to express themselves, I suggest that they paint and write their names on the walls. It is clear that this is something they can do in my playroom, which I call the Free Room, but should not do at home.

This inhibited, awkward, and self-conscious eight-year-old entered the playroom on his first visit and looked around the room guardedly. Then he spoke: "Dr. Dodson, this is the messiest room I've ever seen in my life!"

"What bothers you about it, Franklin?"

"All of those scribblings and drawings on the walls are terrible! Why do you let children do things like that?"

"Because it's fun and they like to."

"Dr. Dodson, you shouldn't let them do things like that. That's why children grow up to be juvenile delinquents!"

This was a sad encounter for me. It was obvious that although the voice that pronounced the words belonged to the child, the sentiments expressed were strictly those of his parents. I noticed too that he spoke of "children" as if he were not a child himself but a miniature grown-up! His stilted, artificial, and nonspontaneous way of expressing himself was a good example of a child who has been taught to keep his feelings bottled up.

Fourth, if a child is not allowed to express his negative feelings in words, they will come out in some form of antisocial action. Let me repeat a story from my earlier book *How to Father* that illustrates perfectly what I'm talking about.

> One Saturday afternoon I came home and went into the bathroom to wash my hands. I noticed the usual vase with flowers in it on the bathroom sink, but this time the vase had a strange yellowish liquid in it. I bent down to sniff it and my suspicions were confirmed; it was not *water!* I be-

*gan to think who might have done it. I immediately elim-
inated my wife and teenage daughter as suspects. I eliminated one-year-old Rusty as a suspect because his aim
wasn't that good. That left only six-year-old Randy. I
hunted him up and confronted him with the evidence.
Randy," I said, "what made you pee in the vase?" "I
dunno," he said, in typical six-year-old fashion.*

*"You must have been mad about something to do that.
What were you mad about?"*

*He finally admitted that he had been mad because his
mother wouldn't let him go to the movies that afternoon.
That's why he did the dastardly deed. So I said, "Randy,
you know you are allowed to tell Mother and Daddy when
you are angry at us. So the next time you are mad at one
of us, tell us you're mad, but don't pee in the vase!"*

This simple incident illustrates the point beautifully. When
a child can express his angry feelings in words, they are over
and done with and out of his system. When a child cannot
express his angry feelings in words he will most likely engage
in some sneaky, antisocial behavior as a substitute for expressing the feelings forthrightly. I can remember one time
when I was seven or eight and very angry at the boy next
door. I lugged his family's garbage can around to the front
porch and dumped it there. (Needless to say, they figured out
who did it, and I had to clean up the garbage!)

Fifth, children who are not allowed to express their negative feelings usually grow up to be adults who cannot express
their negative feelings either. And you would be amazed at
how much time therapists spend in helping patients to dig up
repressed negative feelings and express them. When they can
vent the repressed angry or sexual feelings that cause anxiety
attacks, the anxiety attacks disappear. When they can exor-
cise the repressed angry feelings behind depressions, the depressions fade away. And so on. If you want to keep your
child out of a therapist's office when he is an adult, give him
the precious freedom to express *all* of his feelings as a child.

I have tried to convince you that freedom to express his
feelings is one of the greatest gifts you can give your child.
But there may be some practical problems.

First, you may worry that he will get into trouble by telling
off his schoolteacher, or Sunday school teacher, or Boy Scout
leader, or some other person. Have no fear. Children can

make distinctions very clearly as to where it is safe to express feelings and where it is not.

My three kids have been allowed unlimited freedom of expression at home, yet none of them ever got in trouble for expressing negative feelings anywhere else. For example, in fifth grade, Randy had a music teacher he detested. At home, we often heard about his angry feelings toward the music teacher. Yet not once did he tell the teacher how he felt. If one of my children had gotten in trouble by sounding off at a schoolteacher, I simply would have advised: "Son, at home you can tell us your feelings freely, but it's not wise to do that at school."

Second, if a child is not allowed to express his feelings to his parents, it will be hard for him as an adult to reverse himself and allow his children to express their feelings freely. This has certainly been true for me. Sometimes when I am allowing one of my children to tell me off, a little voice inside my head is saying: "Don't you dare speak that way to me—I'm your father!" This, of course, is not the voice of my scientific training, but the voice of my own father from the past. There is no magical solution to this problem except to keep working away at outgrowing your own childhood hang-ups. The technique of negative thinking, as described in chapter 15, may be helpful in enabling you to get over these hang-ups.

When I am lecturing to a group about the advisability of allowing children to express feelings freely, almost invariably someone will ask: "But what about respect for parents?" Let's define what we mean by *respect*. What many people mean by respect is that when you are very angry with a parent, instead of expressing your feelings out loud you say them silently to yourself. If that is respect, then I don't see that it does anybody any good. My understanding of respect is this: A child respects a parent when she is aware that the parent knows a lot more about life than she does and that the parent is a person of integrity to whom she can look for guidance. I think the question of whether a child is allowed to express angry feelings toward a parent has nothing to do with respect.

Once a parent has made the decision to allow a child to express her feelings, how does he handle them? He may use the discipline method that I call the *feedback technique*. Here is how it works.

Children very desperately want us to understand how they feel. Unfortunately, most children do not get this understanding from their parents. Not that the parents are cruel or unfeeling. Mostly they are not able to let their children know they understand how they feel because nobody taught them how to convey this kind of understanding. Also, many parents have not learned the importance of listening to their children and empathizing with them. The feedback technique can help parents overcome these barriers to parent-child understanding.

The essence of the feedback technique is simple. You are doing three things whenever your child expresses her feelings:

1. Listening carefully to what your child is saying
2. Formulating in your mind what your child is expressing
3. Feeding back to her in your own words the feelings she has just expressed to you

When a parent uses this technique, the child will really know the parent understands, because the child will hear her own feelings coming back to her from the parent. I want to give several examples of situations, first showing how the average parent would handle the situation, and then showing how a parent would do it using feedback.

A fifth-grade girl is very scared about a math test she is going to have in school the next day, and she approaches her mother one evening to talk about it.

Here is the way the average parent would handle the situation:

HELEN: Mom, can I talk over something with you? We've got a math test tomorrow and I'm just scared to death I'm going to flunk it.

MOTHER: Now, Helen, that's ridiculous to think that way. You've had scads of math tests this year and you haven't flunked any of them yet, have you?

HELEN: No.

MOTHER: As a matter of fact, the lowest grade you've gotten on any of them has been a B minus, isn't that true?

HELEN: Yes, but . . .

MOTHER: No buts! All that's wrong with you is a bad case of what I call the Wim Wams! I used to get them myself every once in a while when I was your age, when I thought all kinds of bad things were going to happen to me. And the cure for the Wim Wams is good old positive thinking. Just think to yourself: I know I'm going to do well on this test because I've never done badly on a math test yet. And picture yourself sailing through the test with flying colors. You just work hard at some positive thinking and some hard study and you'll do fine on the exam.

HELEN: Well, if you say so. I'll try it.

It is apparent that the mother has made no attempt to tune in on Helen's feelings, find out why she feels as she does, and communicate to Helen a deep and genuine understanding of her feelings. Instead, she simply dishes out superficial advice and reassurance and thinks she has been of help. She has not. Helen probably feels, deep inside: "This math test is different from the others and Mother just doesn't understand how I feel about it at all."

Now, let's try the feedback technique:

HELEN: Mother, can I talk over something with you? We've got a math test tomorrow and I'm just scared to death I'm going to flunk it.

MOTHER: Can you tell me more why you're so afraid you're going to flunk this test?

HELEN: Well, I know I've gotten pretty good grades on my math tests before, but this one is different. It's what they call modern math and we're supposed to do fractions in ways I've never done before, and I'm scared of it.

MOTHER: This test scares you because it's different from anything you've had before. It's modern math and you have to do fractions in completely new ways, and its frightening.

HELEN: It sure is! I read some of these paragraphs three or four times that tell how to do it and I still don't understand it.

MOTHER: It's awfully scary when you read how to do it a couple of times and still don't get it.

HELEN: It sure is! Could you help me with the really tough parts? If I could understand the principles of how to do it, I think I would be all right.

MOTHER: The thing that really gets you up tight is not being able to understand the principles; is that right?

HELEN: That's it.

MOTHER: Yes, I'll be glad to help you. I didn't have modern math when I was in school at your age, so I may have some trouble understanding the principles at first too. But between the two of us I think we can figure it out.

HELEN: Oh thanks, Mom, you really do understand how I feel!

Note in this example of the feedback technique that the mother does not jump in with superficial reassurance or advice. She takes Helen's feelings of fear seriously, does not belittle them, and by feeding them back to her lets her know that she genuinely understands how she feels. By doing this, she is able to uncover the reason this particular test is scaring Helen: the unfamiliar modern math and her difficulty in understanding the principles involved. Once she uncovers this, she is able to respond to Helen's request for help in understanding these new and difficult principles.

Here is another situation, first as the average parent would handle it:

JEFF [*age five*]: Dad, Bryan [*age three*] is getting into my toys again and messing everything up.

DAD: Well, tell him to stop doing it.

JEFF: I tell him to stop it and he doesn't. Why do I have to have a brother anyway? I just hate him.

DAD: Jeff, that's no way to talk about your brother. He's your brother and the two of you should be loving brothers.

JEFF: That's easy for you to say, Dad, because he doesn't get into your stuff and mess it up. It's *my* stuff he messes up. I'd like to flush him down the toilet so he'd never come back!

DAD: That's just about enough of that! One more word like that about your brother and you're going to be in big trouble with me!

JEFF: But that isn't all he does! Messing up my toys is bad enough, but besides that he's always teasing me. He's always saying "ninga, ninga, ninga" to me.

DAD: Well, he's only three years old. What's so terrible about saying some funny words to you?

JEFF: They're not funny to me! And how would you like it if somebody kept saying the same dumb words to you over and over again?

DAD: Well, remember he's only three and doesn't know any better.

JEFF: He just keeps doing it. Dad, would you spank him so he'll stop getting into my toys and teasing me?

DAD: I certainly will not! But I might give *you* a good wallop, young man, if you don't drop the subject. Now, I'm trying to read my magazine. Why don't you go outside and play?

Jeff's father has made no real effort to understand Jeff's feelings and to communicate that understanding to the boy. Instead, the father's whole attitude seems to be: "I don't want to be bothered with your feelings, Jeff. Now go on outside and play and get along with Bryan the best you can."

Here is the same situation, using the feedback technique:

JEFF: Dad, Bryan is getting into my toys again and messing everything up.

DAD: That must really bug you when Bryan gets into your stuff.

JEFF: That's putting it mildly! It really makes me mad! He's got no right to get into my toys. He's got his own toys to play with and he should leave my toys alone.

DAD: So it just makes you furious when he gets into your toys.

JEFF: It sure does. Sometimes I wish I didn't even have a brother. I just hate him.

DAD: Sometimes you hate him so much you wish you didn't even have a brother.

JEFF: I sure do! I wish I could flush him down the toilet so he'd never come back!

DAD: Sometimes you actually hate him so much you wish you could flush him down the toilet and get rid of him permanently!

JEFF: Right! But there's more to it than that. Besides messing up my toys, he's always teasing me.

DAD: Tell me more about it. How does he tease you?

JEFF: Well, he follows me around and he's always saying "ninga, ninga, ninga" to me.

DAD: What does "ninga, ninga, ninga" mean?

JEFF: It doesn't mean anything. It's just some dumb old words he made up. But it sure gets on my nerves when he keeps saying them over and over.

DAD: So when he says those words it really bugs you.

JEFF: It sure does! Dad, could you spank him so he'll stop getting into my toys and teasing me?

DAD: I hear what you're saying, Jeff. You're so mad at

Bryan for getting into your toys and teasing you that you want me to spank him for it. I understand how mad you feel, but I have to handle the situation in my own way. I know you'd like very much to have me spank him but I'm not going to. But I will do some other things to stop him from getting into your toys and teasing you. I'll give him a Time Out, and then when he's on a Time Out he can't be getting into your toys or teasing you.

Note the totally different atmosphere of this parent-child interaction. The father makes no attempt to talk Jeff out of his feelings. He accepts the fact that Jeff is angry and through the feedback technique conveys *his understanding* of Jeff's feelings back to Jeff.

When Jeff makes the demand that his father spank Bryan, notice how the father makes a distinction between feelings and actions. Jeff would like it very much if his father would spank Bryan. His father conveys to Jeff that he knows how angry and resentful he feels, but that he, the father, is not going to handle the situation by spanking but by other means. But throughout this parent-child interaction it is clear that the father believes Jeff has a right to be as angry as he wishes toward his brother and that he fully understands Jeff's anger.

Another situation, this one involving *irrational* feelings, first as the average parent would handle it:

TIMMY [*age four*]: Daddy, I don't want to go to bed tonight. I'm afraid of the dark.

DAD: Here we go again! A drink of water, a trip to the bathroom, anything to get you out of going to bed. So tonight it's going to be fear of the dark!

TIMMY: But, Daddy, I'm not making it up! It really is scary in the dark!

DAD: Timmy, you've got a night light in your room, so how can you be scared of the dark?

TIMMY: Well, the night light doesn't make it very light, you know. It's still mostly dark in the room. And it's scary.

DAD: Oh, that's ridiculous! Now come on and go to bed.

TIMMY [*beginning to cry*]: But I'm scared!

DAD: There's absolutely nothing to be scared of!

TIMMY: There is too. A burglar could come in.

DAD: No burglar is going to come in.

TIMMY: How do you know? Didn't Mother read the story

in the paper about the burglar that came into the house on Deep Valley Road?

DAD: Yes.

TIMMY: Well, then, how do you know a burglar couldn't come into our house too?

DAD: No burglar is going to come into our house.

TIMMY: But I'm scared he will, and maybe if a burglar |came into our house he'd kill me.

DAD [turning on the overhead light in the room]: There. It's all lighted up in the room now. There's no more darkness in the room so you're all safe. Now you can go to sleep.

TIMMY: But just because it's light in the room, that doesn't mean a burglar can't come in. He could come in right through that window there! Daddy, I'm scared!

DAD [who at this point has had it, having done everything he can possibly think of to deal with TIMMY's irrational fears of the dark and of burglars]: Now, that's enough. I'm sick and tired of hearing about the dark and burglars. They're just excuses so you can stay up later instead of going to bed like you should. So you stay in that bed, young man, and stop your crying. And if I hear anything more about the dark or burglars, I'll come back here and really give you something to cry about! [DAD stomps off to the living room.]

Notice how the father paid absolutely no attention to the boy's fearful feelings. When children exhibit irrational feelings, parents have a tendency to ignore them precisely because they are irrational. Certainly Timmy must have felt very alone, since his father made no attempt to understand his fearful feelings or to deal with them. Instead the father tried to use logical devices to get the child over his irrational feelings, none of which worked. The end result of using logic to try to cope with irrational feelings is that the father felt frustrated and angry at the child.

Now let's see how the same situation could be handled using the feedback technique:

TIMMY: Daddy, I don't want to go to bed tonight. I'm afraid of the dark.

DAD: You're so afraid of the dark you don't want to go to bed tonight, huh? Sit down on Daddy's lap and tell me all about it.

TIMMY: Well, the dark scares me, just scares me awful. I'm afraid all kinds of bad things might jump out and get me.

DAD: The dark is scary to you because you don't know what might be hiding in the dark. You're afraid all sorts of bad things might be hiding in the dark and could jump out and get you.

TIMMY: That's right. And there might be burglars too, in the dark.

DAD: You're afraid that there might be burglars in the dark and they would jump out and get you.

TIMMY: You bet, and crocodiles too. [TIMMY *continues to to list fearsome things, such as crocodiles, monsters, snakes, enormous rats, etc., that might be hiding in the dark and might come out to get him. Each time, his father feeds back the fear Timmy has of that specific animal or person.*]

DAD: I can understand how afraid you are of all of these things you've told me about, Timmy, and how you're afraid they could be hiding in the dark and jump out and get you. But you've got your night light, so it's not really dark in your room.

TIMMY: Yes, but the night light doesn't make it very light, you know. It's still mostly dark in the room, and that's what makes it scary.

DAD: I see. The night light still leaves lots of dark in the room, and that makes you feel scared.

TIMMY: That's right.

DAD: Well, how about this [*turning on the overhead light*]. Now it's all lighted up and there's no more dark. How about that?

TIMMY: Well . . . it is all lighted up, and it's not dark anymore, but there could still be a burglar outside the window and he could come in and get me!

DAD: Even though it's not dark in the room anymore, it still makes you feel scared when you think that a burglar could come in the window and get you.

TIMMY: It sure does! Or a monster could come in through the window and get me.

[DAD *once again feeds back the fears Timmy feels that a monster, a crocodile, a snake, etc., could come through the window and get him. Dad takes all of these fears quite seriously and communicates his understanding of* TIMMY's *fears, although, of course, they are quite irrational. Finally,* TIMMY *seems to have "wound down" and gotten the fears out of his system, in response to his father's sympathetic understanding.*]

TIMMY: Daddy, I guess maybe those things aren't so scary after all. I think I can go to sleep now. Will you tuck me in?

DAD: After we talk about them awhile they don't seem quite so scary, huh? Sure, I'll tuck you in. [DAD *kisses* TIMMY *goodnight.*]

Most parents are completely at a loss as to what to do when their child has irrational fears. They try to talk the child out of the irrational fear by reason and logic, get absolutely nowhere, and usually end up feeling infuriated at the child. But once they learn the feedback technique they have a method at their fingertips for dealing with any irrational fears their child may express. This does not mean that the irrational fear will always vanish. Even after the parent uses the feedback technique the fear may still persist, but the child will be less afraid, because he now feels he has a parental ally against his fear, and therefore he can cope with it better.

The feedback technique is simplicity itself to understand, but hard to put into practice at first, because it runs counter to the way we have been responding to other people for years.

With the feedback technique you show that you understand how your child feels by putting her feelings into your own words and feeding them back.

When using the feedback technique you will typically begin sentences with: "You feel" or, "You feel scared" or, "You feel angry" or, "I'm hearing you say . . ." With the feedback technique you do not ask your child *why* she feels a certain way; you simply accept the fact that she does. You do not bring in your own feelings; you stay with hers. You speak only in response to her; that is, when she expresses a feeling, you feed it back. When she is silent and is not expressing a feeling, you are silent.

When working with parents to teach them the feedback technique, I have a sneaky method I use with fathers. Frankly, many fathers tend to think this technique is for the birds, although they are too polite to say so. I ask them if they have any difficult people they have to deal with at work: customers, colleagues, bosses, etc. If they do (and many do), I try to convince them to use the feedback technique in dealing with these difficult people. I may even say: "Well, you've just admitted that nothing else you've tried has worked with Mr. Gargoyle; why not try the feedback technique! What have you got to lose!" The amazing thing is that if the father is able to use the feedback technique successfully at work, he will really be sold on using it at home with his children.

Here are some examples of the feedback technique with adults. I first learned it many years ago from Dr. Volney Faw, of Lewis and Clark College, who had studied under Dr. Carl Rogers, the originator of the technique. Dr. Faw not only taught us about the technique; he lived it. I will never forget one time when Dr. Faw had just given back a midterm exam, and a group of us were standing around after class waiting to see him. One student burst out: "Dr. Faw, you gypped me!" Think back to your own days as a student and imagine what a typical professor would answer to a comment like that! But Dr. Faw answered: "Tell me why you feel I gypped you."

"I got an eighty-eight on that exam and you gave me a B. I feel that's unfair; I deserve an A."

"You feel very deeply that I gypped you by giving you a B instead of an A, when you got an eighty-eight on the exam."

"You bet I do. I'm a premed student. I need to get the best possible grades I can in all of my courses so I can get into the best medical school, and that grade is unfair!"

"You want to get the best possible grades in all your courses so you can get into a really good medical school, and you feel my grade is just plain unfair."

Dr. Faw went on reflecting the student's feelings in that fashion for about five minutes, and then he said: "Well, I had to draw the line somewhere, and I drew it at ninety. Ninety to a hundred got an A, and eighty to ninety got a B."

At this point the student grudgingly said: "Well—all right!"

Now I am sure the student would not have responded this way if Dr. Faw had not first used the feedback technique to show the student he truly understood how he felt.

Here is another example from the world of adults. I remember standing in line in a bank during the Christmas holidays. In the back of the bank the assistant manager was trying patiently to explain to a woman why Crocker Bank could not renew her loan. The more logically and patiently he explained, the madder she got and the more decibels her voice rose. I thought to myself: "Isnt't it a shame they don't teach the feedback technique to these bankers as well as banking practice!" For had he used the feedback technique, he would have said something like this: "You're just furious with Crocker Bank because we won't extend this note."

Had the assistant manager used the feedback technique for ten or fifteen minutes he might have been able to convince the woman he truly understood how she felt. And only then would she possibly have listened to a rational explanation of why the bank would not renew the note.

You see how it works? People cannot listen to rational explanations *until they feel that the other person truly understands how they feel.* This is true for both children and adults.

Now for an example from the world of children. On a weekend camping trip, when Randy was nine and Rusty was three, Randy was really being obnoxious with Rusty, picking at him and teasing him at every opportunity. Finally I decided some action was called for, and suggested Randy take a walk with me down the canyon. I said: "Randy, you are really being mean to Rusty on this trip. What's bothering you?" Well, finally it came out. "You and Mom love Rusty more than you love me." Of course this would have been a perfect opportunity to use reason and logic and say: "That's not true, Randy. We love both of you equally." That kind of answer would have done absolutely nothing to help Randy's feelings of jealousy and antagonism. So instead I used the feedback technique.

"You feel like Rusty always gets the good side of the stick and you always get the lousy side."

"That's right. You and Mom are always doing good things for him and all you do is criticize me."

"You feel he gets good treatment from us, and you get nothing but criticism."

And so it went. I spent about twenty minutes doing nothing but reflecting his feelings so that he could get all of the envy and jealousy out of his system. When he had wound down, I put my arm around his shoulder and said, "Okay, Randy, let's go on back with the others now."

I won't pretend he was an angel the rest of that weekend, but his behavior toward Rusty was vastly improved. Why? Because he had vented his negative feelings and had them understood and accepted.

Now for a few cautions about this technique. Many parents, when I am first teaching them this technique, say: "I feel so silly doing this. I sound like an echo chamber." Well, naturally you feel silly or awkward or ill at ease when you are learning a new skill. When you were first learning tennis or golf or sailing or bridge did you feel confident and at ease at the beginning? So don't worry. As you become more experienced, you will feel more at ease and the awkwardness will fade away.

The ideal time to begin the feedback technique is when the child is three. By the time your child is ten he has been accustomed to it for many years, and you are an old pro with it.

Be sure you don't repeat the exact words your child has used, otherwise you *will* sound like an echo chamber. Paraphrase your child's feelings in your own words.

Many times parents will come back to me after having tried the feedback technique and say: "It isn't working—Jenny is still scared," or angry or whatnot. This is a misunderstanding of the technique. If you truly feed back your child's feelings, the technique will work *every time*. This doesn't mean he will necessarily make some *outward response* every time. But every time you feed back his feelings he will know that Mom or Dad really understands. And that is always a good thing. Don't expect a *dramatic* change to take place in the child as a result of the feedback technique. Sometimes it will and sometimes it won't.

If I were allowed to teach only one discipline technique to parents, I think I would choose feedback. It is the most powerful way I know for keeping lines of communication between parent and child open, letting a child know that you understand how he feels, giving him the knowledge that his feelings are respected and valued, and offering him a safe outlet for all his negative feelings. In addition, it helps to promote a feeling of *mutual* respect between you and your child.

And it is also a prerequisite for the discipline technique of our next chapter: *the mutual problem-solving technique.*

11

THE MUTUAL PROBLEM-SOLVING TECHNIQUE

From time to time, every family has conflicts between what a parent wants and what a child wants. Many of these can be resolved by the discipline techniques I have already discussed. Others do not yield so readily to these techniques, particularly as the children grow older.

As I previously mentioned, one of the problems with using punishment as a method of discipline is that it simply isn't effective when a child reaches adolescence. The child has lost much of his fear of punishment, and his attitude often is: "Go ahead! Punish me and see if I care!"

Frantic parents often consult me (when a child is eleven, twelve, or older) and say: "I don't know what to do with my child! She used to be such a sweet, obedient little girl, and now I can't control her anymore. She does things I don't approve of and I can't figure out how to stop her!"

Before presenting the mutual problem-solving technique as an answer to this problem, let's see what most parents do when there is a conflict. Here is a typical example: Bill, age fourteen, wears his hair long, in keeping with his crowd's style. Not superlong and down to his shoulders, but much longer than his father approves. There has been conflict between them for several years about hair length, and here is how the father handles the problem:

FATHER: Okay, Bill I know you don't agree, but it's time for a haircut. And I mean a haircut that looks decent, not like a shaggy dog.

BILL: Aw, Dad, you're always giving me a hard time about my hair. Do I complain about your potbelly? Why don't you let me have my hair the way I want it?

FATHER: My potbelly has nothing to do with the question. You look like some stupid hippie instead of like a decent human being who takes some pride in his appearance.

BILL: But, Dad, all the other guys wear their hair long; why can't I?

FATHER: I don't care how many kids wear their hair long. No son of mine is going to look like a circus freak. Now go and get your hair cut!

BILL: What would you do if I told you I was going to leave it just the way it is?

FATHER: I'll tell you exactly what I'll do. You're very fond of playing the stereo with the earphones on—a stereo paid for out of my hard-earned money, incidentally. So until you get your hair cut, it's no more stereo playing for you, young man!

BILL: All right! If that's the way you're going to be, I'll go down and get my hair cut! [BILL *flounces out angrily and slams the door.*]

* * *

What is going on in this little scenario? Bill and his father are locked in a power struggle over the issue of a haircut. The outcome of this family drama is that *parent power wins and child power loses.*

Now let's examine what happens when parent power wins and child power loses. No one likes to be forced to do anything against his will. It is clear that the relationship between Bill and his father has deteriorated. Bill is angry and would like the chance to get back at his father in some way. For example, if a friend urges Bill to try some drugs next week, Bill may try them as an unconscious way of hitting back at his father. Bill's father has "won" the power struggle, but he may have paid a very high price and not even be aware of it. Bill's father may only have seen the outcome as: "Well, I'm glad

Bill finally had sense enough to go get his hair cut." And suppose Bill had been sixteen instead of fourteen? Chances are his father would not have had his way so easily.

Furthermore, since the goal of all discipline is to develop self-discipline—to build a young person who can make his own decisions and discipline himself—how has the father's power play contributed to this goal? It has not. By the threat of forbidding the use of the stereo, Bill's father *forced* him to get a haircut. This action, like all parental power, has done absolutely nothing to promote Bill's inner growth and psychological maturity. It is like a parent saying to a five-year-old: "Now say 'thank you' to Mrs. Farson." The child may say mechanically: "Thank you, Mrs. Farson," but just parroting what you have told him does not enable him to develop true inner courtesy. It's what he learns from you about people that counts, not the rituals you've taught him.

This demonstrates what happens when parent power wins and child power loses. Now let's look at the reverse situation: *when child power wins and parent power loses.* This concerns Arnold, age sixteen, and the family car (in this family there is only one car):

ARNOLD: Dad, the kids are having a big party this Saturday night, and I need the family car to take Karen. Is that okay with you?

FATHER: Son, I'm terribly sorry, but Mother and I are going to a party of our own Saturday night with the Wests.

ARNOLD: But, Dad, I really need the car that night!

FATHER: I'm sorry, son, but adults have certain priorities.

ARNOLD: There you go again—adults have priorities! Don't children have any rights in this family at all? It's supposed to be a *family* car, isn't it? Well, I'm part of the family too, you know! You have no objection to me washing it. In fact, that's one of my regular chores around here. You never wash the car. But at a time when I really need it, you don't take my needs into consideration at all! Taking Karen to the party on the bus is going to be a real bummer.

FATHER: It's simply not true that I don't take your needs into consideration. I wish my father had done half the things for me that I do for you!

ARNOLD: Well, if you really want to do something that's terribly important to me, why don't you let me have the car? Couldn't the Wests take you and Mom to your party?

FATHER: [reluctantly]: Yes, I guess they could.

ARNOLD: Well, then, that's the perfect solution! The Wests can take you and Mom to your party and I'll have the car to take Karen to ours.

FATHER: Oh, I give up. Have it your own way! It's not worth arguing with you. It seems to me I spend most of my time giving in to what you want.

In this scenario, we have a typical example of what happens when parent power loses and child power wins. First of all, Arnold's father has done a good job teaching him that if he persists in whining, complaining, and wheedling he will get his way. Children raised in homes where their power typically wins and parent power typically loses are usually selfish, self-centered, and demanding. Their unconscious motto is "The world is my oyster: give it to me!" Such children are masters at playing on the guilt feelings of their parents to get their way. At their worst, when they become adolescents, they are uncontrolled and unmanageable. One teenager I know, when his father told him to stay home on a school night and locked the front door, simply jumped out the front window, crashing through the glass, and went off to see his friends.

And what are the effects on the parents when parent power consistently loses and child power consistently wins? The parents are furious at the child for triumphing over them. And they hate themselves for not being able to stand up to their child and his demands. They feel ashamed for not being able to assert themselves.

Is there any escape from these two disastrous kinds of power struggles in parent-child relationships! Yes, there is: the mutual problem-solving technique. In this technique, both sides win and nobody loses. Here is how it works:

First, the conflict between child and parent must be clearly identified. The child wants one thing and the parents want something else. That is the problem to be solved.

Second, the problem may involve one parent and one child, or two parents and one child, or two parents and two children, or whatever. At any rate, all those involved agree to try to find a solution.

Third, those involved appoint someone as notetaker. His job is simply to jot down whatever ideas come forth as possible solutions to the problem.

Fourth, those involved engage in brainstorming. This term and technique were invented by Dr. Alex Osborn, who first applied it to generating ideas to solve problems in business. He pointed out that when three or four people sit down to solve a problem, someone will come up with an idea, and someone else will say: "No, that won't work, because . . . ," and this sequence of idea and rebuttal will take place a number of times. The net effect is to inhibit people from coming up with new ideas.

So the first rule of brainstorming is that nobody is allowed to criticize anybody else's ideas. Everybody is encouraged to come up with ideas no matter how far out. There are no limits on the ideas that may be generated. Even though an idea may be extremely impractical, it may stimulate someone else in the group to come up with a different idea that will work.

Explain how brainstorming works to your family. Then each member suggests as many ideas as he can and the notetaker writes them all down and numbers them. There is no special time limit on this, but you probably shouldn't go over twenty minutes or under five minutes.

Once all the ideas are written down, go over them, one by one, to try to find one or more solutions to the problem. The solution must be one that everybody can agree to. If even one person involved cannot accept the idea, it is discarded. There should be no voting, because with voting someone wins and someone loses.

We want unanimous agreement. Then everybody wins and nobody loses. Everybody will be much more highly motivated to see that the decision is carried out than if he had no part in making the decision.

This method of settling disputes is not new. Labor and management have been using it for years, when they sit down at the conciliation table. Good marriages work this way. Only sick marriages operate by the husband's always imposing his power on the wife or she imposing her power on him.

Mutual problem-solving is only new *when applied to parent-child relationships,* because very few parents sit down with their children to solve conflicts in this manner.

Let me give you an example.

Karen was fourteen, just on the verge of fifteen. She was driving her parents up the wall. Here are some of their complaints: "She lies all the time. She cuts school. She's stubborn and self-willed; everything has to be her way. She pals around with the worst element in school. She defies authority: us, her teachers, everybody. She wants to stay out till all hours. She wants to date a man who's twenty-three."

After listening to the parents' concerns, I instructed them in the mutual problem-solving technique. I suggested that the father take the lead in using it. We arranged for a meeting with mother, father, Karen, and me. I stayed in the background because I wanted the father and mother to learn through actual experience how to use the technique.

First the father went around the group and jotted down the problems and complaints of each person. For instance, Karen began by saying that she had to be in by 10:30 on Friday and Saturday nights and that was ridiculous because none of her friends had to be in that early. Her father said that he and her mother were very concerned about her truancy from school. Acting as notetaker, the father wrote down the various problems.

Then the three of them took about ten minutes to brainstorm with ideas that could solve these problems. They came up with about twenty-five ideas. I contributed a few ideas too, of a silly nature, because I wanted to inject a little humor into a rather heavy, emotion-laden scene. For instance, one of my ideas was "Karen can study belly dancing with records, and that will give her something constructive to do at home instead of wanting to go out all the time."

Then they started going over the ideas. Some were ruled out very quickly by one person or another. Other ideas were not rejected but needed to be negotiated. For example, Karen said, "Okay, I'll tell you what I'll do. I'll stop ditching school if you will give me the right to stay out later on weekends." Karen's mother agreed that at Karen's age 10:30 was too early for her to have to come home Friday and Saturday nights. Karen's father was reluctant but went along with it because he wanted to see Karen stop ditching school. Karen's mother proposed 12:00, Karen countered with 12:30, and they compromised at 12:15. Finally Karen's father wrote down the proposed solution: "Karen will stop ditching school, and we will let her stay out till twelve fifteen on Friday and Saturday nights."

Hours of going and coming seemed to be very important to Karen. She wanted the right to stay at a friend's house until 10:00 on school nights. There was some heated discussion about this because the parents objected to Karen's staying out *every* school night until 10:00. Karen said that wasn't the case. She might in reality stay out only two nights a week, but she wanted the *right* to more independence. She resented having to ask "like a little girl" if she could go to Jennifer's house. After some discussion and negotiation, the following solution was unanimously agreed upon: Karen will do her homework before she goes out on a school night. She will say where she's going, and then she can stay out until 10:00.

The parents were concerned that Karen went around with boys they didn't know, and they were particularly concerned about the twenty-three-year-old. They wanted her to bring each boy into the house and introduce him. Karen objected to this furiously. "It's so old-fashioned and embarrassing. The boys will think you're giving them the FBI routine. And incidentally," Karen added, "you don't have to worry about Richard [the twenty-three-year-old] because he's moving to Oregon at the end of next month." Finally, after much talking and negotiation, the following solution was agreed upon: Karen is to bring a new boy into the front hallway and introduce him to her parents. In addition Karen agrees that she will not date anyone older than eighteen.

Hammering out those three agreements took two hours. Would you say the time was well spent? You bet it was, because it cleared up many of the points of difficulty between Karen and her parents. Furthermore, it introduced the whole family to the mutual problem-solving technique, so that they can use it to solve future difficulties.

Next is an example of the mutual problem-solving technique with younger children—in this case, my own.

Randy was eight and Rusty was three when this incident took place. We often went to drive-in movies as a family, but at this particular time some flak had developed. Rusty would ask questions about what was happening in the movie. As soon as Rusty asked a question Randy would shout: "RUSTY, YOU'RE ALWAYS ASKING QUESTIONS AND INTERRUPTING AND MAKING NOISE. HOW DO YOU EXPECT THE REST OF US TO HEAR ANYTHING WHEN YOU'RE TALKING ALL THE TIME?" Randy's outburst was loud and disrupting, and, needless to say, the movie dialogue could no longer be heard at all. After this had gone on for about a month I decided something must be done. I called Randy and Rusty together and said, "Something happens every time we go to a drive-in movie that bothers Mother and me a great deal. Rusty asks a lot of questions in the movie, and as soon as he does, Randy yells at him. The result is that Mother and I have a great deal of trouble hearing and enjoying the movie. Now we need to solve this problem so that all of us are happy about the solution."

Then I explained the way the mutual problem-solving technique works and decided to be notetaker for their brainstorming. Randy immediately came up with a creative idea: "We can get a baby-sitter for Rusty and leave him home." Not to be outdone, Rusty produced his unique solution: "We can get a baby-sitter for Randy and leave him home so he won't be able to yell and bother everybody." The ideas suggested at that first session, which lasted about fifteen minutes, were of the same general caliber. None, of course, were agreed upon by all. At the end of the time, I said, "Well, I guess we aren't able to come up with any ideas which will solve the problem tonight, so we'll try again tomorrow."

In some way that first night served as an emotional catharsis for each of the boys. The second night they began to take it seriously and produce better ideas. Finally we came up with two ideas on which all of us were able to agree. First, Rusty was to try to save his questions and ask them after the movie was over. And second, Randy was to try hard not to make any comments if Rusty forgot and asked a question. You may be thinking, "Well, those are the obvious ways to solve the problem. Why go to all that trouble to come up with perfectly simple solutions like that?" The answer is: Because the boys themselves thought of them. Therefore they were more highly motivated to keep to the agreements than if I had forced the ideas upon them. Now it would be untrue if I claimed that both of those ideas were strictly adhered to at future movies. But things were considerably better. Rusty asked fewer questions and Randy stopped yelling so much.

A situation need not involve great dramatic conflict in order to benefit from mutual problem-solving. The technique is extremely effective for everyday, routine matters too. A father I know who always cooked the family breakfasts on Sundays decided that eggs would be more nutritious for the two children than the pancakes he usually fixed. Five-year-old Martin complained loudly about this decision and said he wanted "something good I can pour syrup on!" But Dad wanted them to have eggs. It took only a very brief mutual problem-solving session before ten-year-old Diane came up with the perfect answer: french toast!

The mutual problem-solving technique can be used any time after the age of five. In the years from five to ten, I recommend it be reserved for complex problems. But from eleven onward, this technique really comes into its own, particularly in the teenage years. Parents who only use "parent power wins, child power loses" or vice versa with their teenagers will be absolutely astonished at how many disagreements and conflicts can be solved by the use of this technique. In the words of the famous Hungarian philosopher Zsa Zsa Gabor: "If you haven't tried it, don't knock it."

This technique has many advantages for both parents and children.

First, it promotes a deeper relationship between the two, since everybody "wins" and nobody "loses."

Second, the child is motivated to carry out the solution, since he has participated in the problem-solving process. The solution has not been forced upon him unilaterally by his parents.

Third, the use of the problem-solving technique develops creative thinking skills in children. In addition, it gives them valuable social skills in learning how to negotiate and handle interpersonal relations. These skills learned at home can be applied at school and later in the world of work. The use of this technique is like both parents and child putting their heads together to solve a challenging puzzle.

Fourth, the use of this technique usually results in a reduction of hostility on the part of the child. Since he must agree on the solution, he is less likely to walk away angry, secretly resolving to sabotage the solution.

Finally, since it is a problem-solving process, the use of this technique often gets below the surface of the "presenting" problem to the "hidden" problems that may lie underneath. As the parents and child discuss the problem from their own points of view, it may become crystal clear which areas of concern are really bothering the child. Once those areas are dealt with, parents are often amazed how quickly negotiations can be worked out and unanimous agreements decided.

In summary, let me remind you that all of the discipline methods we have discussed so far can be used in the early years until approximately ages eleven and twelve. But from then on, the child is simply too old to use methods such as

Time Out, which worked fine when he was a youngster. He is well on his way to becoming an adolescent and then an adult. He should no longer be handled by methods that are appropriate only for a younger child. This is the time when the mutual problem-solving technique comes into its own. I think it is *the* discipline method (along with the family council, which I will discuss in the next chapter) for handling adolescent problems. Naturally it is easier to use if you introduced your children to it at earlier ages than if you suddenly spring it on them at adolescence.

One final word about this technique. If you have carefully tried it as outlined in this chapter, and it results only in dismal failure, then something is probably wrong with the way you are using it. If so, I suggest you consult a professional person—a skilled psychologist or psychiatrist—so that he can help you find out why this technique is not working for your family.

12

THE FAMILY COUNCIL

In a sense, the *family council* can be thought of as an extension of the problem-solving technique to include the whole family. Here is how it works.

Everyone in the family is a member. Even children too young to talk can be included, unless their presence proves to be too disruptive.

The council should meet regularly once a week, at a time when nothing else will be taking place to interfere with its meeting. Missed meetings destroy continuity and the feeling of cohesiveness that is built up over the course of time by the council meetings.

The council has a chairman and a secretary, who are rotated every week. The only limitation of the secretary is that he should be able to read and write, for he will need to keep minutes of the meeting and read the minutes of the last meeting.

The principle of freedom, not coercion, is used. No one is forced to attend a meeting of the family council, and any member may leave a meeting at any time.

How do you prevent any one person or persons from disrupting the council meeting? In a most unusual way! If someone is annoying and disrupts the meeting, anybody who is sufficiently annoyed can leave the meeting. Also, when a member disrupts a meeting, only the chairman can request that person to behave. If he does not behave, others in the meeting may decide to leave.

Open discussion is the order of the day in the meeting.

Anybody in the council may bring up anything he wishes and talk as long as he wishes until he feels he has had his say. If a council member continues to talk and talk and talk, rambling all over Robin Hood's barn, others may get up and leave if they don't want to listen.

Any member (with the exception of the chairman) can bring up any subject he wants for discussion. However, what is brought up must be *a matter of common concern for the entire family.* It should not be something strictly between two of the children, for example. The chairman will rule on whether the subject is truly a concern of the entire family.

What can be brought up? Anything. Problems, conflicts, difficulties, grievances, plans for positive activities, whatever.

As with the mutual problem-solving technique, there must be unanimous agreement on the solutions to any problems brought up. There should be no voting, because with voting, some will win and some will lose. Those who lose will be disgruntled and not motivated to carry out the supposed "solution" to the problem. If you cannot get unanimous agreement at one meeting, try again at the next meeting.

In every smoothly functioning family council you will find the parents making abundant use of the feedback technique. The family council is a marvelous opportunity for children to air resentments and get grievances off their chests before they build up into major problems. And wherever there are grievances and resentments, there you should use the feedback technique!

However, the family council should not be thought of merely as a place to solve problems or air grievances. The family council is also a place to make plans for outings, trips, family activities, and vacations. But the unique thing about the family council is that decisions about these activities will be made in a democratic manner by the whole family, rather than in an arbitrary manner by one or both parents.

It is a good idea *not* to schedule the family council meeting during the weekend, because there is too much opportunity for interference from other activities. A week night seems best. It is also a good idea to plan some family fun (ice cream, a trip to the pizza parlor) immediately following the council meeting. (Remember the positive reward system?)

How do you start a family council? First the two parents should talk the whole concept over thoroughly. Realize that if you decide to adopt such a procedure, you are taking a real risk. You are risking letting democracy into your family structure! Your family may never be the same once you have let democracy in. (And incidentally, the greatest danger to the family council is that the parents may misuse it to manipulate the children to try to get them to do what they want them to do.)

Once you have decided that you really want to use the family council and you feel you have the structure of it pretty clear in your mind, present the idea to your family. Tell them you will have an organization meeting at which you will present your ideas as to how it can be organized. But emphasize that the final decision of how the family council will operate will be made by the whole family.

Then the ideas that I have just described to you will be presented to your family. They may decide they do not want to meet once a week. They may decide they don't want to have a secretary. And so forth. From the very first organization meeting, the rules of the family council will be decided not by mother and dad, but by the unanimous family.

I would suggest that the meetings should be short at first (perhaps fifteen minutes), and then later a half hour or forty-five minutes, as the time is needed. When you have a family of teenagers, you may find the meetings getting quite lengthy on certain issues.

What are the advantages of using a regular family council? Obviously, it helps to settle grievances, rows, and conflicts within the family. But that is very minor compared with the fabulous training your children will be getting in the art of human relationships. If you start it when a child is three and continue it until he is eighteen and leaves for college, he will have had fifteen solid years of training in learning to understand, adjust to, and get along with all of the other members (of varying ages) of his family. He will have had plenty of opportunity to take his turn as chairman of the meeting, and try to reconcile others with opposing points of view. He will have had lots of practice being secretary and learning to analyze what is going on in a meeting.

And I will bet you that when your youngsters grow up and look back on their experiences as members of your family, they will rank the family council as one of the greatest gifts you ever gave them!

13

TEACHING YOUR CHILD ETHICS AND MORALITY

A conscience is not innate. Nobody is born with a conscience, a sense of what is right and wrong, what is ethical behavior. A conscience is *learned*, and children mainly learn their consciences from their parents, and to a lesser extent from their schoolteachers, church leaders, Boy and Girl Scout leaders, and their peers.

There are some people with too little conscience. These are called criminal psychopaths. They are able to steal, embezzle, mug, sometimes even kill with very little feeling of guilt or contrition. These people are not sorry about what they have done or the human consequences of their antisocial acts. They are only sorry they got caught.

It is also possible for a person to have too much conscience, in the sense that he is overburdened with an excessive sense of guilt. I think of a patient of mine who went through agonies of guilt whenever she had even the slightest hostile feelings about anybody in her therapy group. Such people deal far too rigidly and harshly with themselves through their consciences.

Back at the turn of the century, in 1900, many American people followed this pattern. Their lives were governed by the harsh, repressive, Victorian, authoritarian type of conscience.

An analysis of American society today—our literature, our movies, our TV shows, etc.—quickly reveals that the situation that obtained in 1900 has changed radically and drastically. I personally believe that much of the change has been for the good. We have thrown out much of the old, severe, repressive type of conscience—and good riddance to it.

But unfortunately, I believe, we have gone too far to the other extreme. We are now raising too many people who have far too little conscience. You can see this in many places.

Many years ago it would have been unthinkable for children to cheat in the Soap Box Derby. Yet now we have had scandals with children cheating in the construction of the cars, egged on by their parents or relatives. Years ago it would have been unthinkable to find cheating in the Boy Scout organization, since this group stood for the utmost integrity of character. Yet recently scandal invaded the Boy Scout organization, when Scout executives were caught padding their membership rolls. In years gone by it would have been equally unthinkable to find cheating in the Naval Academy or at West Point. Yet we have had scandals involving students in both of these places. There have been recent examples of cheating by premed students trying to get into med school, with no indication that the reliance on cheating would end right there. Ask yourself: How would you like a member of your family to be operated on by a surgeon who cheated his way through medical school?

When I was a student in college, there were people who copied the term papers of other students, but this was a very small group of students and it was done in an unorganized, informal way. Now there are blatant advertisements on the bulletin boards of colleges all over the country for businesses, run by students that will write your term papers for you. From time to time some of the schools may try to crack down on them, but the businesses go on.

Conscience, and a sense of what type of behavior is decent and what type is not, applies to sports also. For example, when I was a college student, no basketball rooters made noise or attempted to rattle a member of the opposing team when he was attempting a foul shot. Today, anyone who follows basketball knows what a different scene it is. When an opposing player is taking a foul shot, the other rooters do everything they can to upset him. They shout, boo, yell imprecations, and may even come prepared with wooden clogs to bang together to make noise. There are equally glaring examples from other sports. What this means is that the concept of decent behavior and good sportsmanship on the part of sports rooters seems to have gone out the window.

Of course, the most glaring examples of the crisis of ethics and morality in the United States are our political scandals. Of the thirty-eight people involved in Watergate, all but one came from one of the supposedly most ethical professions in our society: the law. One was an attorney general of the United States, an office that is supposed to be the peak of those charged with upholding law and order in our country. And one was a President—both forced to step down from office in dishonor. Something has gone terribly wrong with our society when we have to admit to our children that those who are supposed to lead and demonstrate an example of ethics and morality have failed them so miserably.

In my previous two books on child-raising, *How to Parent* and *How to Father*, the idea of teaching ethics and a sense of right and wrong behavior and a sense of values was implicit. I see now that I need to make this kind of approach not merely implicit, but explicit.

Let me put it very forcefully and bluntly. If we as parents have raised our children to age twenty-one, using whatever discipline methods we have chosen to use, and our twenty-one-year-olds do not have an ethical sense, a sense of right and wrong, and of values, then we have failed in a very important part of our job as parents.

What I am trying to outline in this chapter is a set of ethical standards you can transmit to your children, regardless of your own religious orientation: whether you are Catholic, Protestant, Jew, or even agnostic or atheist.

First, be aware of this fact: *The responsibility for teaching my children a sense of ethics and values belongs primarily to me, their parent.* The church, the church school, the public school, may all share in the job, but first and foremost, it is my job as their parent.

Second, you need to be aware of how you can louse up the process of teaching ethics and morality and values to your children. The best way I can do a very poor job of teaching these things to my children at any age is to give them lectures and assail their ears with monologues about the importance of ethics and values.

Third, the most powerful way I can teach my children ethics and morality is by being an ethical and moral person myself and having them imitate me. Let me give you one very simple illustration from a totally different context to show you how powerful is the urge for children to imitate their parents. When my children were younger we ate often in a family-type hamburger restaurant. I ate my hamburgers in a very peculiar way. I took off the top bun and ate just the hamburger pattie with a fork, leaving the top and bottom bun (saving calories so that I could indulge myself from time to time in a brownie for dessert).

Never once did I say to either of my boys: "Eat your hamburger the way Daddy does." But once when we were at the restaurant eating, Randy age nine, said, "I want a fork too." "Go get one," I replied. He did, and proceeded to eat his hamburger in exact imitation of me. As soon as he started to do this, Rusty, age four, said, "I want a fork too!" and did the same thing.

What our children do in trivial things like this, they do in important things such as imitating our sense of ethics and morality, and our values. So this is by far the most powerful way in which we can teach these things to our children.

Fourth, we parents luckily have available a series of books called *Value Tales.* Each one is the story of some value, such as patience, determination, kindness, or believing in yourself, organized around the story of a particular historical figure embodying this value. These *Value Tales* are written by Spencer Johnson, M.D., and published by Value Tales, P.O. Box 1012, La Jolla, California. You can read these books to preschoolers from three on up, and older children can read them by themselves.

Fifth, your dinner-table (or other) conversations can become daily seminars in values and ethics, which are often relevant to the news of the day. Here again, it is most important not to go at this whole issue so heavily that your children will feel: "Jeepers creepers, here come some more lectures by Mom and Dad on ethics and morality." But where it is appropriate, don't hesitate to bring up the subject in connection with what's going on in the newspapers and magazines, or what's happening in your children's school or wherever. But whatever you do, do it with a light touch.

Many of you may feel, "Yes, but what ethical standards *can* we teach to our children that make sense and are on their level of comprehension?" Here are some suggestions based on what I have taught my own children. These are suggestions that I believe a parent who is a member of any religion or no religion could agree with.

We begin with a very simple proposition. Anything you do that hurts another human being or hurts yourself is wrong. Anything that you do that does not hurt another human being or yourself is probably right. For example, if your child has been stealing from the supermarket, you have a logical basis for telling him why that is wrong. It's not just wrong because you, his parent, arbitrarily say it's wrong. It's wrong because the stealing hurts the owner of the store.

In the same way, if you cheat on a test, you are hurting both other students and yourself. You are being unfair to the students who studied for the test but did not cheat, because you are taking unfair advantage of them. And you are hurting yourself because by cheating you are preventing yourself from gaining the knowledge you would get from legitimately studying.

You have to live by this ethical proposition yourself in order to teach it to your children in any meaningful fashion. And then you need to teach it to your child as an overarching system, above and beyond a particular incident. If your child, age six, takes candy from a store and you find out about it, obviously you will want him to take the candy back to the store, or, if he has eaten it, take money to the store to pay for it. But you don't want to deal with just this particular incident. You want to explain to him, without a lengthy lecture, just why it was wrong to take the candy in the first place.

In addition to the first proposition I have set forth that whatever hurts another human being or hurts you is wrong, there is another ethical proposition, which all religious (or nonreligious) groups can agree on. That is the proposition that it is good to do loving things for other people and for ourselves. Included in this proposition is the idea that it is the loving and right thing to do to go to somebody else's aid if that person is being hurt or injured. We have had several recent instances where this principle was violated, where many people were witness to a crime or mugging without even one of them calling the police. The time to teach people such ethical principles is not when they are forty-five years old, but when they are six or seven and another child is being teased or beaten up on the school playground.

It is important for us to know two things about the ethics

and the values we teach our children. First, we need to be prepared for adolescence, when our teenagers will challenge the values we have brought them up on in every way they can. They will challenge them in actual practice in their lives. They will challenge them verbally and vocally, either by criticizing them or deriding them.

Next, it is important and reassuring for parents to know that this challenging of values and ethics by their teenagers is a normal phase of adolescent rebellion. Something would be wrong if they did *not* challenge the values with which they have been raised. Parents are often panicked by this challenge, for it seems to them as if everything they have brought their children up to believe is being permanently thrown down the drain. This is not so. Amazingly enough, when those same adolescents are in their early twenties they will return to the values they spurned in their teenage years.

In dealing with your adolescent's challenge to your values, I think two extremes of position are to be avoided. One is the view championed by many people today (especially young people) that ethics is "doing your own thing." This is complete relativism in ethics. Everybody does his own thing and then everybody will be happy. This view of ethics says that there is no right or wrong beyond the individual person. I profoundly disagree. If you leave it to each individual to decide what is right and wrong, then you can justify anything at all in the name of individual ethics. You can justify any of the atrocities committed under Hitler or under Stalin if it is all right to "do your own thing." The extreme example of this doctrine would be Charles Manson and one of the girls in his "family" deciding that they needed to kill a person out of "love" for that person. The "do your own thing" ethic does not make psychological sense to me.

On the other hand, I think we need to be very careful in dealing with our teenagers not to give the impression that we, their parents, have some exclusive pipeline to the heavens by which we can zero in on an infallible approach to what is right and what is wrong. For example, I can remember my mother saying to me many times, "Well, at least, son, I taught you the difference between right and wrong." During one of my smart-aleck phases in college she said that to me and I replied, "Congratulations, Mother, you have learned something that the philosophers from Plato onward have debated endlessly about!"

I didn't really need to be sarcastic about it, but my sarcasm had a point. My mother was confusing her particular limited views on right and wrong as a middle-class mother living in the suburbs of Baltimore with universal views of right and wrong. That's why I think it is important for us as parents to have our firm views on ethics and morality, but not put them forth as if we knew with absolute certainty that they had universal validity. When talking with our teenagers, I think it is important to preface our statements by comments such as, "Here's the way I see it but you or other people may see it differently," or, "This is what makes sense to me about ethics and morality, but other people may disagree."

14

HOW TO USE
"PARENTAL MUSCLE"

I have covered all but one of the discipline techniques that are necessary to raise children. If you use all the methods I have discussed so far in this book, you will never need to use this last-ditch technique. But because I have dealt with a number of families over the years, particularly those with teenagers, who found it necessary to use this desperation technique, I believe it would be remiss if I left it out.

I am referring to sheer raw power on the part of the parents, or what I call *parental muscle*. I do not believe the use of power, in itself, is necessarily immoral or bad. It is certainly clear from what I have said in this book that I believe mutual agreement is far superior to the stark imposition of power by either parents or children. And it is abundantly clear that I believe it is far better to solve a conflict by negotiation and agreement rather than through power. However, in certain extreme cases, where all other resources have been tried and have failed, I believe we have to fall back on sheer power to bring order out of chaos in the lives of some children.

There is one further thing parents should do before falling back on unabashed power. That is to seek professional help from a psychologist, psychiatrist, or psychiatric social worker. A book can only talk about children in general or families in general. But a professional therapist can deal with your children in particular and your family in particular, and give you unique help no book can.

So before you resort to any of the drastic steps mentioned in this chapter, get professional help.

Almost always, when the drastic step of flexing parental muscle is needed to bring order out of chaos, we are talking about the family with teenagers. Very rarely do younger children defy parental authority in such outrageous ways.

For example, one divorced mother had a fourteen-year-old boy, a sixteen-year-old boy, and a seventeen-year-old girl. She had no control over that family whatsoever. When she asked them to rinse the dishes and put them in the dishwasher, she was answeerd by, "Do it yourself, Pudgy!" When she asked for help with anything around the house, the answer was, "I'm busy," or, "Screw off." It was clear from her description of the scene that the kids were running the family, and she was their unwilling slave.

After talking the situation over with her, this is what we decided would be best for her to do: go on a parental strike.

She told the kids that she could not tolerate the situation where they paid no attention to her requests around the house. So until the situation changed, she was going to go on strike. She was not going to buy any groceries; she was not going to cook any meals; and she was not going to give any money to any of the three of them. She was using her parental muscle of money as leverage for her strike. The three kids thought she was kidding at first. They were so used to having a mother they could boss around, they were dumb-founded at the new type of mother they had to deal with.

At first the three of them tried to outmaneuver her. They scrounged around at friends' houses for meals. They also bummed money from friends to buy gas for their cars. But after about five days, they had had it. They had to face the fact that mother controlled the purse strings and there was nothing they could do about it. I had instructed the mother not to approach the kids but to wait until they came to her. Finally they came to her and said they wanted to have a meeting to discuss the situation. The discussion was hot and heavy. But the mother stood her ground. The upshot of the meeting was that the mother agreed she would start contributing money to the family again and cooking the meals again, provided that they worked out a chart to be put on the kitchen wall specifying the family chores for which each was responsible. From a situation in which mother gave and the kids took, it changed to a situation in which both mother and teenagers contributed effort to make the family situation work. Mother's parental strike had proved the power of parental muscle.

Here is a more extreme example of the use of parental power as a last-ditch measure. I remember one family I worked with who had an eighteen-year-old son. He had dropped out of college. He was not working. He spent most of his time lying around the house getting stoned on pot. Believe me, those parents and I tried all of the discipline methods found in this book to get through to Joey. Nothing worked. He had even come in with his parents to see me twice, and then dropped out. Finally, the father had had it. He said, "Look, we've tried everything with Joey, and nothing has worked. He's not going to college and he's not working. I think we should kick him out of the house." This shocked the mother. "But he's our son—what a terrible thing to do!" I agreed with the father. I pointed out to the mother that they were not doing Joey a favor by subsidizing him to get stoned day after day. Reluctantly, she agreed.

The father gave Joey one more week. He said to him, "Look, Joey, if you were going to college I'd be happy to pay for your room and board so you could get an education. If you don't want to go to college and prefer to work now, that's okay too. But I can't allow you to just sit around the house and do nothing except get stoned. So if the situation hasn't changed in a week, you'll have to get out."

Sure enough, nothing changed in a week, and Joey left. At first he went over to his grandmother's and mooched off her for three weeks, until she got disgusted with him and kicked him out. Then he mooched off a variety of friends, staying at their houses until they also got tired of him and asked him to leave.

Finally he got a job pumping gas. Life forced him to do this, because he had run out of people who would feed him, give him a place to sleep, and put up with him. A year before, he would have considered pumping gas beneath him, but now he felt lucky to get the job. He managed to find a single room for rent, and rented it, cooking his meals on a one-burner hot plate he bought. About eight months later he had saved up enough money to graduate from his rented room to a small apartment, which he furnished with wooden boxes and makeshift furniture and posters. He had stopped getting stoned because he had decided he wouldn't be able to keep his job if he did, and he needed the money from that job.

About a year and a half later he concluded he had had enough of pumping gas. He knew there were better ways of making a living and he planned to head toward them. He had always been good in math, and so he decided he wanted to be a computer programmer. Rather hesitantly he went back to see his father and told him he had decided to go back to college and study computer programming. He wanted to know if his father would take him back into the house if he returned to college. Would he! The father was tickled pink. The boy went back to college, graduated in computer programming, and got a job in the field.

As I view it, the turning point in that young man's life was the day his father kicked him out of the house!

In over twenty years of clinical practice, I don't think I have recommended to more than three or four sets of parents that they kick a youngster out of the house. But there are times when such a drastic, last-ditch exercise of sheer parental power may be necessary.

Let me summarize what I am saying in this chapter. With children younger than teenagers there should almost never be any need to use such extreme methods as I have described in this chapter. Even with teenagers, the use of the feedback method, the mutual problem-solving technique, the family council, and other discipline methods should handle almost any problem that comes up. If these methods do not take care of things, then the family should seek professional help.

I felt I needed to include this chapter because other books on discipline do not, in my opinion, deal realistically with what the parent is to do when the teenager absolutely refuses in any way, shape, or form to obey reasonable parental authority. For example, in one book that stresses active listening, in all the incidents quoted when the parent says, "Son, let's sit down and talk things over," the son obediently sits down to discuss the problem. But what do you do when the teenager says, "Screw you!" refuses to talk over the problem, and stomps out of the house? Or if you are that father who forbade his fourteen-year-old son to go out and locked the front door, and whose son them jumped through the window, crashing through the glass, to go meet his friends? How can parents handle this kind of ultimate situation?

My answer is that in all such extreme cases of defiance of parental authority the parents must make use of parental muscle in some form that will bring leverage on the teenager to begin obeying parental authority. For until a teenager is willing to obey, you have chaos in the house instead of a family.

The use of sheer parental power is drastic surgery, and is not to be undertaken hastily, ill-advisedly, or lightly. But there are times when it may be necessary.

15

THE ART OF
NEGATIVE THINKING

So far we have talked about how to teach your child desirable behavior or help him get rid of undesirable behavior. Both of these imply that there is something wrong with what the child is doing. Now we come to something almost completely ignored by experts writing on the subject of discipline. Suppose the child's behavior is perfectly normal and appropriate for his age, but because of the parent's own hang-ups, they find their child's perfectly normal behavior grating on their nerves? This can happen to either or both parents.

I think, for example, of a father who consulted me about his only child, an eight-year-old boy. The father was unusual in his ability to be objective about the situation. He said, "I've read a lot of psychological books on the subject, and from all I can gather Donald is basically a normal eight-year-old. And probably if I knew years ago what I know now about children his age I might have decided never to have children. But I didn't make that decision then, so I'm stuck with the situation now. The things he does, like running around the backyard screaming and yelling with his friends, or going through the house and slamming doors, or leaving the remains of peanut butter and jelly and Cokes around the kitchen, or riding his bike through the front yard—these things bug me. I know it's normal for him to act this way, but it bothers me anyway. I guess I really expect him to be quiet and sedate like an adult instead of feisty and rambunctious like an eight-year-old boy. So what do I do about it?"

Here was a clear case where the father realized that there was nothing really wrong with the boy's behavior. The problem was not in the boy, but in the father's feelings. The father wanted his son to behave like an adult, which he was not, instead of like an eight-year-old boy, which he was. So in answer to the father's dilemma I taught him the art of *negative thinking*.

Ever since the publication of Dr. Norman Vincent Peale's book *The Power of Positive Thinking*, back in the late 1950s, millions of people have tried to think positively to change their attitudes toward themselves, their jobs, their spouses, their customers, special situations with which they are faced, and almost anything else you can think of.

I agree with Dr. Peale in the goal he is asking people to pursue. It's a good thing to be able to think positively about yourself, your spouse, your children, your job. But I disagree emphatically with the means by which he urges people to get there. He suggests that people set up positive images in their minds and concentrate on bending their thoughts in a positive direction. The catch is that only a very few people are able to do this. When most people find themselves gripped by an intense fear or a deep depression, positive thinking simply does not work. Positive thinking is not powerful enough to deal with the deep unconscious forces of a person's mind.

So, instead, I advocate using what I call negative thinking. Here is how it works. Many years ago, a psychologist, Dr. Knight Dunlap, was learning to type somewhat late in life, at age thirty-five. He found he was making a persistent error. When he wanted to type "the" he kept making the mistake of typing "hte." If he had tried to use positive thinking to correct his error, he would have tried to think positively about typing "the." He would have pictured the right letters coming out instead of the wrong ones. But since he was an experimentally minded psychologist, he did a little experiment with himself. He deliberately typed the mistake "hte" about two hundred times. When he went back to trying to type "the," he found he had no trouble doing it correctly.

Here is how he corrected his error. He consciously wanted to type "the," but unconsciously, and against his conscious control, "hte" kept coming out. So he took the involuntary

and unconscious error and put it under his control by deliberately doing what he wanted to avoid.

Using this principle, Dr. Dunlap worked with people who
were learning to type, play the piano, master Morse code, or
other mechanical activities. I have extended Dr. Dunlap's
original concept to the area of feelings and emotions. I teach
it to people as a technique to use to get rid of undesirable
feelings and emotions and replace them with positive and desirable ones. Perhaps an example will make clear how this
works.

I remember a twenty-seven-year-old patient who came to
me initially because of feelings of shyness and inadequacy.
When I first saw her she was working as a file clerk. In one
of our early therapeutic sessions she remarked rather offhand-
edly, "I know I'm not very intelligent, but I guess that's a
cross I'll just have to bear." I could tell by talking with her
that she *was* intelligent, so I gave her an intelligence test. She
came out at the eighty-third percentile, meaning she was
more intelligent than eighty-two out of one hundred people
her age and less intelligent than seventeen out of one hundred
people her age, a very good score. Do you think she was de-
lighted at the results? Not at all. In fact, she actually thought
I had fudged the results to make her look more intelligent
than she really was!

In the course of trying to find out why she had such difficulty believing she was intelligent, we soon discovered the
reason. One of her mother's favorite words for her was "stupid." She would say things to her like, "That was a stupid
thing to do," "How could you be so stupid?" "You never do
anything right," "You'll never hold a job more than twenty
minutes; you'll make some dumb mistake." These negative
parental tapes originating from her mother, and now running
in her head, caused her to downgrade herself and her intelligence.

My goal was to get her to achieve positive feelings about
her intelligence. But I did *not* do this by telling her to try to
think positively about it. The negative tapes in her head were
too powerful for that. Instead, I used negative thinking. I had
her look at herself in the mirror for five minutes every morning and deliberately exaggerate all the negative things her
mother had said about her. I had her say things to herself like
"Margaret, you know how stupid you are. You're just lucky
your boss doesn't know how dumb you really are or he'd fire

you. You make so many dumb mistakes at work you deserve to be fired." I had her say the same kind of things to herself while driving to work and driving home at night. She was to deliberately exaggerate all of the negative feelings her mother had planted in her mind about her intelligence.

What happens in a situation like this is that as long as the negative tapes in her mind are allowed to operate silently, they are very powerful and prevent her from feeling positive about her intelligence. But when the negative tapes are placed under her conscious control and deliberately exaggerated, she begins to feel how absurd they are. Sooner or later it is as if a little voice within her begins to say, "Ridiculous! All this stuff about how dumb I am is baloney! I am really intelligent." And after three or four months this began to happen to Margaret. She began to revolt against the putdowns of her mother's negative tapes. One of the first outward signs of this process was that she decided to enroll in a legal secretarial course. When she completed the course she got a much higher paying job as a legal secretary.

Then we began working on Margaret's appearance. When she first came to see me she looked like Miss Mousy Brown. Her mother had done the same hatchet job on her appearance that she had done on her intelligence. She said things to her like, "You're all skin and bones. You can practically see your ribs sticking out. Your legs look like pipe stems. You need to put more meat and potatoes on yourself and fill out more. You're so skinny no man would look twice at you." We used the same type of negative thinking on these parental tapes.

Once again, after a few months, the little voice inside Margaret began to rebel against her mother's putdowns. She began to use makeup and dress more attractively. One day she came in for her appointment looking positively sexy. Immediately I knew she was really making headway and beginning to feel good about her appearance. Soon she had acquired a boyfriend, and not too long after that she was ready to terminate therapy.

Here was a young woman who began therapy thinking of herself as (1) not intelligent and (2) not attractive. By the use of negative thinking she was able to clear away the negative tapes in her head and realize she was both intelligent and attractive. She was now thinking positively about herself. But she did *not* achieve this by trying to use positive thinking and

saying, "I am intelligent" or, "I am pretty." She used negative
thinking to erase the negative tapes in her mind and to find
good feelings about herself.

Now let's return to the father of the eight-year-old boy. If
I had tried positive thinking with him, I would have told him
to say to himself, "My son is a wonderful boy, and I must
have positive feelings toward him even though he does lots of
normal eight-year-old things that bug me." This would never
have worked. For I would have been asking him to sell himself the illusion that certain of his boy's actions did not grate
on his nerves. And this would be doomed to failure.

So I instructed him in negative thinking. I had him go off
by himself once a day, or talk out loud to himself as he was
driving to or from work, and practice negative thinking. I
had him deliberately exaggerate the things about his son that
got on his nerves. I had him say things such as, "My son has
no right to act like a normal eight-year-old boy. He knows it
gets on my nerves. He must act like a sedate little adult, disguised to look like an eight-year-old boy. He must talk softly
and quietly at all times. He must ride his bicycle primly and
sedately, like an elderly lady. Above all, he must not act like
an eight-year-old boy. My nerves are too fragile and too
precious to stand his acting like a normal boy of his age. And
he must at all costs respect the fragility of my nerves. Or else
I will have a nervous breakdown and spend the rest of my
life in a mental hospital." The father was told to really ham
it up in expressing these feelings, and throw in some humor if
he could.

I would not be telling the truth if I said that as a result of
using negative thinking the father reversed his attitudes and
was able to accept his son's normal boyish behavior
completely. However, the use of negative thinking did enable
the father to desensitize himself considerably to things that
had previously driven him up the wall. Now he was able to
regard them as relatively minor irritants. Not only could he
work on this while driving to and from work, but whenever
his son did anything at home that got under his skin, the father could retreat to his bedroom and use negative thinking
to reduce his irritation level.

Don't expect negative thinking to change 100 percent of
your attitudes toward a child who bothers you. But if you
succeed in changing only 50 percent of your attitudes, you
are that much better off than when you started.

Here is another case from my clinical practice wherein a parent was able to change attitudes in his relationship with his son through the use of negative thinking. The son was thirteen. The father wanted to have an intimate father-son talk with him about sex. He felt it would be very helpful, since his son was in early puberty. Although the father's intentions were good, he had great fears of having such a talk, due to his own repressed upbringing. He confided his problem to me.

"I don't want my son to go through the agonies I went through when I was a teenager," he said. "Particularly about masturbation. The subject of sex was always hush-hush in our house, and I don't want it to be that way in my own family. I want my kids to be able to come to me or my wife with sexual questions when they have them. And I want us to have an open kind of atmosphere about sex in our family. But when it comes right down to it, I'm scared witless to bring up the subject because of my own hang-ups. I think I'd rather face combat in war than initiate a talk about sex with my boy."

After listening to the father's dilemma I explained negative thinking to him and suggested he try it to overcome his difficulty. I explained that he had negative parental tapes running in his head which said to him something like this: "It's vile and dirty for you to talk about sex with your son, so keep away from such a subject." I told him to exaggerate these tapes and say things to himself like, "You're a wicked and sinful father to even be thinking of talking with your son about things like sex and masturbation. You're an evil-minded old man to even consider such a thing. Those subjects are just plain dirty and you know it. Confine your talks to 'safe' subjects, like the Boy Scouts and schoolwork. It will be absolutely devastating to your son to have you bring up a disturbing and upsetting subject like sex."

The father faithfully practiced his negative thinking and finally reached the point where he had rebelled enough against the stupidity of his negative parental tapes to be ready to talk with his son. I asked him how he felt about it. "Still scared to death but I'm determined to do it now. I hope my son doesn't know how scared I am." "On the contrary," I said, "I think it's very important to tell him just how scared you are. Don't pose as being calm and unruffled because you're not. Level with him and tell him you don't want him to go through the miseries you went through in adolescence. But because of your parents' attitude it was very hard for you to talk with him about it and you feel scared to death to initiate the conversation."

He did this and found that it actually helped. His son said that he too found it hard to talk to anyone about sex, and this created an instant bond of understanding between the two of them on this subject. The father covered aspects of sex in general, intercourse, contraceptive devices, and masturbation. When he got to masturbation, he discovered that his son had already been masturbating for about a year and feeling very guilty about it. So when his father told him it was a normal thing for adolescents to do, and that he had done it himself when he was a teenager, this reduced the son's guilt feelings considerably.

Negative thinking is something that may be particularly helpful to a stepparent. You may be a man who has married a woman you love, and in the process find you have acquired two or three children. This is a difficult enough situation to handle at best. You may be suddenly stepfather to a four-year-old boy, a nine-year-old girl, and an eleven-year-old boy. "Instant parenthood" is not easy! Even so, you find you can learn to cope with the four-year-old boy and the nine-year-old girl. But you and the eleven-year-old boy strike negative sparks with each other.

If you were completely honest with yourself, you would have to admit that you simply don't like the boy. There may be many reasons for this. You may have had no children yourself and therefore not be used to their ways. Your expectations of their behavior may be unrealistically high. Or the boy may be a little brat whose mother has let him get away with murder, even though she did not do this with his younger brother and sister. Or there may be nothing you can specifically put your finger on—all you know for sure is that you don't care much for him.

What can you do in a case like this? If there are aspects of his behavior that are clearly undesirable, you and your wife can agree how to work together on these. Then you can use the discipline strategies in this book. But if the real problem is not the boy but your feelings about him, then you can use negative thinking.

Take whatever aspects of his behavior rub you the wrong way and deliberately exaggerate them to yourself. Say things like, "He contradicts me and argues with me. How dare he do that! Doesn't he know that no eleven-year-old boy has the right to contradict me or argue with me? After all, doesn't he realize I'm a junior executive in my company? Doesn't he have respect for my superior wisdom and intelligence? And particularly when he pointed out that mistake in physics I made Tuesday evening. He had absolutely no right to do that! He should have kept his mouth shut!"

And so it goes. The stepfather may never succeed in genuinely and deeply liking the boy, but at least he can minimize his dislike.

Whether you have stepchildren living with you all the time, or only visiting every other weekend, if you have one that you have taken a dislike to, negative thinking can help you.

The problem of stepparent-stepchild relationships is particularly difficult if you acquire the stepchildren as adolescents. Adolescence is a period of rebellion anyway. It's not a comfortable period for a natural parent, and it is likely to be a particularly difficult time for a stepparent. When a child is younger there may be many things you as a stepparent can do to handle undesirable behavior. But when you acquire a child who is in the midst of adolescence the number of things you can do to handle undesirable behavior or lessen friction in parent-child relationships is much more limited. Here again, negative thinking may be one of the most powerful techniques at your disposal to enable you to survive your stepchild's adolescence.

Whether you are a natural parent or a stepparent, when you find certain aspects of your child's behavior grating on your nerves it is extremely important for you to know what "normal" behavior is for a child of his stage of development. (For example, a child in the stage of first adolescence, between the ages of two and three, or a child in the stages of preadolescence, between the ages of eleven and thirteen, is generally very difficult to get along with.) If his behavior is what would *not* normally be expected of a child of his age, you need to use discipline strategies to change his behavior to a more satisfactory level. But if his behavior *is* what could normally be expected from a child of his age, then you need to change *your* attitudes as a parent.

The trouble is that many parents do not know what they can expect of a two-year-old, a four-year-old, a five-year-old, an eight-year-old, an eleven-year-old, or a teenager. There are two main sources of information that can help a parent to distinguish "normal" from "abnormal" behavior at every stage of a child's development. One source is my own two previous books. *How to Parent* describes the normal behavior and development of children from birth to age six. *How to Father* takes the chronological story still further and describes the growth and development of a typical normal child from birth to age twenty-one.

The second source of information on the normal development of children comes from the Gesell Institute. They have produced three books that are a great boon to all parents. *Infant and Child in the Culture of Today* describes the growth and development of children from birth to age five. *The Child from Five to Ten* describes normal children in those years. Finally, *Youth* describes the normal growth and development of children from eleven through sixteen. These are really invaluable books for a parent, for without them you have little information to help you distinguish between when your child is being hard to cope with because he is going through a difficult stage and when he's being difficult just because he's being difficult! Without this knowledge, you don't know whether to try to change your child's behavior or your own attitudes.

If you try negative thinking to deal with your negative feelings toward either a natural child or stepchild and find that it does not appreciably change your feelings, then you may need professional counseling or counseling for yourself and the child, or perhaps even for the whole family, in order to improve family feelings and interactions.

Negative thinking is not merely a very helpful technique in parent-child relationships, but a very powerful tool that you may find of help in conquering a wide range of personality problems. For further information on this, I refer you to the chapter on negative thinking in my earlier book *The You That Could Be.*

16

PARENTS HAVE RIGHTS TOO!

When I was a boy growing up, my mother and father would frequently say to me, "Children should be seen and not heard." Fortunately, this type of antiquated thinking about children and child-raising has passed from the scene.

But my parents had an advantage over parents today. My parents, like today's parents, and parents throughout history, made mistakes in raising their children. But my parents were blissfully unaware that their child-raising mistakes could have any effect on their child's future life. They went right ahead and made their mistakes, free from the guilt feelings that plague so many parents nowadays. Some parents of past generations may have raised their children with all the psychological finesse of bulls in china shops, but they were self-confident bulls!

Many parents today lack this self-confidence. On the one hand, the popularization of psychology has taught parents the importance of effective parenting skills in raising children to become well-adjusted adults. On the other hand, as I have pointed out previously, no one gives parents the training they need to help them raise their children wisely.

The result of this paradox is that America today is The Land of the Uneasy Parent. Again and again, anxious parents ask psychologists, psychiatrists, and pediatricians, "Did I do the right thing?" Or, "If I do such and such with my child, would that be wrong?"

Here are some typical comments from worried parents:

> *I was too busy to take the baby out one day, and I felt I had failed him. I mentioned it to the pediatrician, and he said, "Believe me, Mrs. T., by the time he is married he'll have forgotten all about it." I had to laugh to myself, but I did feel better.*

> *My son was in bed with a cold. I had lots of things to do and I felt guilty being out all day while he was cooped up in the apartment with just the cleaning woman for company. So I canceled my lunch date and zipped through my beauty parlor appointment and grabbed a cab home and rushed into his room and said, "Okay, I'm ready now. What will we play?" And he said, "I don't know about you, Mom, but I have homework. Can't you find something to do?"*

> *My friend had a fight with her husband in front of their five-year-old daughter. She's very psychiatry-minded, and she's been worried sick about its effect on the child.*

Schoolteachers and principals cannot help but notice this uneasy attitude of parents. Here are the comments of a principal:

> *They feel so guilty. They worry about whether they're doing the right thing with their children and they suspect they're not. Fully as much of our time is spent with parents as with the children. They call me at home incessantly. They talk about the school and their children and the school and their children.*

These uneasy, guilty feelings lead many parents today into unconscious contracts with their children. This is the way it reads: "Since I feel guilty and I'm not sure I'm doing right by you, I will try to make up for it by giving up my rights and freedoms as a person and devoting myself to you. That way I can atone for any mistakes I am making in raising you."

A psychiatrist in Scarsdale, New York, comments on this phenomenon: "The parents here are slaves to their children. They are constantly involved, car-pooling them or supervising them or planning for them or talking about them."

I think this whole situation is very unfortunate. Whenever a parent feels ineffective and gives up his rights and freedoms in order to cater to his child's whims, deep down he feels as if he has been taken advantage of (even though he has done it to himself). These feelings only rebound and cause him to be angry at the child, which makes him even less effective as a parent. And the vicious circle goes on.

I hope I made it abundantly clear in the earlier chapters of this book that I believe children have the right to be treated with respect and understanding. I believe a child has the right to be treated like a typical child of his age and stage of development, and not expected to be able to behave like an adult. A child has the right to his feelings and the expression of those feelings.

But I believe that parents also have certain rights and feelings, and that it is a mistake to ignore or neglect them. The parent who is sure of his own rights and freedoms and is not hesitant about exercising them is a far better parent than the one who feels so guilty and unsure of himself that he constantly tries to appease his child to make up for these feelings.

Therefore, in order to establish justice, insure domestic tranquillity, promote the general welfare, and secure the blessings of liberty for ourselves and our posterity, I propose this Bill of Rights for Parents:

1. *You have a right to your own feelings and the right to express those feelings to your children.* I have stressed the importance of allowing your children to express their feelings to you. But it would be an unfortunate one-way street if it stopped there. You have an equal right to express your feelings, both positive and negative, to your children. Many parents go around tight-lipped, full of negative feelings about something their child has done but afraid that if they express their feelings it will somehow be bad for the child. Bah, and humbug! Feel free to say things such as, "I've just had it up to here with your smart-aleck behavior today, Todd, and I think you'd better keep out of my way the rest of the day."

2. *You have the right to be the authority in your home.* I know of divorced parents who have, in effect, asked their children's permission to remarry. I think this behavior on the part of a parent is sheer madness. Of course there are certain things the children should be consulted about, or even have a voice in, but not an issue such as this.

Children who know they can push wishy-washy parents around are in for a tough time when they become adults and discover that life does not treat them that way. And down deep the parents feel shame and disgust at themselves for allowing their children to run the show. For example, many parents will allow teenagers to talk on the telephone for interminable amounts of time, even though people complain to them about not being able to reach them by phone. Or a parent may allow a teenager to play his stereo at an unpleasant, ear-shattering level without forcefully telling him to turn it down. Or parents may be willing to make inconvenient, last-minute changes in their plans when their teenager postpones certain decisions until the very last minute. Tolerating a child's unpleasant and rude behavior is not good for either parents or children. Your feelings as a parent should be (although you do not necessarily need to put it into words): "This is my house and these are my rules for behavior in my house."

3. *In the hierarchy of family loyalties and priorities, you have the right to have your marriage come first, and your relationship with the children come second.* In my opinion, too many families in America today are child-centered rather than marriage-centered. I do not think it is psychologically healthy for a marriage to revolve around the children. The marriage should maintain its own independent center of gravity, and the children will inevitably benefit from a happy, stable marriage.

4. *You have the right to take periodic vacations from being a parent.* We assume that it is a good thing for a father or mother to take an annual vacation from work every year. And many people take regular vacations from their jobs every weekend. Can you imagine how stale you would get at your work if you did not take some time off?

But what about the job of being a parent? Is there an accepted custom that encourages mothers and fathers to take regular vacations from that difficult and time-consuming job? No, there is not. For most mothers and fathers, parenthood is something that is always with them. I think this is unhealthy.

There is a psychological rhythm to life: work and play, job and vacation. We grow stale at our jobs if we go too long without a vacation. The same thing is true in spades about parenthood. That's why I believe that, every so often, mother and father should leave the children with a grandparent or baby-sitter and take off for the weekend. Alone together they do not have to play the roles of mother and father and can enjoy themselves as just husband and wife.

I think it is a good idea for parents to get away from the children one night a week and enjoy dinner out or dancing or a movie or whatever, just by themselves. I encourage parents to take the whole family on a yearly vacation, but I think it is good for the parents sometimes to take a week's vacation by themselves. I want to make it clear that I happen to enjoy taking vacations or weekends with my children and family. But I also think it's important for husband and wife to get away by themselves at times. As Kahlil Gibran says in *The Prophet*, "Be together, but let there be spaces in your togetherness."

5. *You have the right to make mistakes in bringing up your children.* So many of today's parents seem deathly afraid of making mistakes in child-raising. Yet what can we expect but mistakes when we are so unprepared for the job? And even if we were all well-prepared with a Ph.D. in child psychology, we would still find ourselves making on-the-job mistakes with our own children. I can attest to the truth of that.

Before I became a parent, I used to be very critical of parents. "How can they botch up so many things in raising their children?" I used to say. After I became a parent myself, my point of view changed radically. I learned that even if a parent has a Ph.D. in psychology he will still go through a learning process in raising his own children. And that learning process will include plenty of mistakes! Now I am very pro-parent and very sympathetic to the difficulties of the job of parenthood.

Consider what happens when we are learning any new skill, whether it is playing bridge, playing golf, riding a motorcycle, playing the piano, or anything else. We learn by making literally thousands of mistakes. Why should learning the complex skills involved in raising a child from birth through adolescence be an exception to this rule? We should take it for granted that we will make mistakes and not berate ourselves or feel guilty about it.

During the time of the Protestant Reformation, a friend of Martin Luther's, Philipp Melanchthon, wrote to him, saying he was worried about his sins. He was not sure he had confessed all of his sins to God; he was afraid he had inadvertently overlooked some. Luther wrote back, reassuring him with a phrase that still rings strikingly down through the centuries: "Sin bravely," he said, "but believe more bravely that God forgives you." So I say to you parents: "Blunder bravely! Go ahead and make mistakes, but believe more bravely that, on the whole, you are doing a good job of raising your children!"

6. *You have the right to pursue your own career and interests.* You may be a mother or father, but that is a secondary role in your life. First and foremost, you are a person, with your own interests and needs to fulfill.

It is psychologically unhealthy for your life to revolve around your children. It is psychologically healthy for your life to revolve around the fulfillment of your own needs, wishes, aspirations, and talents, as long as your children are cared for and their needs are met. But if you don't meet your own needs, you are not going to meet theirs!

7. *You have the right to be irrational.* At times children are irrational, teenagers are emphatically irrational, politicians are irrational, movie stars are irrational, judges are irrational, psychologists and psychiatrists are irrational. So why should parents be the only human beings on the face of the earth who demand of themselves that they be rational and logical all of the time?

To give you but one example, this means that a parent has the right to say to her child: "I have no rational reason to want things done this way, but I just do. So please respect my irrational feelings." Or, "I know it's irrational but it makes me feel uncomfortable when you do thus and so. So please respect my irrational feelings and don't do it."

It is normal for all of us to have irrational feelings from time to time. Expect this, make allowances for it, and stop thinking that parents have no right to feel this way.

8. *You have the right to be a fallible, imperfect human being.* This means that you have the right to have bad days, to be cross, illogical, biased, dogmatic and opinionated at times; to be furious with your children at times; to feel like pampering yourself at times; or to be uptight at times. After all, can we really expect ourselves to shed all of our common human faults and foibles and acquire immaculate and perfect personalities when we become parents? No, we cannot. As parents we have a right to be the imperfect human beings that we are.

9. *You have the right to preserve your sanity.* Any parent

who stays at home all day with kids, especially preschoolers, has the right to take time alone without the children in order to preserve her parental sanity. The constant company of children, especially young children, is psychologically wearing on most adults. Not too long ago a women's magazine ran an article entitled *Why Young Mothers Feel Trapped*, and invited other mothers to write in and relate their own feelings and experiences. The response was overwhelming. Over fifty thousand mothers responded, telling how they felt trapped by their children.

You can find time alone for yourself in many ways. You can hire a baby-sitter two days a week for a few hours or half a day. When your youngster is three, you can enroll him in a good nursery school. You can organize a play group with a few other mothers. You can get away for vacations with your husband. Or just get away by yourself. However you do it, you have the right to protect yourself from coming down with a bad case of cabin fever. You have a right to preserve your sanity by taking time alone without your children.

10. *You have the right to be yourself.* I have repeatedly stressed in this book and my other books that each child is unique. He is born with a unique combination of genes that cannot be duplicated in anyone else on this planet. And he has the right to be the unique person that he is and not be squeezed into some artificial parental mold that does not fit him. Allow him the freedom to be himself and you will raise a happy and psychologically healthy child.

The same reasoning applies to you as a parent. You too have your own unique temperament and personality. It is fine to read books or take courses in child-raising, but in the final analysis, you have to filter the information you get from such books or courses through the lens of your own personality. After all, it is you who are raising your child. So don't try to raise your child Dr. Spock's way or Dr. Dodson's way or Dr. Gordon's way. Listen to whatever Dr. Spock or Dr. Dodson or Dr. Gordon have to say to you, but raise your child *in your own unique way.*

You can't really be anybody else anyway. So have the courage to be yourself—as a husband or wife, as a worker, and, above all, as a parent!

17
WORKING MOTHER

The time is 1947. Mrs. Homemaker has made breakfast for her seven- and ten-year-old boys, packed their lunches, and waved good-bye to them as they trudge off to school. She will occupy her day with a varied round of homemaking tasks: doing the laundry, cleaning, shopping, perhaps having late morning coffee with a neighbor, then attending a PTA committee meeting after lunch. She will hurry home from the meeting, in time to greet her children when they return home boisterously at three o'clock. She will make them a snack, hear a few interesting snippets from the day's activities, and send them off to play.

A pleasant and nostalgic picture. But one that is not true to life for many of today's mothers. Because today Mrs. Homemaker has often been replaced by Mrs. Working Mother.

Mrs. Working Mother may be on her way to her job before her children leave for school. Or if they are preschoolers, she may drop them off at a caretaker's house or a day-care center on her way to work. She will not be there when they return home from school. A relative, a grandmother, or an aunt may take over. Or a paid caretaker or baby-sitter.

Here are some figures that show the radical changes that have taken place in the last twenty-five years.

In 1975, 47 percent of mothers of children under eighteen were working. Thirty-nine percent of mothers of preschoolers under six were working. Fifty-five percent of mothers of children between six and seventeen were working. And the numbers and percentages of working mothers is increasing every year.

Some people may be alarmed that the number of working mothers is increasing. Others may applaud it. But whatever attitude you take toward this situation, it is a fact that must be reckoned with. Unfortunately, it is a fact that is virtually ignored in almost all of the books on child discipline. Advice on discipline is still directed to Mrs. Homemaker, circa 1947. This is fine for approximately half the mothers in America. But what about the other half? Mrs. Working Mother is the Invisible Woman of the child-rearing books. I want to try to correct that omission.

Of course in one sense all mothers work. And work hard. But in this chapter when I refer to a working mother I mean one who works at a job outside the home and gets paid for it. And I mean one who works not because she *has* to for some financial reason, but because she really wants to.

Incredible as it may seem in this enlightened age, there are numbers of people who will say, in all seriousness, "But why should a woman *want* to work outside the home?" These same people would think *you* were off your rocker if you asked them, in all seriousness, "But why would a *man* want to work outside the home?"

I am dedicated to the idea that people are missing a great deal if they do not find part of their self-fulfillment through the joy of parenting. But it should be obvious that neither a mother nor a father can find *all* of his other fulfillment through parenting. Part of their self-fulfillment, at least at some stages of their life span, needs to be found through productive and useful work. This does not have to be paid work, but it sure helps the family budget more that way! So I believe firmly that *both* mother and father have a right to self-fulfillment through productive and useful work at an outside job.

In times past, father found part of his fulfillment through work that lasted until his retirement. Mother found hers through being a mother and homemaker, as a volunteer worker, and then as a grandparent. Here are some figures to show why part of that picture is rapidly changing. Women today have, on the average, nearly twenty more years of life than was common in their grandmother's day. The average woman has about forty years still ahead of her by the time her last child is ready for first grade. In the face of this new and unprecedented life span, it is not hard to see why many mothers today choose to work after the children have entered school. Or to begin working even sooner. A woman no longer needs to think in terms of devoting her entire life only to her family. Of course this longer life span is not the only factor in the changing role of the mother, but it is a major one.

If someone should ask me, "Do you think a mother should work?" I would answer the same way I would answer the question, "Do you think a mother should breast-feed or bottle feed?" I would say, "It is entirely up to the mother. It is her choice. A mother should not be pressured into either breast-feeding or bottle feeding. And, in the same way, a mother should not be pressured into either staying home or working."

Let me attempt to dispel a few of the myths that have grown up about the working mother:

MYTH No. 1. *The children of working mothers are bound to have psychological problems. Therefore, a mother who works outside the home is harming her children.*

False. There is absolutely no hard scientific evidence to support this well-circulated myth. Sure, children of working mothers have psychological problems. But so do children of stay-at-home mothers. The mere fact that a mother works outside the home will not *in itself* cause her child to become neurotic or have problems. Countless women are demonstrating that it is possible to combine motherhood and an outside job with no detriment to their children.

MYTH No. 2. *Any bad behavior on the part of the child must be due to the fact that his mother is working.*

False. Many working mothers (and other people as well) are past masters at the art of conclusion-jumping. And if their youngster starts acting up in any way, at home or school, they are apt to blame it on the fact that they are working.

For example, a mother of a ten-year-old took her first full-time job. Three months later, when the boy was eleven, his ordinary, pleasant behavior began to change. He was sassy and belligerent around the house, he was disruptive at school, and suddenly became very difficult to get along with. The mother immediately assumed that this sudden change was his response to her taking a job. I would not assume that at all. I would guess that his behavior was typical of any child entering the stage of preadolescence (ages eleven and twelve) and that he would have behaved pretty much the same had she stayed home. If the child were younger than eleven, I would look into what might be going on at school or elsewhere that might be affecting him, rather than jump to the conclusion that the mother's working was causing the problem.

MYTH No. 3. *Only a neurotic woman would want to leave her home and work outside at a paid job.*

False. It should be obvious to any sophisticated observer that neither the office nor the home has any monopoly on neuroses.

Some ardent traditionalists convey to mothers that they are practically ruining their children's lives if they leave the home to work. Some militant feminists, on the other hand, imply that a woman who does *not* work is a traitor to her "sister-hood" and is knuckling under to the male chauvinist pigs. I say, "Bah and humbug" to both types of extremists. If a woman is happy and content being a stay-at-home mother, let her stay at home. If a woman is happy and content being a working mother, let her get a job.

This is a decision that must be made individually by each mother as a unique person. As Dorothy Whyte Cotton puts it so well in her book, *The Case for the Working Mother:*

> No two working mothers are alike. No two stay-at-home mothers are alike. . . . Just as staying home will not auto-matically make a mother "good," neither will going to work automatically make her "bad." One thing is certain: no clear-cut pattern of what a mother should do, or be, exists to fit all mothers.

From the point of view of the optimum development of the child, here are what I consider to be the ideal arrange-ments which meet the child's basic needs and allow the mother to gradually enter the world of work outside the home. But once again, every situation is different and every family must arrive at its own solution.

During the first three years of life very complicated develop-ments are taking place in the child's basic personality structure and his intelligence. Ordinarily these developments are best presided over by a mother or father as a full-time caretaker.

But when the child is 3 he can be sent to a nursery school

(which operates on a half-day schedule, as compared to a day-care center, which operates on a full-day schedule). He can start out two or three days a week and work up to five days a week. After the youngster is psychologically acclimated to nursery school and feels secure there, the mother can get a part-time job, and she can continue to work part-time until her child enters first grade.

When the child enters first grade and the stage of middle childhood, he then becomes much more involved with his peers and much less involved with his parents. When he comes home from school, he typically grabs a snack and zooms out again to play. He will be visiting other kids' homes, riding his bike, skateboarding, playing games, and doing other things that do not need close motherly supervision.

As soon as the child has entered first grade and become comfortably adjusted to it, the mother can confidently take on a full-time job because the child has far less need of her. Sometimes a mother can begin a full-time job when the youngster is in kindergarten. Of course she will need to find a good caretaker or some form of after-school care for the child, because of the short kindergarten day.

I want to remind you that I am speaking in general terms, and that there will be all sorts of exceptions to what I have just said. So please do not take this as a set of iron-clad instructions and feel guilty if your particular arrangements for combining work and parenting are different from those I have just outlined.

In her first three years, your child needs you to provide her with both the security of a deep emotional relationship and intellectual stimulation. This is in her first three years. But she does not need such a close maternal relationship when she is six or eight. If you constantly hover over her, you will eventually have to deal with the problems of an overprotected child.

Mothers need to begin gently working themselves out of a job by encouraging the independence of the child from age three on. The best mothers are those who make themselves dispensable rather than indispensable.

This overall philosophy of child-raising should help you decide when it is important for you to be at home with your child and when you can leave for an outside job without damaging his psychological well-being in the least.

Now let me try to answer some of the most important

questions working mothers have asked me about raising their children.

1. *I have a two-year-old girl and I must work for financial reasons. Should I get someone to take care of her in my home or send her to a day-care center?*

This question cannot be answered in the abstract. It all depends on what child care is available where you live. There are excellent day-care centers and there are absolutely awful ones. You may have an easy time finding a competent person to take care of your little girl in your home, or you may have a very difficult time finding someone. So it all depends. But, in general, I tend to lean toward a caretaker in the home rather than a day-care center for this age child.

2. *How can I find a good caretaker for my child when I am working?*

First of all, don't choose your child's caretaker by interviewing just one woman. By talking to several, you can screen out the people you would *not* want to hire. But before you make your final decision, you need to see the potential caretaker *in action* with your child. Only by seeing a sample of how she relates to your child can you realistically decide how she would handle your child if you hired her. So before hiring her on a final basis, spend several days being at home with her while you observe how she interacts with your youngster.

What do you look for? You want to pick up "vibes" from her behavior that she is warm, loving, easygoing, tender, and flexible in handling your child. She could be twenty or fifty or anywhere in between; age is irrelevant. Don't necessarily be impressed if she tells you she has had twelve years' experience in taking care of children. She may have had only one year's experience twelve times!

Ask for at least two references, and be sure to check them out. You will be glad you did, because you will learn a great deal from talking with other parents who have employed her.

Don't be unduly impressed if she tells you she majored in psychology in school. Your child won't be able to tell what she majored in. What counts is how she relates to your child, not what books she's read or what courses she's taken.

Even after you have hired her, if you get any hints from your child's behavior that things are not going right during the time he is with her, check into the situation. Drop in unexpectedly sometime to check things out. If you find she is *not* doing an adequate job, don't hesitate to get rid of her and find someone else.

How can you find such a person? Word of mouth is an excellent way. Ask other parents, your minister, your doctor, or the principal of your school. You can advertise in your local paper. You can also use an employment agency, but personally I think the first sources are better.

In many cases your best bet may turn out to be a middle-aged grandmotherly type whose own children have grown up, but who genuinely likes children and delights in being around them.

You may be lucky enough to find a good caretaker for your child among your relatives—a grandmother or aunt, for example. On the other hand, it may very well be that leaving your child in the hands of any of your relatives would be a recipe for Psychological Disaster! If you do find a suitable caretaker in a relative, insist on paying her, unless she declares that she would be insulted for you to do so. In most cases, unless a relative is being paid to take care of a child, she will consciously or unconsciously feel she is being imposed upon at times, and that is not good.

3. *How do you find a good day-care center for a preschooler?*

As I mentioned in answer to question 1, do not decide too quickly whether to send your preschooler to a day-care center or have him taken care of by a person in the home. Some children will work out better in a day-care center, some will be happier with a single caretaker.

But let's suppose you have decided on a day-care center. How do you go about finding a good one? The sad fact is that most mothers choose a center solely on the basis of geographical convenience. I am appalled by this, but it is true. I assume, however, that you want to use your intelligence and wisdom to select the best possible place for your child.

Some centers are incredibly bad, with incompetent teachers, an inadequate program, and a woefully inept knowledge of the psychology of the preschool child. But the center itself may be freshly painted and look spic and span, very impressive to the casual visitor in terms of its physical appearance!

If you live near a college or university, preferably one with a program in preschool education, you may be able to get a recommendation for one or more day-care centers. If not, you may be able to get a psychologist or psychiatrist in your area to recommend a good place.

You may, in the end, have to resort to researching day-care centers in the yellow pages of your telephone directory. You will probably find them listed under the heading "Nursery Schools." By the way, you will often see a school include in its advertisement the words "State Licensed." This impresses some naive mothers, who think to themselves, "That must be a good one, because it's licensed by the state." What these mothers don't know is that *all* nursery schools and day-care centers must be licensed by the state!

Pick out four or five centers and then take the time and trouble to visit each of them. Sit in on the classes and see what's going on. Notice what kind of rapport the teacher has with the children and how she treats them. Is the atmosphere of the class warm and friendly, or harsh and rigid? How many children is each teacher responsible for?

You do not need to be professionally trained in preschool education yourself to size up the. "vibes" in a classroom. I think that after you visit several centers, sit in the classrooms, and talk to the teachers and directors, you will be able to decide which one is best for your child. Incidentally, if a center does *not* allow you to see a classroom in operation, I suggest you immediately cross that school off your list.

4. *Sometimes I feel so guilty being a working mother. Am I short-changing my children by working?*

This question brings squarely into focus what is undoubtedly the chief enemy of the working mother: GUILT. My answer to this question aims to reduce the guilt of a working mother. So if you still feel guilty after reading it, there is a breakdown in communication somewhere and you are not getting my message!

Working mothers do tend to feel pangs of guilt from time to time because they fear they are not spending enough time with their children. But I have tried to make clear that it would be foolish to rate how good a mother is (working or stay-at-home) purely on the basis of how much time she spends with her children.

She can spend a lot of time with her children overprotecting them. That surely does not make her a good mother. She can spend a lot of time yelling and scolding them. That does not make her a good mother. She can spend a lot of time letting her children manipulate her and thus teaching them to be spoiled brats. That does not make her a good mother. Enuf said?

I have tried to point out that what makes a good mother is love, plus her ability to teach her children desirable behavior rather than undesirable behavior. A working mother can have this love and ability just as can a stay-at-home mother.

So a working mother should try to get out of her head the parental tape that tells her: "The amount of time you spend with your children is the sole criterion of whether or not you are a good mother." The use of negative thinking (chap. 15) can help you do this.

Incidentally, there are a lot of stay-at-home mothers who spend relatively little time with their children. They are off in a whirl of volunteer community activities, and their children see little of them. And yet, interestingly enough, these women do not seem afflicted by the guilt that plagues the typical working mother.

The guilt of the typical working mother is often due to the conscious or subconscious thought: "I want to get away from my children—they're driving me up the wall." I do not condemn such a wish at all. I think it's very normal for a parent to feel this way. But millions of American mothers think it is abnormal or "wicked" to have such feelings. However, whenever we are cooped up most of the day, with one person or several persons, it is normal to want to get away from that other person. Anyone who has gone on a one- or two-week backpack trip with one or two other people will know exactly what I mean.

So I want to say to all of you working mothers: It is completely normal to want to get away from your children from time to time. And this is a perfectly valid reason (among others) for taking a job outside the home.

Guilt feelings do not produce good parenting. Guilt feelings tend to make working mothers try to make up for being away from their children by overindulging them and by being afraid to be firm with them when they need firmness. The guilty mother is also the natural prey of the child who has learned how to manipulate her, and this is not good either.

Your question also asked: "Am I short-changing my

children?" The one situation in which a working mother may be doing so is when she works full-time during the first three years of her child's life. During this time, a child needs at least one constant caretaker with whom she can form a deep emotional relationship, as a foundation for the emotional relationships throughout the rest of her life. If you or the father are not available throughout the working day to fulfill that role, who will do it?

You may be lucky enough to find a really wonderful woman to act as your child's substitute mother during those first three years. But such a person is not easy to come by. Furthermore, suppose after taking care of your baby for a year, she moves away to another city? This will have a very upsetting effect on your baby. This possibility is something that many working mothers never think of, but you would be wise to take it into account. Obviously you, your child's mother, are not going to move away from her any time during those first three years. But you cannot have that absolute certainty with someone you hire.

Of it you go the day-care route instead of hiring an individual caretaker, you quickly are going to find that there are very few good ones. Unfortunately the United States lags way behind many other countries, such as Sweden, in providing working mothers with really top-notch day-care centers staffed by well-trained professionals.

There are exceptions to what I have just said, of course. I can speak only in generalities. You may be able to find very adequate care for your child during her first three years of life equal to what you yourself could give her. But, as a generalization, I would hazard the guess that you would probably not be able to. This is why I suggest that, if at all possible, you do not take an outside job until your child is three.

But if you take a part-time job at the time your child is three until she enters first grade, and then take a full-time job, there is no reason for you to feel guilty about being a working mother, or to fear that you are short-changing your child. In fact, if you are a working mother and use the discipline methods discussed in this book, you may find that your mothering ends up being far superior to that of many stay-at-home mothers who do not have this information about effective teaching methods with children.

5. *I am about to take a full-time outside job and I have a*

feeling that the emotional impact of this on my six-year-old boy will be negative. Is there anything I can do to get him to take a positive outlook on my working?

There certainly is. Remember the positive reward system (chap. 3)? Associate something positive *for him* with the fact that you will be working full-time outside the home. Tell him that this will enable the whole family to have more money to do things they want. Then each week, give him either a certain sum of money (say, a dollar) or buy him some toy or special thing he would like. Many mothers tell their children that by working they will be putting aside money for their child's college education. But this means little to a six-year-old. However, a dollar a week or more for an older child, or a special toy each week is something he can understand in the here and now. A few weeks of this and he will be feeling very positive about your working!

Also, I think it is important for you to take your child to see where you work and what you do there. Then your job becomes a real thing to him that he can be interested in and feel positive about. I once overheard one school-age child say proudly to another: "See that newspaper? My mother writes stories for that paper!"

So if your new job means that good things happen to him, your child is bound to feel positive about it.

6. *Can I use my teenagers to supervise my younger children in the late afternoon before I get home from work?*

You can, but I would strongly advise against it. Even if you pay them, it will probably work out badly. The reason is simple. Two children from the same family have all sorts of subterranean jealousies built into their personalities. These ambivalent feelings are bound to prevent effective supervision of the younger children by the older ones. You can hire a teenager from outside your family to do the job, but don't use one of your own.

7. *I feel so rushed and harried all the time, working full-time outside the home, but also responsible for the children and the household. What can I do about this?*

This is the complaint of many working mothers. Jean Curtis, the author of an excellent book, *Working Mothers*, having interviewed over two hundred mothers in the course of her research for the book, had this to say: "Almost all the working mothers I interviewed for this book had one thing in common: They were overworked and tired."

The answer is to sit down and wisely plan your time and organize your life. (It helps to involve your husband in this also.) I think it is safe to say that most people do not plan their time or organize their work. That is why there are numerous books for business executives on how to do just that. Sad to say, I do not know of any published book on time management for the working mother (although a friend of mine, Sid Love, is working on just such a sorely needed manuscript). Meanwhile, although it is not a book specifically addressed to working mothers, you will find *How to Get Control of Your Time and Your Life* by Alan Lakein (New American Library) very helpful.

Once you make the effort to plan and organize your time, you will be amazed at how much this will take the hurry and rush out of your life.

8. *I'm a working mother with teenagers. I've told them they are not to have their friends over when their father and I are not home, but it doesn't work out that way. Our home becomes the target house for other teenagers in the late afternoon. How can I put a stop to this?*

Begin by using the mutual problem-solving technique (chap. 11) and see what happens. If that does not produce the desired results, then you could use the following strategy.

Tell your teenagers that you all know what the problem is, and you are going to trust them not to have anyone over when you are not there. Then, if you find out that they are disobeying your instructions and violating your trust, tell them this: "You have violated my trust, and so I will need to get a college boy to take care of things in the late afternoons until we get home from work." They will scream and complain, of course, but pay no attention. After three weeks or so, tell them you will give them one last chance to prove that you can trust them on their own. If they justify your trust in them this time, fine. If not, bring back the college boy.

9. *How can I keep a feeling of closeness with my preschool children when I am away from them part of every day working?*

Just because you are not with them physically does not

mean you cannot be with them psychologically. First of all, you can phone them, which takes only five minutes of your time. Second, you can send them a postcard or a little note. Preschoolers get little mail, and it is always thrilling for them to get something that's really addressed to them.

Best of all, probably, is to use a tape recorder to foster closeness. You can tape cassettes anywhere (on your way to and from work, for example) or in your room before you go to bed, and mail them to your preschoolers from the office. You can read a story to them, you can make up a story of your own, you can talk with them about your job and what you are doing, you can talk with them about what you look forward to doing with them on the weekend, you can ask what they're doing at their day-care center or with their caretaker, you can tell them you love them.

In short, through the medium of a tape cassette you can tell them just about anything you could tell them if you were with them in person. And one big advantage of the tape cassette is that your youngster can play it over and over again, as much as he wants to. This is particularly helpful when he is home sick and needs the comfort of hearing your voice and knowing you care for him.

10. *I don't see any real reason why my three kids can't empty the dishwasher and tidy up the house by the time I get home at six o'clock, but they are not cooperative. What will motivate them to help me?*

The positive reward system (chap. 3) is your answer. I don't think you're going to get them to do these things without some kind of reward to motivate them.

11. *My nine-year-old daughter calls me at work with all her problems and my boss doesn't like it at all, to put it mildly. In spite of my telling her "emergencies only" she treats everything as an emergency. What can I do?*

Obviously your daughter is missing you, and her avenue of seeking more contact with you is the phone calls. Tell her to separate her calls into two groups: true "emergencies," which need action immediately, and calls about problems that do not need immediate action. Then allow her to phone you at the office for "immediate action" emergencies, but tell her to use a tape recorder to tell you about other problems she wants to talk over with you. This will enable her to get some emotional catharsis by talking about the problems. Then you can listen to the tape when you come home and are making dinner, and can talk things over with her either then or following dinner.

If your daughter should continue to abuse the privilege of phoning you at the office, tell her that if it's not a true emergency, you will be forced to hang up the phone on her. Once this happens a few times, she will stop deluging you with calls.

12. *I don't want to work full time, but I'm discovering that part-time jobs are hard to find. What can you suggest?*

You will find Joseph Cooper's book *A Woman's Guide to Part-Time Jobs* (Doubleday) very helpful. But you may find no good part-time jobs available at the time you are job hunting. So you have two other options open to you. First, carve out your own job. Go to several employers where you have salable talents and try to convince them to use your talents on a part-time rather than a full-time basis. In this way, you are creating your own part-time job. Second, you can volunteer your services free one day a week, and use this way of getting your foot in the door to promote yourself into a part-time paid job.

In closing this chapter I want to say: Mother, if you really do want to work, go to it! You'll be a better mother if you do than if you grimly stay home and wish you were somewhere else. Arrange your home situation so that you know your youngster is happy and well while you are away. I've given you the best guidelines for doing this that I know. Take care of your health, because being a working mother takes a lot of energy.

Enjoy your productivity and enjoy your family!

18

THE SINGLE PARENT

I hope that none of you married (even happily married) people make the mistake of skipping over this chapter or the following chapter on stepparenting because you feel it doesn't apply to you. Perhaps it doesn't.

But if your spouse is away on business a great deal, or in the service for long periods of time, or is suffering from a lengthy illness, you are also in many ways a single parent, although you are different from those who are single through divorce or death. I believe that all parents, whether married or single, can find something in these two chapters that will be useful to them, whether now or in the future.

I am sure you have gathered by now that I think parenting is one of the most joyous things that can happen to you in life. I hope you have also gathered that I think parenting is a complex skill that needs to be learned. Most people have no training in this skill and that is what makes it hard for them.

If parenting is hard for parents in an intact family, single parenting is much, much harder. If parenting in an intact family is like hiking up a mountain trail, single parenting is like hiking up that same mountain trail with a fifty-pound pack on your shoulders. There are many reasons why this is so. I will try to make them clear in this chapter.

Basically, there are three kinds of single parent: First is the widow with children. Second, the divorced mother with children. Although different in some ways, they have much in common. I speak of the divorced *mother* with children since it is almost always the mother who gets custody of the children. If you are a widower with children or a divorced father with custody, this category applies to you as well. The third kind of single parent is the divorced father (or, in rare cases, a divorced mother) without custody of the children.

These different groups of people have one thing in common: The first thing they must do to become good single parents to their children is to learn how to be a good parent to the child within themselves. That child is hurt, suffering, wounded, angry, and in desperate need of emotional support. They have to learn how to take care of the child within before they can do a good job of single parenting their own children.

Consider what happens psychologically to every widow, widower, or divorced parent. Researchers who have studied the subject of psychological stress have concluded that the loss of a spouse through death or divorce is the most stressful event that can happen to us. This means that every widow, widower, or divorced person is like a town that has been devastated by a hurricane. Your entire life-style has been wiped out and you have to begin immediately the work of creating a new life-style for yourself and your family.

Here is how one widow describes the experience of her psychological hurricane:

When that protective fog of numbness had finally dissipated, life became truly terrifying. I was full of grief, choked with unshed tears, overwhelmed by the responsibility of bringing up two children alone, panicked about my financial situation, almost immobilized by the stomach-wrenching, head-splitting pain of realizing that I was alone. My psychic pain was such that putting a load of dirty clothes in the washing machine, taking out the vacuum cleaner, making up a grocery list, all the utterly routine household chores, loomed like Herculean labors.

I was alone. Alone. Without Martin. Forever. And I didn't know what to do. I was beset with problems, some real, most imagined. I did not know how or where to start to put my life in order.[1]

And these are the words of a divorced mother describing how the breakup of her marriage affected her:

My daughter says she doesn't have a family, only a mother.

She wants a daddy and a baby and a crazy, raucous, family dinner hour. My heart saddens. I want those good feelings for her.

Something is missing.

I am missing the familiarity of one man's body, the warmth of him beside me.

I am missing my old friends, family. They wonder, and sometimes pull away. . . .

Rhythm is interrupted. Permanence is gone. So is security.[2]

Here is how a divorced father describes what it felt like when the psychological impact of his divorce hit him:

During those first three or four months after my divorce I thought I'd go batty. No wife and kids to greet me when I came home from work. I'd walk into my tomb-like apartment, and the silence nearly killed me. The first thing I would do was turn on the radio to a talk show so I could hear someone else's voice. I even started talking to myself to keep from feeling so lonely.[3]

In addition to contending with the psychological hurricane that uproots your familiar life-style, when your marriage has been broken by death or divorce, you have to deal with an overwhelming sense of personal loss. You may be confronted with the death of a spouse. You may be dealing with the death of a marriage. Even if the divorce was mutually agreed upon, or even if it was your idea, you will still have to contend with a sense of loss, and that loss will probably be more than you had expected.

In the late 1930s there was a tragic fire at the Coconut Grove nightclub in Boston, in which hundreds were killed. About the only good thing to come out of that tragic event was a research study headed by Dr. Erich Lindemann. He and his associates studied the reactions of the survivors whose loved ones were lost in the holocaust. Dr. Lindemann coined the term *grief work* for the psychological mourning that needs to be done by a person who has suffered the loss of someone important to him.

Dr. Lindemann found that many people resisted doing their grief work. They refused to go over the clothes or personal effects of the person they had lost because they did not want to experience the unhappiness this would bring. They tried to maintain the "stiff-upper-lip" position. These were the people who were most ineffective in coping with their psychological loss. The people who adjusted most successfully were those who allowed themselves to experience and express all the psychological pain they felt in reaction to their loss.

This research study may throw some light on Jesus' statement in the Beatitudes which has puzzled many people: "Blessed are those who mourn, for they will be comforted." I think Jesus was saying that unless we allow ourselves to mourn, to experience directly our grief and suffering, we cannot find psychological release and comfort.

Here is how a widow describes her grief work:

> One of the chores of grief involves going over and over in one's mind the circumstances that led to the death, the details of the death itself. Endless dwelling on the dead person. Memories are taken out and sifted. Finally the widow accepts the fact that her husband is dead. This is the reality. And talking about it helps make it real.[4]

Grief work takes time, and it cannot be rushed. But the heartening thing about it is that if you *do* allow yourself to feel your hurt and grief and suffering—*if you do your grief work*—the time will come when it is over and you are once again capable of happiness. It helps a great deal to know this in advance. As one widow put it:

> I am convinced that if I had known the facts of grief before I had to experience them, it would not have made my grief less intense, not have lessened my misery, minimized my loss, or quietened my anger. No, none of these things. But it would have allowed me hope. It would have given me courage. I would have known that once my grief was worked through, I would be joyful again.[5]

In addition to dealing with a hurricane-swept lifestyle and an overwhelming sense of loss, you will also need to begin building for yourself a new self-image.

If you are a widow, chances are that much of your self-image was entwined with that of your husband. When he died, part of your self-image died also. The more dependent a person you are, the more this is true. The more independent and self-reliant you are, the less this is true. But to some extent, it is true of all widows and widowers: The loss of your spouse means the loss of at least part of your self-image. The very derivation of the word *widow* makes this clear. It comes from the Sanskrit, and it means *empty*.

The same thing, in a different way, happens in a divorce. Your self-image receives a terrible blow. The spouse you married has conveyed this message to you: "You are no longer desirable to me as a person." Even if you took the initiative in dissolving the marriage, you still received this message. Amazingly enough, in any divorce, *both* husband and wife end up feeling rejected. "It's as if I threw out one half of myself when I threw Bob out," said one divorcee.[6]

Every divorced person has to struggle to overcome a sense of being inadequate as a self. That's why it is important to establish new relationships with people who value you and find you worthwhile.

In your marriage relationship, only a part of the person you potentially are was brought to the surface. Now other parts of your personality must be discovered and used. You must go through a difficult period in which a new self-image is born. This isn't any easier than the grief work. You will need to break old psychological molds. It will be good for you to experiment with new hobbies or sports or activities that you may have considered in the past but never tried.

In addition to coping with the shattering of a lifestyle, a sense of personal loss, and battered self-image, you must also contend with a fourth psychological stress: loneliness. For a widow or a divorced parent the loneliness is ever present and gut-wrenching. One widow put it this way:

> It's depressing as the backyard of hell. That's where I am.[7]

Your loneliness is something you carry around with you, wherever you go and whatever you do. Someone is missing. It may be a beloved husband. It may even be a hated spouse. But right now there is no other significant person in your life to whom you belong. And even when you are with other people, the fact of your aloneness intrudes upon your awareness. The world seems to come organized in twos, but you are only one.

When you add up all of these agonizing stresses, it is no wonder that the little child within you is a wounded and quivering lump of negative feelings. He feels hurt, devastated, bewildered, abandoned, angry, and alone. So before you can do an effective job single parenting your own children, you must learn how to parent that unhappy little child in you and get him to feel better. How can you do this?

The wisest thing you can do for yourself at this time is to get professional counseling. When going through a divorce or the experience of widowhood there is no better way you could spend money on yourself if you have it to spend. If you have managed to save up some money for a rainy day, *the rainy day is here!* Spend it on therapy for yourself. If you are a widow and have received some life-insurance money, don't put it all in a tax-sheltered investment. Use part of it for therapy. Many people spend money for marriage counseling, but few are wise enough to invest in "divorce counseling." Yet I think that ideally *every* person going through a divorce should receive counseling. It is the most beneficial thing you could do, not only for yourself but for your children.

Almost any city of some size has low-cost clinics where you can get counseling if you cannot afford the fees of a psychologist or psychiatrist in private practice. You may be put on a waiting list for a while, but if you are patient you will eventually get the counseling you need.

One single parent describes what her therapy meant to her in the midst of this enormously stressful period of her life:

> My therapist, a woman, was a source of strength from the first visit. She gave me a feeling of security. Suddenly I felt safe enough to talk. I no longer had to spill out my distress to an unresponsive pad of lined paper. The psychologist listened. And slowly, patiently, she guided me out of the maze of anxieties I had lost myself in. Together we examined my fears. As I talked about them, many disappeared. Others, I began to realize, were manageable. It was a great liberation.[8]

If for some reason you are not able to get professional counseling, you can do two things on your own.

First, since you have undergone the loss of a spouse, and with it an emotional support system, you can begin to build a new emotional support system for yourself. How? For example, Parents Without Partners, a non-profit organization, has chapters throughout the United States. (Incidentally, they publish a very fine magazine, *The Single Parent*, which you will find helpful to read.) I would suggest you join their local chapter. If you are a woman, don't go there just to meet men, although you will meet some. Go there to meet *other women*. Take your time and find three or four women you feel are on your "wavelength" and get to know them better. Have them over to your house or apartment. You might even want to organize your own little "hot line" of these four or five people. Then you could phone each other whenever you felt overwhelmed and in desperate need to talk to someone. The organization of your own "emotional support life line" group might be the single most important thing you could ever do for both yourself and your children during your first year of widowhood or divorce.

Second, you can get your feelings out in whatever way you find satisfying. The more primitive the way, the better it is. For example, when you are alone in your house or apartment, take a pillow and beat the bed or sofa with it, letting out your feelings of anger and hurt and grief. Here's how one single parent let out some of her feelings:

> *One evening I was working late. Feeling terrible. Sorry for myself. Angry at the world. Wounded. Bewildered. I didn't know what to do. Another woman was still there. I asked her to come with me. "I have to scream," I explained idiotically. It was after six and the building was practically empty. I called the elevator. Pushed the button for the top floor. And I started screaming. Long wailing screams. No words. Like an animal. I pushed the hold button and kept on screaming. I felt an enormous relief, the kind of exhausted peace one has after vomiting. And the lump in my throat was gone. My throat was sore and raw. I felt as if I had had surgery. My companion put her arm around me and said, "I'm going to take you home now."*[9]

One single parent used an old towel, systematically knotting it up and ripping it to pieces while putting into words the feelings that were tearing her apart.

Once you have put yourself on the road to recovery by helping the hurt and angry child inside you, the job of single parenting becomes much less overwhelming. You can then concentrate on the job of single parenting your children.

Your first task is to free yourself from some old myths. The first myth is that broken homes inevitably produce children who have psychological difficulties. There is absolutely no scientific evidence to support this old wives' tale. Yet I have heard teachers and principals and other people who should know better repeat their versions of this myth.

I have attended psychological conferences with a teacher and principal about a child I had in therapy, and heard the principal or teacher say, "Of course, he comes from a broken home." When they heard these words the other people nodded sagely, as if that explained the whole thing. Sometimes when I have been at such conferences involving a problem child from an *intact* home, I have been tempted to say, with Olympian wisdom, "Well, of course, he comes from an intact home." So let's throw away, once and for all, the idea that a child from a single home is necessarily handicapped psychologically.

The second myth is that parents from intact homes naturally and inevitably do a good job in raising their children. Many of them don't.

With these myths dispelled, let's look at the three main categories of single-parent homes: widows, divorced mothers with custody, and divorced fathers without custody.

The balance of this chapter will consider each of these categories individually, examining parenting problems unique to each category and giving specific suggestions to aid each group of single parents in dealing most effectively with their children.

I am well aware, of course, that these are not homogeneous catagories. Consider a widow whose husband has died and left no insurance and no will, who is working as a secretary and just barely making ends meet to support two grade-school children in a town of forty thousand in Ohio. This woman is by no means in the some life situation as a widow whose husband has died leaving her a large insurance income and a family business, who is raising two teenagers in Baltimore, Maryland.

Consider a divorced mother whose ex-husband has fled the state, sends her no child-support checks, and shows no interest in their two preschool children. This parent is obviously not in the same life situation as a divorced mother of two preschoolers whose ex-husband lives twenty minutes away, sees the children regularly, and sends his child-support checks equally regularly. Consider the divorced father without custody whose ex-wife is cooperative and flexible in his visitations with the children. This man is certainly not in the position of the divorced father without custody whose ex-wife immediately hangs up the phone when he calls his school-age children and makes it as difficult as possible for him to see them.

Each of these situations is very different from the others. Yet these single parents must each face many common problems of child-raising and discipline, and meet other life challenges in common.

First of all, let me point out that the children of single parents are first and foremost *children*. They go through exactly the same developmental stages as children in intact homes. Secondly, the discipline techniques for raising children are the same whether you are dealing with two parents or a single parent. The positive reward system, contracting, Time Outs, the feedback technique, the mutual problem-solving technique, and the family council work with children from both kinds of homes.

And now let's look at the parenting problems confronting the three main categories that single parents fall into: widowed mothers, divorced mothers with custody, and divorced fathers without custody.

Widows as Single Parents

Your first job in relation to the children is to prepare them for your husband's death, if you and he know it is coming. This is not an easy job because our whole culture does as much as possible to turn away from the reality of death. Therefore, you will have to overcome your cultural conditioning which urges you to dodge the fact of death.

Your most effective weapons in helping your children face their father's impending death are courage and the truth. Above everything else, tell them the truth, regardless of their age. Children can face an unpleasant truth much better than the pervasive feeling that you are hiding something from them. You know your children. Adjust the truth that you tell them to their level of understanding. And don't be afraid to say, "I don't know," if they ask you something you can't answer.

If your husband dies unexpectedly, then your first job with the children is to help them face the reality of his death, which has come so abruptly.

Whether expected or unexpected, when your husband dies, your most important job is to help your children mourn him. Since many widows shirk their own grief work in order to avoid the pain of mourning, it is no wonder they have trouble in helping their children mourn. In fact, it comes as an absolute surprise to many adults that children even *need* to mourn the death of a parent.

As one perceptive widow put it:

> *I knew that Buffy and Jonny missed their father terribly, but at the beginning I did not realize how much. And what I did not understand and what nobody told me was that children have to work through their grief too. When they were babies, I read dozens of books on child care, but none of them ever told me anything about helping children cope with the fact of death, helping children accept the death of a parent. This should be changed.*[10]

Most children find it very difficult to mourn. Unless they have been raised to express their feelings freely, as I advocate in this book, children generally tend to clam up when experiencing intense emotions. Their feelings of shock, loss, abandonment, hurt, and anger seem so overwhelming that they are afraid to express them. You, as their parent, can help them in two ways.

First, share with them your own feelings of unhappiness, hurt, loneliness, abandonment, and even anger that their father, your husband, has died. This will make it easier for them to express their feelings to you.

Second, use a variation of the feed back technique with them. As you will recall, in the ordinary use of the feedback technique you feed back to the child only the feelings he has actually expressed in words. In this situation the child may have expressed no feelings at all about his father's death. But you know that he is holding his feelings inside him.

And so you feed back feelings that you know must be there but which he has not actually expressed. Depending on his age and level of understanding you can say, "I know you must feel just awful about Dad's death. One day you have your dad, and the next day he is dead of a heart attack. You must miss him very much." If he does begin to express some of his feelings in response to your gentle psychological probe, fine. Continue to use the feedback technique to draw him out. But if he only nods and clams up and makes it clear he does not want to talk about it, drop it for the time being. Try it again at a later time.

If your child persists in clamming up about his father's death, do not force him. Even though it is psychologically best for him to mourn and get his feelings out in the open, respect his right to choose psychological privacy and *not* talk about it.

One of the reasons it is important to help children do their grief work is that if the child is not able to do this, then when he grows up he becomes afraid to love. He is afraid that if he dares to love another person, that person may also be taken away from him like his father. (And it should not be too surprising that widows also who do not do their grief work are often afraid to love, and therefore shy away from deep and meaningful relationships that could lead to remarriage.)

So the first important job to accomplish with your children is to help them do their grief work.

The second most important thing for you to do is to create an order and structure to your life, if it doesn't already have one. If you already have a job, continue working at it. The fact that you *have* to get up in the morning and you *have* to turn out certain work in connection with your job is psychologically good for you. This reminds me of a patient I had once in Oregon who illustrated this truth. I was treating him for depression. He came in one week for his regular appointment and said, "You know, Doc, for about ten minutes this morning I wasn't depressed! You know when? When I was cleaning the frost off my spark plugs so I could start my car. I was so busy concentrating on cleaning the spark plugs I forgot about being depressed!" Work can do the same thing for the widow who is hurt and depressed and lonely. Work can give order and regularity and structure to your life.

If your husband has left you so well fixed financially that you do not need to work, I would still recommend that you get at least a part-time job. This will force you to involve yourself in the world of adults and prevent you from confining your life to the tight little circle of your family.

You may think of your children as a tremendous burden to carry on top of your psychological feelings of raw distress. In one sense they are undeniably a burden on you. But in another sense you can thank God for the burden! For their demands on you, like the demands of a job, will force you to keep going. Coping with your children will help take your mind off your own problems. Your children will be your anchors time and time again when your emotions are riding on stormy seas.

So both a job and your children help create the stability and structure your life needs at this time.

Third, even more than if you were a parent in an intact family, you need to make definite provision for regular time away from your children. If you are still in the grief-work period and are not ready to start dating again, then your time away from the children might well be spent with other women. Other widows and divorced women are much more likely to understand your situation than married friends. Once again, Parents Without Partners is an excellent place to find such friends.

You can also find time away from your children, depending on their ages, by hiring a baby-sitter twice a week for a few hours or a half a day. This will give you time to go shopping, to a movie, or just the chance to luxuriate in doing nothing. If all of your children are in school, is is easy to get away by yourself for part of each day. Be a good mother to your children, yes. But don't be a slave to them.

When you have done enough of your grief work to be ready to begin dating again, you will have to contend with a new problem in parenting your children: *guilt*. No matter how much your intellect and logic tell you that it's time for you to have men in your life again, you may experience irrational feelings of guilt as if by dating you would be neglecting your children. You may also irrationally feel that, by dating, you are betraying your dead husband. Even if before he died he specifically told you that he wanted you to marry again! To combat these irrational feelings I suggest you use negative thinking (chap. 15).

Talk to yourself something like this: "Helen, how could you be dating again? You are a terrible person! Not only are you being disloyal to Bill, but you are neglecting the children's needs. You have only so much love to give, and if you share it with the men you are dating you will have just that much less love and affection to give to your children. So nip this dating phase in the bud! Give up men entirely and devote yourself completely to the care of your children until they are all twenty-one." By putting these irrational guilt feelings into words and saying them out loud to yourself, you will lessen their hold over you.

There is another problem you will have in raising your children. It is easier for me to describe this than to tell you how to solve it, since I do not know your individual situation. It is the problem of providing a male image or a father surrogate in your children's lives. This is more of a problem for a boy than a girl, but it is still a real problem for both. A boy needs a man to identify with and model himself after, and he does not have that, since his father is gone. A girl needs a woman to model herself after, and she has that in you, her mother. But she also needs a father surrogate to serve as a model for the man she will ultimately marry, and she does not have that.

What can you do about this? Perhaps there is an in-law or a relative—a grandfather or perhaps an uncle—who can play an active male role with your children. In rare cases a male friend can do this. This person can be invited over to dinner or picnics. He can take the children to movies, take them fishing or camping, take them to sports events, go swimming or sailing with them. If you cannot find such a person in a relative or friend, there is an alternative that single women rarely think of. If your children are preschoolers or in middle childhood, you could hire a high school or college boy, carefully selected, to do things with them two afternoons a week or one weekend a month. I suggest you find someone who is capable of doing many things, particularly things your children may not know how to do, such as swimming or playing baseball or football or basketball or fishing or camping or backpacking. They will enjoy learning to do new things with this male figure.

A man you are dating cannot play this kind of role with your children until you and he have settled down to a steady relationship. And I recommend you not bring the men you are dating into your children's lives very much until you feel ready to settle down to a steady relationship with one of them.

Which brings us to your last task as a widow and single parent. And that is not to make a career of widowhood. Here is one example:

A memory flashed through my head. A scene at an airport. I was waiting for my flight to be announced. A woman

sat down beside me. Small, well-dressed, somehow birdlike.
"Good morning," she said, "I'm Mrs. Wendell Willkie."
Even then I was horrified. Her husband had died years be-
fore. But he was still providing her identity!

It was a chilling flashback. I thought to myself, "I'm not
Mrs. Martin Caine. I'm Lynn Caine."[11]

So I assume that after you have finished your grief work
you will begin to forge a new self-image that will be different
from the self you were when you were married. As part of
that new self-image you will begin dating again, which may
lead to a new marriage.

At this point you will have to contend with mixed feelings
your children will have toward the person you choose to
marry. I'm assuming you are not foolish enough to
contemplate marrying a man who does not get along with
your children. That way lies disaster. So I'm assuming that
your children and your prospective husband basically like
each other. However, no matter how much your children like
their prospective stepfather initially, they will still be torn by
mixed feelings. On the one hand, they want a new and stable
male figure in their home and in their family. They need one.
But on the other hand, they probably have idealized their father, as children typically do after the death of a parent. This
means a clash between their idealized image of their father
and the real-life, down-to-earth image of your fiancé. In such
a clash of images, your fiancé loses.

In addition, although they may even have asked you,
"Couldn't you marry again so we could have a new daddy
like other children do?" they have probably had you all to
themselves for several years and they don't want to give that
up. So they see your husband-to-be both as someone who will
add to their love input and as someone who interferes with
their love input from you.

Inside your children's minds is a complex, mixed tangle of
irrational and contradictory feelings toward him. Although he
and your children got along beautifully before you married
him, once you marry him, he may suddenly become the target of what to him is some bewildering and unwarranted hostility from them. This is one of the ways they try to solve the
dilemma of their mixed feelings. So what you can do for this
man is to help him not to take this hostility personally, and

help him understand your children's confused and irrational feelings.

It would be a great help for you to invest in four or five sessions with a professional counselor for you, your new fiancé or husband, and your children. As long as these ambivalent feelings exist only in your children's unconscious minds, they can come out only in disguised forms. But a trained professional can help all of you lay your feelings out on the table to look at. Once the feelings are out in the open they can be talked about and worked through.

Finally, I have one small but important suggestion. Almost always, when a parent remarries, the newly married couple leave immediately after the wedding for a honeymoon. Nothing could confirm more the children's dire suspicions that when you marry they will lose a great deal of you. Have you not proved this, since the very first thing you do after marrying your new husband is to go off and leave them? So instead of taking off on a honeymoon immediately after your marriage, I suggest you wait a week. This may seem a small thing to you, but it will be greatly reassuring to your children.

One last word. This chapter deals basically with single parenting. It does not deal with parenting problems that arise when a new husband, who is now a stepfather for the children, enters the scene. I strongly suggest you read the next chapter, Stepparents and the Blended Family, before embarking on a new marriage. It will help you become much more aware of the psychological booby traps for children that can exist in a new marriage.

The Divorced Single Mother with Custody

Let's begin by assuming the least complicated situation for you: one in which your ex-husband does not hassle you in any way. He sends his child-support payments regularly and he visits the children regularly. It would be too much to expect that you and he would be able to talk over problems concerning the children so that both of you can work on the problem together. That would be the ideal situation, and a few divorced couples manage to achieve it. But they are very few.

Assuming that you are not being hassled by an ex-spouse, what problems do you face as a single parent?

First is the economic problem. In twenty years of counseling divorced couples I have known only three divorced single mothers whose standard of living was not drastically reduced after the divorce. Those three lucky women had ex-husbands who were so well fixed financially that the divorce had no real effect on the children's standard of living. But for most divorced single mothers the opposite is true. Many of them are almost literally pinching pennies and worried sick about supporting themselves and the children.

The worst thing of all is that very few of these mothers had any inkling that their finances would be so tight after the divorce. This is partly due to the general ignorance among married people about what divorce is really like—legally, financially, and emotionally.

In my work as a psychological counselor of divorced people, I have come to the conclusion that our society needs a profession of financial counselor to divorced persons. Such a counselor would help you as a divorced mother to draw up a list of your salable talents, or find a way to get yourself trained for a new occupation, learn how to write résumés and do job interviews, perhaps even learn how to go into business for yourself. Since the profession of financial divorce counselor does not exist, I suggest you find someone who could fit this description (a lawyer, a CPA, a businessman, someone at an employment agency, an executive hiring service, a family friend) and get him or her to help you with this task. Because 99 chances out of 100, the money you have coming in from child support, alimony, or your employment is nowhere near enough to support you and your family decently. And if you are worried sick about family finances it is obviously going to interfere with your ability to do a good job of parenting.

The more things you know how to do for yourself, the better off you will be financially. If you check out nearby colleges and adult education programs, you will find courses in how to take care of your own car and make simple household repairs, such as fixing a leaky faucet and doing simple electrical repairs. If you can't find such a course, you will be amazed at how many how-to books are available at your local library. One of the best is *I Took a Hammer in My Hand,* the woman's build-it and fix-it handbook by Florence Adams. This book covers such topics as home carpentry repairs, plumbing, electricity, automobiles, and how not to get taken on car repairs.

If you are short of money, you can learn how to use the good old barter system.

You begin by listing every conceivable skill you have to trade, and then find somebody who will exchange that skill for something you want. Here are some examples.

You can exchange babysitting with another mother so each of you can get away from your kids now and then.

If you play bridge well, you can exchange bridge lessons for the use of a washing machine twice a week.

If you're a good cook, you can exchange a fine meal for having that leaky faucet fixed.

Not only is the barter system an excellent way to save money, but it gives you a chance to meet some interesting people as well. A divorced patient of mine once decided to try the barter system. She had a big lawn that needed cutting; she also had a typewriter and was a good typist. She found a struggling, after-hours author who was happy to mow her lawn in return for her typing his manuscript. Unfortunately, he never sold the book, in spite of her excellent typing. But there is still a happy ending to the story; He is now not only cutting the grass, he's also painting the house and living in it as her husband.

Second, I say the same thing to you that I did to the widow who is a single parent. You have custody of your children. And no doubt you think to yourself at times, "Why couldn't *he* have custody and see what it feels like—it's overwhelming!" It's natural for you to feel at times that the children are a burden, natural to wish sometimes that you could give them over to their father and be rid of them.

And yet those children are blessings in disguise! Because when you are meeting the demands they make on you, when you are helping them with their lives, this takes your mind off yourself and your own terrible feelings. Your children and your job give a structure to your life, and you need that structure, especially when the devastating feelings of the early aftermath of divorce hit you.

Third, you, like the widowed single parent, need an emotional support system in your life. You will have to face the shocking reality that many of your old married friends will quietly drop you. The wives are usually too insecure and prone to view you as a threat to their marriages. (And often they are quite right. Most divorced women, as well as widows, have the unsettling experience of receiving sexual propositions from husbands who were friends prior to the divorce.) You will soon discover that you are a fifth wheel in the married circle of friends with whom you once traveled. A single parent widow expresses her bitterness at making this discovery:

> *I was really stricken when I found out that a very dear friend had not invited me to her annual Sunday-after-Thanksgiving dinner. This had been a tradition among our little group for a good ten years. There were eight of us, four couples, who always got together for dinner on that Sunday night. The year after Martin died, I wasn't invited. In my naïvete, in my self-centeredness, I thought at first that the dinner had been canceled because the hostess thought I would be too sad. But no, the dinner had been held. Instead of the Caines, another couple had been invited. Lynn Caine, widow, was no longer a desirable dinner guest.*
> *After that I became conscious of being left out of other gatherings of people whom I had always considered good, dear friends. I became rather bitter about it.[12]*

It is a shocking experience to find that you seem to have suddenly become an invisible person to your former circle of married friends. But you will have to face it. This means that your emotional support system must come from new friends you meet who are divorced or widowed, single parents like you are.

One of the things you will discover as a single parent is that there is a whole minority subculture in America of people like yourself, with different problems, different goals, different feelings, and different lifestyles from the mainstream culture of married couples. This subculture of divorced persons and single parents is invisible to the culture of married couples. If you continue to see friends in the married culture, you will often discover that they simply do not respond when you begin to talk about your feelings and problems as a divorced person and single parent. The reason for this is often patently obvious. The couple's own marriage is shaky and it upsets them to think that what you are talking about might one day happen to them.

So go to Parents Without Partners, Solo Parents, or other organizations of divorced people or single parents. If you are the outdoor type and like hiking and camping, you can join the Sierra Club (national headquarters: 530 Bush Street, San Francisco, California 94108) and go on hikes or trips with the Sierra Singles section of the club. They also have very easy hikes you can take your children on. In all of these organizations you can form new friendships. No married person can really deeply understand the problems you face as a single parent. Only another single parent can.

Meeting other single men can help also. You do not have to look at every man as potential Husband Material. You and the man might become good friends to each other (which is important) without becoming romantically involved. Here's what one divorced mother told me:

> *I think the thing that helped me the most was beginning to talk with divorced men. I mean really talk. Gut-level talk. I hadn't had the opportunity to do that before. You find they are suffering traumas too. You know it intellectually but you don't really know it until you talk to them. Somehow it was comforting to me to know that other men were going through this as well as women.*

Of course, when you are ready to begin dating again, men will become an important part of your emotional support system. How to meet desirable men is the subject for a book in itself, but let me offer a few hints. First, there are the singles organizations I've already mentioned. If you are lucky, your job may offer an opportunity. If you are in a one-person office, you may have a terrific job but it's not going to help you much to meet men.

Out here on the West Coast we have two excellent ways of meeting men. One is a singles newspaper called the *National Singles Register*. Many divorced women are afraid to put an ad in this paper for fear they will meet weirdos or creeps. Their fearful fantasies, however, have little relation to the high quality of men and women you can meet by placing or answering ads in this paper. My divorced patients, both male and female, have been very successful in meeting singles through this newspaper. One widow who was a patient met a professor of philosophy at UCLA, whom she later married. If you are on the West Coast and interested in finding out more about the newspaper, you can write for a sample copy to *Na-*

tional Singles Register, P.O. Box 567, Norwalk, California 90650.

We on the West Coast also have a new technique called video-dating. You are interviewed for five minutes on video tape. Clients can then see one another's video tapes. If a man is interested in meeting you, you are informed of that and have the opportunity to see *him* on video tape, and vice versa. If the interest seems to be mutual, you are introduced to one another. Such a technique makes a great deal of sense to me as an effective way for simpatico singles to meet.

I see I'm writing as if all you had to do was to immediately join a hiking club or try video-dating or put an ad in a singles newspaper. And of course it's not that easy. For you have to overcome a four-letter enemy named FEAR in order to start dating again. Fear that a man may not find you desirable. Fear of the unknown. This fear may wear many disguises, and one of them is often called, "My child needs me and that's why I don't want to date yet."

One of my patients had been divorced for almost two years and had made no effort to get back into circulation. Ann was thirty-two, attractive, educated, and scared as well as scarred. A messy divorce had left her ego bruised to the point where it hardly existed. Although she was lonely and part of her wanted to meet people and start going out, she insisted that her seven-year-old daughter needed her. Ann had got to the point where she had convinced herself that her daughter couldn't do without her. (Although actually both of them needed time away from each other.)

The ski club at the corporation where Ann worked offered a weekend trip for very little money, and I was finally able to persuade her, reluctantly, to go. She left her daughter with an aunt who lived nearby. She told me the next week, "I worried about Cindy all the way up on the bus Friday night. But by the next morning, when I got on the slopes, I started enjoying myself for the first time in so long that I hardly thought of her at all, to be honest. It was really great going away. I think it practically saved my life. And I met a very nice guy who's taking me out to dinner this week, and Cindy enjoyed the time at her aunt's. So I guess you're right. It really is good for *both* Cindy and me to get out."

Fourth, you are probably going to be overwhelmed by feelings of inadequacy, particularly in the early stages of divorce. Even if you were not happy with your husband, at least he was *there*, and you could talk over with him your feelings and problems about raising the children. It always helps to have somebody to back you up about a decision regarding the children, when you are unsure. But now you are alone.

There are two things that can help you combat your feelings of inadequacy: information and "informal group therapy."

You would not feel so inadequate about raising your children if you had your own personal psychologist to advise you. In a sense, by reading this book, you have me to fulfill that role for you.

But a book is never as good as a real live person, and if you can at all afford it, I suggest you find a psychologist or psychiatrist you can have as your own special consultant. Not as someone you go to for therapy, but someone you might consult perhaps once or twice a year when you feel you need to, especially about your children.

Married couples often get together for different social events—meetings, informal dinners, coffee klatches, or parties. One of the usual topics of conversation at these gatherings is children. This is what I call "informal group therapy." Because the couples say things to each other like, "George is so obnoxious at that two-year-old stage that sometimes I could just kick him down the stairs!"

"Hey, that's the way I feel about Russell. I guess it's normal to feel that way, huh?"

If parents did not have an opportunity to meet this way, they would really have little chance to find out how other people raise their children. They would not know what chidren are like at different ages, what problems other parents face, and what feelings other parents have about their children, such as frustration and anger. This informal exchange gives parents a chance to ventilate their feelings and experience the emotional support of the group.

You as a single parent need this kind of informal group therapy with other single parents. They may be your friends or people you talk to at meetings of single-parent groups. You will find such sharing invaluable in raising your children. It will help greatly to reduce your feelings of inadequacy.

Fifth, one problem the widowed single parent does not have to contend with that you probably do is that of guilt feelings about the breakup of your marriage. The widow did not have any choice in becoming a single parent. You did, in most cases (unless the divorce was completely your husband's idea). Either way, your guilt feelings will cause you to feel, from time to time, "This whole divorce was a dreadful mistake. We should have stayed together!" Incidentally, this is one of the important reasons to seek out marriage counseling or divorce counseling. If you go through a period of professional counseling and *then* decide that your marriage is dead and cannot be revived, you are much less likely to feel guilty than if you never had counseling.

You are going to find that guilt feelings tend to interfere with the wise handling of your children. You may be tortured by needless self-blame, such as, "Look what I have done to my children through this terrible divorce!" And this may tempt you to overindulge or give in to your children at times when you should be firm. It's as if you are saying to yourself, "I have done a terrible thing to my children by putting them through this divorce; the least I can do is to pamper them a bit to make up for it." Such guilt feelings do not help you do an effective job of parenting.

Guilt may also strike you an agonizing blow in the pit of your stomach when you begin dating again. One divorced single parent puts it this way:

> I work all day, and then when I start getting dressed for a dinner date and have to leave my four-year-old with a sitter after I've already been gone all day, I feel so selfish and so guilty, especially if he starts crying as I go out the door.[18]

Your intelligence may tell you that you need to date and have a social life. But your guilt feelings may be saying to you, "No, you must stay home and devote yourself totally to the children." Here is where negative thinking (chap. 15) can help you rid yourself of this irrational guilt so that you can feel free to fulfill yourself as a person and do a good job of raising your children.

Sixth, you will have to contend with dreadful feelings of loneliness. These can strike you anytime, anywhere. You will probably find them a constant companion until you ultimately marry again. Your best way of coping with loneliness is to rely on your emotional support system and establish your own special "hot line" with other divorced or widowed parents.

Seventh, you need to know how to handle your children's feeling about the divorce. In the same way that children tend to clam up about the death of a parent, they also tend to clam up about their feelings about divorce. I suggest you reread the earlier section of this chapter where I suggested ways for a widow to draw out the children's feelings about their father's death. You can use exactly the same methods to bring out your children's feelings about the divorce.

I can assure you that underneath their quiet exteriors they are feeling angry, hurt, and abandoned. In many ways, a divorce is like a death. It is the death of a marriage and the death of a family. Your children need to mourn the loss they feel about the death of the family.

There is one unpleasant thing you will have to live with. Since you are the parent with custody, your children will probably tend to take out their feelings of anger at *both* parents on you. Learn not to take this personally. And help them to mourn in the same way that I suggested a widow help her children. One helpful tool for you to use is a book entitled *The Boys and Girls Book of Divorce*, by Dr. Richard Gardner. This is written for children to read, but not all at once. It can be the basis for several helpful discussions with them.

There are two different ages when divorce hits children the hardest, ages three to six and the teenage years, which are the years of the "family romance." During these years a little boy falls romantically in love with his mother and wishes his father would vanish so that he could have her all to himself. (A little girl feels the same thing in reverse.) The whole sequence of events takes place again during the teenage years, only this time sexuality becomes an added ingredient in the feelings.

So what happens if a divorce takes place when a little boy is four? It is as if his secret wishes, to possess his mother all to himself and to have his father vanish, have caused the divorce to happen. His wishes have actually come true. The little boy feels very guilty, believing that he has caused the divorce.

If a divorce occurs during the times when the "family romance" is in process, your children will have an extra set of ambivalent or guilty feelings that you will need to help them work through.

Your children will suffer from the lack of a male figure in their lives in the same way that children of a widowed parent do. Reread the suggestions given earlier in this chapter for solving this problem. They apply here as well.

When you do find a man with whom you develop a deep relationship that is leading toward marriage, you will discover that your children will have mixed feelings toward your husband-to-be, which I have already described in the section on the remarriage of a widow, and you can cope with them in the same ways that I have described. Your children will want a new father surrogate in their lives, but on the other hand they have had you all to themselves and will hesitate to give that up.

I would also suggest you read carefully the next chapter, Stepparents and the Blended Family, so that you will know some of the psychological land mines to be avoided when you enter into a remarriage.

So far we have discussed your situation as a single parent assuming that your ex-husband is not hassling you. But he may be doing exactly that. He may be moving around or have moved to another state to make it more difficult for you to get your child-support or alimony checks. And legally it may be very difficult for you to do anything to correct this situation. I think it is a national disgrace that the average length of time divorced fathers actually pay child support is fourteen months.

Or he may see the children very irregularly, perhaps twice a year, or not at all. My professional experience has given me the impression that a high percentage of fathers in the United States are not truly involved with their children. Since this is true for intact families, it should come as no surprise that so many divorced fathers simply fade out of their children's lives.

Or your ex-husband may play a very active but unwanted part in your life by hassling you and the children. He may be bad-mouthing you to the children or telling them lies about you. He may be hassling you personally in a thousand ways, phoning you, coming over to the house without asking permission, following you on dates. Even threatening your life. Or actually making attempts on your life.

Any one of these hassles is difficult to live with. It is hard enough being a single parent. You need extra hassles from your ex-spouse like you need a recurring case of poison ivy. Again, if you can afford it, some professional counsel may be of great value in helping you to cope with these hassles. If you cannot afford professional help, you need to discuss your problems and relieve your feelings with your emotional support system of special friends.

To cope with some of the more extreme of these hassles, you may need legal advice. You may even be forced to change your residence and keep the new one a secret from your ex-spouse. When you tell your children what you are doing, and why, simply tell them the truth. Explain the situation in terms appropriate to their age level and level of sophistication. To preschoolers you can simply say, "Daddy is being so mean to me I have to move to a new place to live. And I can't tell Daddy about it because then he will know where we live and can start being mean again." With grade-school children or teenagers, you can go more into the specific reasons why you feel that taking the drastic step of moving is your only solution.

If your ex-husband never comes to see the children and they ask why, again, I advocate that you tell them the truth. If you dream up some cover story for him, and the children find out later that you have lied, you will have destroyed your credibility with them. Depending on their age and level of sophistication, you could say something like this to them: "Any father would want to come and visit such really neat kids. But your father has his own psychological problems. He's so wrapped up in them that he doesn't come to see you kids. I really feel sorry for him because of what he's missing."

In summary, I want to remind you that you have a lot going for you as a single parent, which you may tend to overlook when things get rough. First, your children's love for you is a great psychological reservoir to draw upon. Second, the psychological methods for raising children effectively are the same in a single-parent family as in a two-parent family. Third, if you are well informed on all the material in this book, you will know far more about raising children than most parents in two-parent families do. All these factors put together mean that you can do a better job of raising children in your single-parent family than most parents in a two-parent family can. So take heart, and feel confident that you will succeed.

The Single Parent Father without Custody

I put the father rather than the mother in this category because it is rare for the single father to have custody. It is true nowadays that more and more fathers are getting custody. That is technically true, but it does not mean that more divorce judges are looking at the question of custody from the point of view of the welfare of the child. This is an intelligent way of looking at it, but unfortunately it does not prevail in our divorce court system. This system is one of the most sexist organizations in the United States. For example, there was a famous case in California in which a known prostitute was awarded custody of the children, provided that she did not bring her customers around when the children were present. Incredible, but true.

Men get custody of their children in only a small percentage of cases, as low as 2 or 3 percent in some states. Or as one attorney put it to me, "The only way a father can get custody is for him to have two eyeball witnesses who saw the mother standing over a dead body with a smoking gun in her hand, and have the ballistics match up. Otherwise the mother will get custody."

So when you hear that "more and more fathers are getting custody these days," it's like saying 53 out of 1,000 fathers used to get custody and now 62 out of 1,000 are getting custody. And the real reason that more fathers are getting custody is that more women are giving up the children to the fathers! The mother doesn't want to be bothered with custody of the children, so she hands them over to the father.

That is why I indicate that the parent without custody is usually the father. Let's talk about the situation.

Let's assume you have the easiest situation possible: one in which your ex-wife is not hassling you.

What is your post-divorce trauma, and how does it differ from the post-divorce trauma of the mother with custody? Marriage with children involves two roles: spouse and parent. The custodial parent loses only one role, that of spouse. The parent without custody loses both roles. Now if the father without custody is not particularly involved with the children anyway, the loss of the full parental role is no great thing to him, and he eventually joins the ranks of the dropout fathers. But if his children mean a great deal to him, then the loss of full parenthood comes as a shattering blow. Here is how one father put it:

> . . . what has happened is that I've become a weekend father and sometimes only a Saturday father. It is not because I want it that way, but it's what often happens after a divorce. My ex-wife and I quarrel constantly when we're together— more than we did before the divorce, and that's no good for the kids. But, Lord, how I miss them through the week. I once saw them seven days a week—now I only see them for two days or not at all if I have to be out of town. I really love those kids, and it just tears me apart when I have to say good-bye to them.14

As a father without custody you will have to go through the same feelings of loss of spouse that the mother with custody goes through, plus the dreadful experience of the loss of your children on a full-time basis. You will have to do your grief work about all of these things, and it is a painful, horrendous job. So all the things I said earlier about the grief work that a widow or a divorced mother needs to do apply to you also.

If you can afford it, divorce counseling will probably be of great help to you, particularly in dealing with the aftershock of divorce. You too will need to build up a new emotional support system for yourself. Find friends who are also fathers without custody—people who can truly understand your situation.

I know of one divorced father who asked a married couple with children, friends of his, if he could eat dinner with them one night a week. They agreed to this arrangement, and then, every so often, he took their whole family out to dinner in return. He told me that he really looked forward to that one night a week. He was very lonely, and this experience gave him a feeling of belonging to a family once a week.

With regard to your handling of the children, I suggest you read the chapter Divorce, Remarriage, and Blended Families in my book *How to Father*. This chapter covers extensively the situation of the divorced father without custody. The following are some of the highlights from this chapter.

First, I want to stress the fact that it is actually possible for you to have a better and deeper relationship with your children as a divorced father than you had in your previous family situation. For one thing, when you see your children you will be totally free of the push-and-pull that may have been going on in front of the children when you were married. For another thing, you may be inclined to put more time and effort into your relationship with your children as a divorced father than you did as a married father. It has been the experience of many fathers that they first really began to know their kids after a divorce.

> *Tim, a twenty-seven-year-old teacher, said, "I'm a better father today than I was a year ago when I was married. Sure, I only see the kids on weekends, but now I pay attention to them. I listen to what they say and feel. As a matter of fact, I didn't spend all that much time with them when I was home. Usually all I wanted to do was watch football on television: my body was home but my mind was elsewhere. Now we talk a lot more, and for the first time we're getting to know each other."[15]*

As a divorced father your relationship with your children begins with the terms of your visitation, as set down by the court. Here I want to advise you about a psychological land mine that many fathers unwittingly run into. Most judges like to dispense visitation privileges to the divorced father by granting him "reasonable visitation."

Reasonable visitation is a snare and a delusion, and only a stupid lawyer would let you fall for that one. The very fact that we have such a legal concept as reasonable visitation shows the sex-biased nature of the courts. If the mother with custody *is* reasonable, you will have reasonable visitation. But if she is not, you will quickly find out that reasonable visitation means whatever visitation she decides to dole out to you. Can you imagine what would happen if a judge awarded "reasonable child support" to a divorced mother? The court would resound with her cries of indignant outrage, and rightly so.

So do not accept reasonable visitation. Get your visitation rights pinned down specifically. Here is a schedule of visitation worked out by one father who had a fifteen-year-old boy and a nine-year-old boy. He took both boys out for dinner one night a week. He had a flexible visitation schedule with the fifteen-year-old that allowed them to get together whenever it was mutually agreeable. He took the nine-year-old boy out every Friday night to the movies or a sports event. He had the nine-year-old every other weekend. He also had him for one week of the two-week Christmas vacation, one week of the Easter vacation, and one month in the summer. These were the regularly scheduled visitation times. In addition, allowance was made for spontaneous visitation when it was agreeable both to the mother and the child or children.

When you establish a definite schedule of visitation such as this, it gives a structure and order to your relationship with the children. They will know just when they can count on seeing you. This will give them something predictable to look forward to. It will also give you something to look forward to, particularly in those first desolate months of separation.

I strongly suggest you provide your children with some kind of "second home" that is theirs and theirs alone when they come to visit you. If you live in a house, you can set aside a special room that is theirs and nobody else's. If you live in an apartment, which is more likely, hopefully you can afford to rent an extra room for them, over and above what you need. This can be their room, fixed up with things of their own choosing—clothes, or toys and playthings. This becomes their home away from home. If this is beyond your financial resources, then fix up some special corner of your apartment as a "mini-room" for them. Here they can maintain a strong feeling of "territoriality." It will be very important to them to have a second home, however small, at your apartment.

I think it is safe to say that very few fathers know much about how to relate psychologically to their children, regardless of their ages. That's why it is so important for you to make a real effort to study and understand your children and the psychology of handling them. If you have the information in this book at your fingertips, you will be light-years ahead of many fathers in intact homes.

It may be best in the beginning of your visitation with the children to plan ahead of time a general outline of what you are going to do. It may also be best to start in low gear, spending just a few hours with them at first, and then working up to longer periods of time. Plan activities that will not require you to talk a great deal with each other, such as a movie or a sports event, rather than activities that do require a great deal of talk, such as going out to dinner.

As one patient of mine put it, "There I was with my two-year-old and my four-year-old last Saturday. After I had taken them to the zoo I didn't know what to do with them. What can you do with a two-year-old and a four-year-old?" This was a man who had spent very little time with his children when he was married. He had pretty much left the care of the children to his wife. So when he was faced with interacting with them for long stretches of time he felt inadequate and actually panicky.

So do your homework. Take the time to read up on the psychology of children and how to handle them. It will pay off in rich emotional dividends for you and your relationship with your kids.

One helpful thing is to have each child bring a friend along. This will ease the general emotional atmosphere greatly and take much of the heat off you. Many divorced fathers get worn down emotionally from the demands the children make on them. But with a friend along, the children will relate together easily and naturally, and you will not feel the pull of emotional demands focusing on you. You can have each child take a friend along on nearly anything you do—a visit to the zoo, a museum, a movie, a sports event, a camping trip, a visit to the beach.

Adolescents pose a special problem for the father without custody. The adolescent generally wants to be with his peer group and not with his father or mother. Nevertheless, it is important that you maintain contact with your adolescent while you are single and separate from him. Depending on the adolescent and his tastes, here are some things you and he could do together: go to the movies (particularly R movies, which he cannot get into by himself), go to sports events, go motorcycle riding, fishing, camping and backpacking, or sailing. If your adolescent is a girl she may enjoy all of these activities, as well as being taken out to a nice restaurant for lunch or dinner.

You may find that your late adolescents (ages eighteen to twenty-one) will begin to turn more and more to you for help with such things as choosing a college, selecting a vocation, and handling miscellaneous problems connected with making the transition from school to "real" life. If you have established the custom of regularly having dinner with them, it will be easier for them to bring up some of these problems.

So far we have been assuming that your ex-wife has been

cooperative in your child visitation and has not been hassling you. If so, count yourself fortunate. The sad fact is that if you are a father who loves his children and your ex-wife knows this and is bitter and vindictive, she can cause trouble for you in ways you wouldn't dream possible. I know of a divorced lawyer whose children were late adolescents. He was relentlessly harassed by his ex-wife for four years of pressuring phone calls, demands for more child support and alimony than she was entitled to, trying to embarrass him in public meetings, and hauling him into court at every possible opportunity. Finally he decided that enough was enough. He actually gave up his law practice in Los Angeles and moved to San Francisco, where she couldn't get at him. But he does not get to see his children very often.

A line of defense you may be forced to use is to have no communications with her in person or by telephone regarding the children. She can lie in court with a perfectly straight face about such communications, where there is no witness. A letter will not do the job either; she can claim she never received it.

The only completely safe form of communication is a telegram or night letter, with a confirmatory copy to you. She cannot talk her way around that one.

As a second line of defense, you may sometimes, or perhaps all the time, take a witness with you when you visit the children. If you go to pick up the children some night and find nobody home, it's your word against hers, unless you have a witness with you. And your word against hers in a courtroom will get you exactly nowhere. The basic principle of all of these measures is simple: Unless there is a witness to any communication between the two of you, you are lost in a court of law (particularly a sexist divorce court, which is almost always biased against the father).

I once had a patient whose ex-wife had been doing everything she could to thwart his visitation with his six-year-old girl. One day she phoned him and said she wanted to talk over some things with him and suggested they have lunch the next week. He agreed, and at lunch she informed him that she wasn't going to let him see the little girl during his half of the Christmas vacation. "I just think you're a bad influence on the child, and I think it's better for you not to see her at Christmas." Then she added, "And it's too late for you to do anything about it in court before Christmas." "But it's not too late for me to take you to court about it after Christmas," he replied, and that's what he did.

He told me about his testimony and her testimony on the witness stand: "It was absolutely incredible. The only thing our two versions had in common was that we both agreed we had lunch at the Aladdin Restaurant on December 18. I testified as to what was really said. She fabricated a complete web of lies, claiming I had threatened physical harm to my little girl if she disobeyed me, and other figments of her prolific imagination. From that time on," he said, "I never talked with my ex-wife without a witness present." Don't think such a scene is incredible; it could happen to you.

The court can safeguard your right to visit your children. The court cannot prevent your ex-wife from bad-mouthing you and poisoning the minds of your children against you.

If you face any of these obstacles in attempting to see your children regularly, your best strategy is to take a long-range view. See my answer to question 9 in chapter 25, Middle Childhood, which discusses this problem. Even though your wife may bad-mouth you to the children, they will see the real you when you visit them. And no matter how vicious she is or what she says about you, do not retaliate in kind and attack her to the children. This can only boomerang.

Simply be yourself. No matter what she says, your children have a firsthand perception of you as a loving, kind, understanding, fun person who is their father. And as they grow older your ex-wife's vindictive tactics will often backfire and hurt her in their eyes. They experience you as a nice person, but she tells them you are an awful person. When they get old enough to assert themselves against her, usually as adolescents, they will begin to stand up to her. They will tell her what they feel you are really like, as opposed to what she has told them about you.

If you are saddled with a vicious and vindictive ex-wife, you may have to endure constant guerrilla warfare to see your children. Even though this is a most unpleasant situation, the end result will be worth it when your children are eighteen and out of her clutches and you can relate to them directly and lovingly.

So there it is, single parents, whether you are widowed, or a divorced mother with custody, or a divorced father without custody. There is no doubt that it is much harder to be an effective single parent than an effective parent in an intact family. It is even harder if you have an ex-spouse hassling you.

But in spite of these things, you can still lead a rich and fulfilling life as a single parent. You can raise children who are as happy and psychologically healthy as children brought up in an intact home—or even more so. Here are the moving words of a twenty-one-year-old whose parents divorced when he was sixteen. This boy testified to the excellent job that single parents can do in raising a child:

It sounds funny to say, but I think the divorce was a really good thing for all of us. It gave my parents a chance to grow, especially my father. Right after the divorce he went back to school and got a master's degree in journalism and now he's really into something which is incredibly satisfying to him. He's thrown off twenty years of the crap of being a businessman, and he's really happy. So is Mom. It's been harder for her, I think, because she's a woman—but she's looking good, travels a lot, and is starting to go out again. I've got a fantastic relationship with both of them now, especially my father. . . . It almost feels strange to have that good a relationship with him now, considering how we used to fight all the time. Neither of them understood me.[16]

When you turn out a child like this you can smile happily to yourself, knowing you have made your own unique contribution to the destruction of the myth of The Maladjusted Child from a Broken Home.

19

STEPPARENTS AND THE BLENDED FAMILY

In the preceding chapter I said that single parenting is harder than parenting in an intact family. Stepparenting is also harder, but in a different way. This does not mean that stepchildren, in a blended family, are bound to be more unhappy or maladjusted than children in a biological family. In fact, I know of children in blended families who are happier and better adjusted than many other children. But it takes knowledge and skill to achieve this, and that is what I hope to furnish you in this chapter.

Personally I think that stepparents are the most neglected parents in America. In many ways our society acts as if stepparents do not exist. Have you ever been to a PTA meeting, a child's piano recital, or a high school graduation and heard the presiding person say, "Welcome, parents *and* stepparents"? I never have. Everybody knows we have Mother's Day and Father's Day. But where is Stepmother's Day or Stepfather's Day?

If you turn to the literature on child-raising, you will find the same glaring omission of stepparenting. There is no mention of stepparents or the stepchild in Dr. Spock's original book, and this omission has not been corrected in his new revised edition. In the new edition you can find out about many others things, but not a mention of the stepparent or the stepchild.

Dr. Thomas Gordon's *Parent Effectiveness Training* is an

excellent book, and has helped thousands of people to become better parents. But once again, absolutely no mention of stepparenting. His new book, *P.E.T. in Action*, suffers from the same omission. In another good book on parenting, Joan Beck's *Effective Parenting*, you can find advice on how to pick a pediatrician, the sleeping problems of babies and young children, how to get the most fun for your toy dollars, how to help a shy child, and many other things. But once again, if you read the book you would have no idea that there were such things in America as stepparents and stepchildren.

The vast neglect of stepparents is very sad because, contrary to the impression you might get from reading books on child-raising or attending school meetings, *stepparents do exist*, and there are a lot of them! Here are some statistics.

In the United States, one out of every three marriages is a remarriage, and in one-third of these remarriages, *both* spouses have children from a previous marriage. It is estimated that there are 15 million children under eighteen living in stepfamilies. There are an estimated 25 million husbands and wives who are stepfathers and stepmothers. As of now, *one out of six children in America is a stepchild*. By 1980, based on present divorce and remarriage projections, *one child in every four* will be a stepchild. Why do practically all books on child-rearing ignore the stepparent and the stepfamily? I think it is because people (even psychologists and psychiatrists, who should know better) unconsciously assume that *parenting and stepparenting are the same*. They are not! And I will spend the rest of this chapter describing the unique world of the stepfamily, pointing out the psychological booby traps that you may run into as a stepparent, and telling you how to make your stepfamily a happy one.

The stepparent is, first of all, a parent. And like all parents he is a child psychologist and a teacher. This means he needs information on child psychology, especially the different psychological states of development from birth to age twenty-one. Second, he needs information on teaching methods (what some people call discipline) that are effective with his children. This you can find in the first sixteen chapters of this book.

So the basic skills of the child psychologist and the teacher are as necessary for the stepparent as they are for the biological parent. But these parenting skills are exercised in different ways in the biological family and in the stepfamily. An English teacher will need certain fundamental teaching skills wherever he teaches. But he will certainly teach English differently (or he will be unsuccessful) to teenagers in Pakistan than he will to teenagers in the suburbs of Chicago.

Let's start with some basic definitions. *A stepparent is a person who has married a spouse with one or more children.* A stepfamily or a blended family is a *household unit where a stepchild (or several of them) lives or is a regular visitor.* A stepparent could also be defined as an *instant parent.* Biological parents have more time to adjust to parenthood as their children grow up from babyhood. Stepparents are catapulted into parenthood, trying to manage suddenly in the role of parent to an eight- or ten-year-old, or all sorts of combinations and permutations of ages and sexes. If parenthood is a complex and difficult skill (particularly without any training), instant parenthood is much, much harder. When I think of the problems of instant parenthood, I think of one of my previous patients, Susan.

Susan was a woman who had remained single until the age of thirty-two, at which time she married a man with two teenage daughters, thirteen and fifteen. After five months of marriage she came to me for help, at the end of her rope. She cried throughout most of the first interview.

"I love Andy very much," she said. "He's a wonderful man and I think we have a terrific relationship, emotionally, intellectually, sexually, and in every way. But those girls are eroding my marriage, and I've got to do something about it or everything that's important to me will go down the drain."

She went on to say that the children would swing back and forth between being cooperative and being sullen. "I try so hard to be a good mother to them, and what do I get? Flip remarks and sullen looks, that's what I get. And when one of them said to me last week, 'You're so finicky and picky about everything, I wish we lived with our real mother,' that was it! I just couldn't take it anymore.

"I blew my stack and called her every name in the book. And you know what? Their real mother is an alcoholic! How's that for laughs? I'm just a cook and a housekeeper and a washerwoman, with little help or thanks from them. I feel I'm being used, and Andy just sits back and lets it happen. I ask him to help me with them, and all I get from him is, 'Oh, they're just being normal teenagers.' Then I get so angry at him it frightens me. I feel my relationship with those two girls is like a time bomb ticking away and sooner or later it's going to blow up my marriage.

"I guess everybody has twenty-twenty hindsight. But when I married Andy I thought everything was going to be really super. Of course I knew that it was a package deal. The two girls came with Andy. But I didn't think that would be any real problem. They seemed like nice kids, and I was sure we were all going to be very happy. Believe me, I had no idea things were going to be so difficult!"

This is the testimony of many, many stepparents: "I was totally unprepared for the actual realities of coping with life in a stepfamily." One stepparent put it this way: "It's like being plunked down, a stranger, in the middle of rural China, speaking the wrong language and yet torn all the while by too many people asking unanswerable questions."[1] A stepmother commented: "I found that being a full-time working mother was nowhere as difficult as being a part-time stepmother."[2] A stepfather described stepparenting as "like trying to learn to swim from the deep end rather than the shallow."[3]

What makes stepparenting so hard, and why are so many people unprepared for the difficulties they encounter in managing children in a blended family?

First, the people involved usually have no training in parenting skills. Of course, the parents of a biological family usually have no training in parenting skills either. But as parents and children grow up together, emotional bonds are forged that help to smooth over the rough edges of the parents' deficiencies in parental skills. This holds true for both parents and children. Children will tolerate bloopers from their parents that they will not tolerate from outsiders. And parents can be more tolerant and understanding of their own children's faults than the faults of other children. As one father put it, comparing his biological son with his stepson, "I know Timmy is an obnoxious little rat sometimes, but he's *my own* obnoxious little rat!"

So lack of training in parental skills in the biological family can often be smoothed over by other factors when people have grown up with one another. But when you are a stepfather or stepmother who is woefully ignorant of parental skills, this lack of knowledge will stick out like a sore thumb when you attempt to handle your stepchildren.

Second, most stepparents do not realize it until they are actually in the situation, but the blended family is an incredibly more complex set of emotional relationships than the biological family. As someone has said, "There are too many people in a second marriage."[4] Indeed there are. A blended family contains one of the most intricate sets of emotional relationships you can find. The relationship and the feelings of a mother toward her own child are quite different from those toward her stepchild. The same with the stepfather. The feelings of a child toward his natural mother and father are different from his feelings toward a stepmother and stepfather. And the same is true of the feelings of the stepchildren in the family toward the biological children, and vice versa.

The emotional relationships in the biological family are much less complex. If life in a biological family is like playing a game of chess, life in a blended family is like playing five games of chess simultaneously.

Third, the blended family is permeated by jealous and ambivalent feelings. Of course jealousy exists in the biological family too. Siblings are jealous of one another. A parent may be jealous of his own child, feeling that his spouse pays more attention to the child than to him.

But this is nothing compared to the jealousy that exists in the blended family. It's as if each person, parent or child, goes around with one eye out to see if someone else is paying more attention to another person in the family than to him. Stepmothers or stepfathers may feel that their marital relationship is being wrongfully intruded upon by one or more of the children. A child may feel that a stepmother is taking away his father from him, and vice versa.

Not only are there more jealous feelings for both parents and children to cope with, there are more ambivalent feelings. If the truth were really known, both stepparents and stepchildren feel ambivalent about each other. This is one of the things stepparents are not usually expecting, and it hits them with a shock when they realize that their feelings are not what they are "supposed" to be. Instant parenthood does not mean instant love.

A concerned stepfather asked his spouse, "Don't you love my children?"

"Not yet, Roy," she answered. And she later commented to

friends, "They're not even the type of people I would choose for friends outside the family."[5]

The plain fact is that with very few exceptions we cannot feel the same about somebody else's child as we do about our own. This is especially true for a mother. Psychologically it is simply impossible for her to have the same feelings for another child as she does for one that she carried within her own body, gave birth to, and raised. I think it is important for every stepparent to come to terms with these ambivalent feelings. Unless you can accept it as an emotional fact that *it is normal to have ambivalent and mixed feelings toward your stepchildren*, then you are still in the world of pretense rather than the world of reality.

One stepfather expressed his ambivalence this way: "I like the kids as people all right. I just resent the fact that they exist!"[6]

And a stepchild summed up his feelings about how to deal with the jealousies and mixed feelings swirling around him this way: "You are like a politician caught by a bunch of reporters. All you can honestly say is 'No comment.' "[7]

The following analogy might help us understand the basic cause of the jealousies and ambivalent feelings seething within a stepfamily:

> *The stepfamily might be considered analogous, psychologically, to what happens physically in organ transplants. The most common cause of failure in transplants, as we know, is quite simple: the body responds protectively and rejects foreign tissue. Medical measures are taken to keep this from happening. Psychologically, the danger of similar pathology exists in the merged family situation.*
>
> *The stepfamily brings with it foreign and inexperienced ways of communicating within groups of people. At the same time the relationships are tender and tenuous. The comforts of the "never-go-away" constancy of the biological family are not present.*[8]

Fourth, the blended family will always be haunted by ghosts from the biological family.

Some of these psychological facts are difficult for adults to understand, for they seem so irrational. It is a fact, however, that almost all children wish their parents would get back together again, no matter how unhappy the marriage was. I had a ten-year-old boy in therapy whose parents had been divorced for six years. He was getting ready to fly back East to spend a month with his father in the summer. He said, "Maybe my father will come back with me, and Mom and Dad will get remarried." I said, "Jerry, what makes you say that? You've heard your mother and father yelling at each other over the phone. You know how they hate each other. Why in the world would they want to get married again?" "Well," he replied somewhat sheepishly, "maybe they could fall in love all over again."

This wish that his parents could get back together is a psychological fact that permeates every stepchild's life.

No matter how bad or ineffective his parents are or have been, each stepchild feels that they are *his* parents and nobody can replace them. And he is right, psychologically speaking. So to a certain extent, a stepchild will experience a stepmother or stepfather as an intruder, someone who is trying to take his father or mother away from him. The story of young Donny exemplifies this very clearly:

Mother told him one day when they were driving in the car, "I have wonderful news. You're going to have a new Daddy. Uncle George and I are getting married next month."

Donny thought of his Daddy out in California. He wondered if he'd still see him as much. A kind of sadness and panic began inside him. Then a hope. He said, "Maybe Uncle George won't want to get married."

Mommy laughed. "Sure he will, Donny. It's something we both decided."

"Well, you didn't ask me! I don't want a new Daddy, I don't want Uncle George."

"Of course you do, Donny," Mommy said. "You'll see. We're going to move to a new house. You'll go to a new school. Just wait. Everything will be marvelous."

"I don't want a new anything. I just want us to stay the way we are. I hate Uncle George!"

Donny's mother was stunned. She loved George, and she was certain Donny liked him.

"Donny, of course you don't hate Uncle George. Don't you understand? Life is a lot easier for us now."

She proceeded to paint a rosy picture of the future. The better it sounded, the more confused Donny got. He did like Uncle George, but he didn't want a new Daddy. He already had a Daddy and he wanted him back.[9]

Stepchildren tend to idealize all biological parents, particularly one who is dead. No stepparent can possibly measure up to this kind of idealized parent. And the stepparent soon feels the stepchild's hostility because he does *not* measure up and because he is presuming to take the place of the idealized parent. Here is a good example: A psychoanalyst who was also a stepfather described his early months with his stepchildren as "hell." He had moved into the house where the children had been living with their mother. "They had an absolute unconscious need to get rid of me. . . . They very much wanted a father. But they idealized their father, who was dead. There was no way in which I could have measured up."[10]

So the idealization of a natural parent is something a stepparent will simply have to live with until he is able to establish his own unique relationship with the stepchild.

One legacy the ghosts of the departed parents inevitably leave behind is the mistakes they have made in raising the children. One stepmother felt she was "standing on the ruins of someone else's life, and paying, paying, paying, for their past mistakes."[11] When you are raising your own biological children, even when you make mistakes, at least you know they are your own. But when you become a stepparent, the Stepmother Stork may deliver to your doorstep a shy, withdrawn five-year-old; a nasty, uncontrollable, sarcastic eleven-year-old; a Goody Two Shoes nine-year-old, who boasts, "I said, 'thank you' twenty-seven times this weekend, more than any of the other children"; or a sullen, defiant adolescent, who knows just where your weak spots are and proceeds to hit you there. And it is your job as a stepparent to learn to love and discipline these instant children whose problems you had no hand in shaping! It is no wonder that one stepmother wrote these lines:

> *Whatever way you look at it,*
> *You can't recycle other people's children. . . .*
> *Look here, I say.*
> *You handed me the empty pages*
> *Of a book I never wrote.*[12]

Fifth is the problem of constant, unremitting attacks by an ex-spouse against one or both of the parents, using the children as pawns. It is frequently a mother, rather than a father, who indulges in this kind of vindictive warfare. And the ways in which the children can be used as pawns in the gigantic game of Hit Back Against Your Former Mate are almost endless. Any stepparent who has suffered through years of this will know exactly what I mean. It is like Chinese water torture, with constant drip, drip, drip, of aggravating actions by the ex-spouse funneled through the children. It gets so the stepparent wonders, every time he goes to pick up the children, "Well, what will it be now?" Or as another stepparent said, "Hostility comes with the weekend!"

Sixth, whereas the roles of the biological mother and father are clear and well defined, both in the family and outside it, the role of the stepparent is fuzzy and unclear. On the one hand you are not the stepchild's parent because he has a parent, either living or dead. And you can never take the place of that parent in the child's mind. On the other hand you are more than just a friend who happens to live in the same house as the child. So what are you, exactly? One stepmother put her reaction to the unclear nature of her role in these words:

> *I am the sound of one hand clapping.*
> *I play tennis without a ball and golf without a club.*
> *In this game, they've changed all the rules.*
> *And they never admit I'm playing.*[13]

A stepmother has been defined as "a bird that sits on another bird's eggs."[14]

The role of the biological father or mother comes ready-made. But the stepparent must carve his own role out of a very ambiguous situation. We will talk about how to do this later in the chapter.

Although many of you are already stepparents, some of you may be only contemplating a marriage that will make you a stepparent. Naturally you want to know what factors will most affect your chances for success in getting along with your stepchildren. The three most important considerations are:

1. Did your prospective spouse's marriage end in death or divorce?

2. Are you already a parent?
3. What are the ages and sex of the children involved?

Death or divorce. In popular fiction the new stepparent is pictured as winning the hearts of the grieving children and walking with them into the sunset of a happy ending. Don't you believe it! The expectations of stepparents are often high and unrealistic. Because they are helping by coming as new stepparents into a sometimes tragic situation, stepparents often have a tendency to expect gratitude from a stepchild. Biological parents usually have learned not to expect gratitude from their children (unless they are very foolish and unrealistic). But stepparents often feel deep down, whether they put it into words or not, "Look at all the things I'm doing for this child. The least he could do is show a little gratitude." This attitude ignores the following facts:

• A dead parent is more likely to be idealized. The remarriage of the remaining parent is seen as an act of disloyalty by the child. The child is likely to become hostile and regard the stepparent as a usurper.

• Statistically, divorces occur sooner than death, so the children involved in divorce tend to be fewer as well as younger. As I will explain in detail later, younger children seem to have an easier time adjusting to the new situation.

• Divorced parents generally remarry within a shorter period of time than widowed parents do. The child has had less time to adjust to life with a divorced single parent, so that he has fewer intimate emotional patterns of family living to give up.

• If the parents are divorced, the child will usually have an alternate place to visit or live if things get rough for him in his present home. No such safety valve is provided for the child whose other parent is dead.

Are you already a parent? As I have said many times, parenting is a complex skill. Unfortunately, it is not taught to parents in any systematic, careful way, but is learned haphazardly by trial and error. If you have children of your own, you have probably learned the hard way that children are definitely not like adults. At times they lie, steal, and cheat. They can often be messy, noisy, and dirty. They are egocentric, thinking first and foremost of themselves. They can have a genius for embarrassing you in public. And so on and so on. If you have had children, you know all this—and more—to be true. But if you haven't had children and you become a stepparent, you may feel as though you've been hit in the face with a wet flounder when you are suddenly confronted with the less pleasant aspects of children's behavior.

Roger was a forty-year-old bachelor when he married Anne, a charming woman eight years younger, with three children under nine. He confided to me recently: "I never knew that three children could make such a racket. Just the sheer noise those kids make overwhelms me! It's rough on Anne too, because it upsets her that they bother me. I actually find myself working late at the office so I can escape them. I don't tell Anne that, of course. I come home after I'm sure they're in bed. I just can't take that bedlam. As much as I love her, sometimes I wonder if the hard fact is that I was a bachelor too long to take on that rowdy crew."

Even if you have had children of your own, it takes a lot of adjustment to get used to new stepchildren. But it takes even more if you have never had any of your own, because you do not really know what children are like. You will probably expect them to exhibit a level of maturity that is totally unrealistic. And you will probably not know the teaching skills you need to in order to cope with them. You will be like a man who has only had a dog as a pet and suddenly has to cope with three monkeys in the house. Unconsciously you keep expecting them to behave like dogs, and they don't. So you haven't the faintest idea of how to train and handle them.

Age and sex of the children. Generally the stepchild/stepparent adjustment works best when the children are very young or are young adults. Probably the most difficult age is when the children are teenagers. Teenagers in the biological family are in a state of rebellion as a normal part of their development. Which means they may be belligerent, uncooperative, sassy, and downright defiant. This behavior is hard enough for the biological parents to handle, but when you mix up these same psychological ingredients in the situation of a new stepparent it spells T-R-O-U-B-L-E.

When the children are between three and six or are teenagers and are presented with a new stepparent of the same sex, a special kind of difficulty can be expected to arise. At these two age levels, children are in the stage that I call the family romance, as I mentioned earlier. (I suggest you consult my book *How to Father* for a detailed discussion of this important stage and how to handle it.) In the family romance, children want to oust the parent of their own sex so that they can have the remaining parent all to themselves. Between the ages of three and six, the child's sexual feelings are not developed fully because his sex glands have not yet matured. But in the teenage years the feelings of the family romance are powered by the emerging sexual impulses of puberty.

Although the family romance is a normal stage of development in the biological family, it can turn sour when a stepparent enters the scene. A stepson can become very hostile to the stepparent who is taking his beloved mother away from him. The little boy of three who announces to his mother that he wants to marry her when he grows up feels very threatened when a man comes along and actually does marry her. He feels displaced and shoved out. A teenage girl who openly flirts with her father has abnormally strong feelings of jealousy when someone else receives her father's affection. Here is how one stepmother describes her stepdaughter's reaction to the wedding:

> For my stepdaughter, our wedding was a shock. Every little girl may want to marry Daddy, but not every little girl gets a new dress, new shoes, and flowers in her hair to watch Daddy marry somebody else. She sailed into the registry office like the mother of the bride. She had organized everything. There were enough potato chips, the flowers had come on time; she could enjoy herself. After the ceremony was over, she stumped out, a little girl with a dough-face and knee socks that were too tight. "I take thee . . ." She broke off. "I knew all the words," she said bitterly, "and nobody asked me to say anything."[15]

So if you marry a parent with a child in either the three to six phase or the teenage phase of the family romance you will need to deal with the child's feelings of jealousy and hostility. You will find the feedback technique I described in chapter 10 especially helpful in dealing with these feelings.

But regardless of the child's age, you will have to expect a certain amount of hostility. The sooner you get to know the

child, the greater the likelihood that both of you will eventually be able to make a good adjustment to each other. For
this reason, it's a good idea to get to know the child in the
early stages of the courtship, especially if you feel that you
are in courtship and not just a casual relationship. Knowing
the child's bad points probably won't keep you from wanting
to get married, but it will prepare you for the problems.
Knowing the child's good points will help you to develop loving feelings sooner.

A friend of mine, Carrie, fell in love with Jack, who was
divorced and had a seven-year-old son named Billy. Carrie
had never had any children of her own. She told me, "Although Billy and I got along well from the beginning, I knew
it was going to be rough. He even told me that he wished his
mother and father would get back together again, which
made me feel like a real interloper. Nevertheless, over the
couple of years Jack and I went together before we got
married we would take Billy on picnics and to the park, and
we gradually got to be pretty good friends. But the week before the wedding, I could tell he had some anxiety about the
marriage. He began to kid me about the fact that stepmothers
are supposed to be very wicked, and he wanted to know what
awful things I was going to do to him once I got to be his
stepmother. He was deliciously horrified when I told him I
was going to feed him toad's eggs and frog's legs with lemon
sauce. He squealed and hollered and shuddered and said, 'Oh,
that's *gross!*' We all laughed, and Billy seemed to feel reassured that everything was going to be all right."

Clearly, you not only need to woo the parent, you also
need to woo the child. Here are some suggestions.

Don't rush the relationship. If you try too hard at first and
go too fast, the child will back off. Wooing a stepchild is
similar in many ways to the formula for wooing a very beautiful and sought-after woman. You take her out (dinner,
movies, theater, skiing, sailing, a walk on the beach, or whatever). You are attentive to her and charming, but you make
no physical move toward her at all. You do not even try to
kiss her. Since this approach is the exact reverse of what she
is accustomed to, with men constantly pressing her physically
and trying to get her into bed, she will usually be nonplussed.
Finally, she will begin to make advances to you, and then at
that point you can respond to her advances. This kind of
low-key approach is ideal for wooing a stepchild. Be friendly,

but not overfriendly. Do not try to hurry the relationship along. Here are examples of two stepparents who tried to rush the relationship:

"I'm your new mother," said the stepmother.
"The hell you are," said the thirteen-year-old stepchild.[16]
Another stepmother rushed much too fast into trying to have a love relationship with her nine-year-old stepson.
"I love you," she said.
"Bullshit," said the boy. "You don't even know me."[17]

By contrast, here is a stepmother who took things easy, using a low-key approach to build a relationship with her young stepdaughter:

> *Helene, a stepmother with a very young stepdaughter who would barely speak to her, found a picture of the child's dead mother. She had it framed and gave it to the little girl. Together they found a place for the picture in the child's room. She spoke to the child about her loss, about how much the child must miss her mother.*
> *"You know, the heart has a lot of sections," she said, "and it grows while you grow. There will always be a section of love in your heart for your mommy that will never go away. But you have other sections in your heart, for the love you have for your daddy and your sister and brother. As you grow older you will learn to love other people too, and there will be even more sections in your heart."[18]*

After that conversation the child started warming to Helene.
And here is some wise advice from a fifteen-year-old boy on how a stepparent should approach a child or teenager and attempt to build a relationship:

> *You have to ease into it. It's sort of a strange relationship. Here is this other person, and they're coming into your life whether you like it or not. And you're going to get along with them whether you like it or not. Because you have to. I think it should be made as easy as possible because if people come on too strong you just can't handle it.[19]*

Bring a gift, but not the first time you meet the child. It looks too much like a bribe (and it probably is). Whatever you get, don't make that first gift too expensive. Ask your spouse-to-be what the child or teenager likes, and be governed accordingly. As you get to know the child better and learn his interests firsthand, you will be on surer ground in getting things for him.

It's generally harder to find suitable gifts for teenagers than for younger children. But here are some suggestions, depending on the taste and interests of the teenager: Take a sports fan to a game he would enjoy; give him two tickets (so he can take a friend) to a rock concert; take him to a good R-rated movie that he can't get into by himself. Then, of course, there are special gifts you can give him if he is a surfer, scuba diver, backpacker, motorcycle enthusiast, etc.

Let's suppose you have met your prospective stepchild and have tried your level best to get along with him. Perhaps he may make it all too plain that his feeling toward you is one of dislike. Suppose your feelings toward him are mutual. What then?

It will help if you can learn to look at the problem of your relationship from the child's point of view. Remember, I said that all children are egocentric, seeing the world as if it revolved around them. The child is not thinking of you in terms of your relationship with his father or mother. He is thinking of you purely in terms of your relationship with him, a disturber of his status quo. He is afraid of you, even though you are bending over backward to please him.

At times like this the feedback technique is very helpful. You will find a detailed description of it in chapter 10.

I suggested the feedback technique to Alan when he was having difficulties with his prospective stepson, Greg. Greg was a hostile eleven-year-old, so hostile, in fact, that Alan was considering breaking off his engagement.

"I even went so far as to tell Amy that unless that brat would live with his grandmother or go off to boarding school, I didn't think we should get married."

"What did she say?" I asked.

"She just said that he would get used to me in time and that he was just shy. Shy! That little monster is about as shy as Jack the Ripper! Frankly, I think she's just papering over a real problem for us. If she admits it's a problem, then we may break up. And she doesn't want that. Neither do I, of course, but he's her kid, and he's not nearly so bad with her. So what am I going to do now?"

I told Alan about the feedback technique and described how it worked. The next week he came in and told me how he had used the technique and what had happened.

"Frankly, it surprised the hell out of me, but I've got to admit that feedback technique really helped a lot. Of course, things are not perfect by any means, but they're a whole lot better."

I asked what happened.

"First of all," he told me, "I got tickets for the Rams game. It wasn't easy but I got them. I know Greg was happy about it, because he's a football nut. But he acted like going to a Rams game was just some ordinary thing, even though it was the first one he'd ever been to.

"The day didn't start out too well. He hardly talked to me in the car driving to the game. I asked him if he wanted a hot dog and a drink. He said he wanted a hot dog but no drink. So I waited in line about twenty minutes to get a hot dog for him. After I leave the line and bring him back the hot dog then what does he do? He decides he wants a drink after all! So I grit my teeth and get back in line. But it takes so long, I miss the opening kickoff."

"But what about the feedback technique?" I asked.

"Oh, yeah, I'm getting to that. About halfway through the second quarter the Rams intercept a pass and run for a touchdown. It was beautiful. So I say to the kid, 'Wasn't that great?'

" 'Yeah, I guess so,' he says.

" 'I thought you liked football,' I said.

" 'Sort of,' he says. 'It all depends.'

" 'Depends on what?'

" 'On who I'm with.'

'Well, Doc, I don't mind telling you that at that point I felt like strangling the kid with my bare hands. I felt like saying, 'Why you ungrateful little rat, after all the trouble I went to to take you to this game, you give me that kind of crap in return!' But I didn't say those things. Somehow I controlled myself and remembered the feedback technique.

"I tried to put myself in his shoes and see the situation through his eyes, like you told me. And I said to him, 'Greg, it sounds as if you like to watch football better with some people than with others.'

"When I said that it was like I had turned a key in a lock on his mind. Right there in the middle of the game he started to tell me about his mixed-up feelings. It was really weird. But each time he told me some of his feelings I used the feedback technique to play them back to him and let him know I understood how he felt. And after we had talked a while the real bone crusher came out. Believe it or not, somehow Greg had gotten the idea that I was not going to let him visit his father anymore after I married Amy. I don't know where he got that idea. But he actually thought I was going to take over his father's place lock, stock, and barrel. When I told him that his father would always be his father and that he could call him or see him whenever he wanted and that I had no intention of trying to take over his father's place, you could almost see the relief on that kid's face."

The feedback technique is not only good for a situation like this. It is also one of the indispensable discipline methods for handling all of the feelings, particularly the mixed ones, that crop up between stepparents and stepchildren. The feedback technique is ideally suited to handling the intricate labyrinth of feelings that exist within the stepfamily.

One of the wisest investments you could make *before* you marry, become a stepparent, and set up a blended family is to have a few sessions with a professsional counselor (psychologist, psychiatrist, or psychiatric social worker). A skilled counselor can help you bring to the surface the relationship problems your blended family will need to face, and teach you some ways of facing them. I would recommend this to *all* people who are planning a marriage that will make them a stepparent.

If you are a parent with a child who seems to be unhappy about your prospective remarriage, you must realize that children just don't like changes. And acquiring a stepparent is bound to bring changes! A child in a single-parent household has usually had to take on more responsibilities than a child in a two-parent family has. This is particularly true for a girl in a motherless home and a boy in a home without a father. Girls who have become "Daddy's little housekeeper" or boys who have taken on the role of "the man in the house" are not always willing to relinquish the special feeling of being wanted, even if the extra chores are not always thrilling. When an outsider enters the scene and assumes these responsibilities, the child has feelings of being replaced.

Fourteen-year-old Eric began getting in trouble at school about six months after his mother married. Where once he had been outgoing and friendly, he was now sullen most of the time. His mother brought him to see me. As I was introduced to him and inviting him into my office, his mother suddenly grabbed him by the arm and practically dragged him into the office, as though she feared he would run away if she let go. When she saw he was safely in the office, she relinquished his arm. "I'll see you in an hour," she told Eric as she left.

It was not a good beginning. I began by explaining to him that it was strictly his mother's idea to escort him into my office in that fashion. Eric replied that this was typical of her lately; she just didn't trust him. As soon as he realized I was sympathetic and not an ally of his mother's, he opened up and started talking about why he felt hostile toward his stepfather. His stepfather wasn't mean to Eric. He tried to be his friend. But the trouble was he tried too hard sometimes. Before his mother remarried, Eric used to help her with the groceries. He always used to grumble about it. His new stepfather, hearing him complain, started carrying in the groceries. He was totally unaware that Eric did not like this one bit. "Every time I see him do that, I want to hit him," Eric muttered. "That used to be *my* job and he took it away."

I understood completely. Eric felt he was being replaced. A child usually feels resentful when another person takes over some of his tasks, even the unpleasant ones, especially if he is not consulted in the matter. Because it makes him feel less necessary. It infringes on his territoriality.

The child in a single-parent home not only has extra responsibilities but often receives extra attention. Sometimes a single parent is lonely and, especially if the child is older, makes a confidant of the child. A special kind of bond grows up between them. As one ten-year-old said of herself and her mother: "It seems to me like we're more like sisters than mother and daughter." When the parent remarries, the child's status changes from special friend back to child, and the child resents it.

If you think a person doesn't act differently toward his or her children when a spouse is around, just recall the last time you were alone in the car with your child. You carried on a conversation with him. Then remember the last time you were in the car with your spouse and that same child. You probably talked to your spouse and ignored your child for most of the conversation. This is a normal thing to do, but you can't blame the child for feeling left out, especially if this is a new spouse with whom he does not yet feel at ease.

These are just some of the problems and mixed feelings a child faces when he acquires a new stepparent. If the remarriage involves stepsiblings, the feelings and concerns multiply. What are the new children like? Will I be able to keep my own room? Will I have to share my bike? Will Mother like them better than me?

Children feel very competitive toward their own siblings for parental attention. But rivalry among stepsiblings is even fiercer. All of these things cry out for the use of the feedback technique (chap. 10), the mutual problem-solving technique (chap. 11), and the family council (chap. 12). All these techniques are of enormous help in enabling children to ventilate their feelings, especially mixed and irrational feelings, to resolve disputes between stepsiblings, and to have a weekly democratic forum at which family conflicts can be ironed out.

Although the family council is helpful for any family, it is especially helpful for a stepfamily. It helps both parents and children bring bothersome feelings out of hiding into the open. It is a safe way for both parents and children to ventilate angry and jealous feelings and get them out of their system so that loving and positive feelings can take their place. It provides a regular opportunity for settling disputes and conflicts within the family. And it serves as an orderly forum within which the two original families can learn to blend their different life-styles into a new family with its own unique style.

Especially in the early months of a newly blended family, I feel that the family council meetings should be held regularly, once a week. Extra meetings can be held whenever a member of the family calls for one. It is important for the children (and sometimes the parents!) to learn to let everyone have his say without being interrupted. Emotional accusations should be avoided whenever possible. One way to accomplish this is to teach the children to state their own feelings without telling someone else what to do. Suggest that they avoid the word *you* as the first word in a sentence. "I felt hurt when you scratched my records by piling them up on the stereo," is easier to take than, "You scratched my records piling them on the stereo, and you'd better not do it again."

It is vitally important that all decisions made in the family council be unanimous. Do not vote. If you vote, there is always someone who wins and someone who loses, and that does not promote the family harmony you seek. If you can't get unanimous agreement at one meeting of the family council, that issue will have to be held over until the next meeting.

Here are some more questions people ask about getting married and creating a stepfamily:

1. *Should I ask my child's permission to marry?*

I have already given my opinion on the answer to this question in chapter 16. I believe strongly that under no circumstances should you ask your child's permission to marry, regardless of the age of the child. It puts a heavy psychological burden on him. Don't do it.

2. *Should you invite the children to your wedding?*

When the children involved are between the ages of three and twelve, I believe you should include them in the wedding unless they make it clear they do not want to attend. If this is the case, respect their wishes and let them stay away. If you don't ask them to come, even though they say nothing about it, they will probably feel hurt and left out. If you have teenagers to consider, simply ask them if they want to come. If so, invite them. If not, let them stay away.

3. *Where should we live?*

If it is at all possible financially, find a new place to live. It may mean changing schools for the children. It may mean some financial sacrifice for you. But it will be worth it. Here's why. The prior occupation of a house confers a certain power of territoriality upon the children and parent who live there. They tend to regard the house as "my house" and make the other stepchildren (and even the parent) feel like outsiders. Here is an example.

When Ed married Sandra, it was a second marriage for both. She was a widow; he was divorced. Her two daughters were both in college and came home only on vacations. He had married late in life and his sons were younger, ages twelve and sixteen. For reasons of economy (her husband's insurance had paid off the mortgage) they moved into Sandra's house.

From the beginning, Ed felt uncomfortable. He was a large

man and felt awkward surrounded by the delicate antique furniture that Sandra preferred. He brought with him a few of his favorite furnishings—a large worn leather chair, three heavy oak bookcases, and a collection of American Indian wall rugs. They looked totally out of place, even though one of the rooms was supposedly his den. Ed suggested redecorating, but Sandra would have none of it. "I love this kind of furniture," she said. "I wouldn't feel right living with any other kind."

When his sons came to visit, it was uncomfortable for everyone. They had to be reminded constantly not to put their feet up on the fragile furniture and to look out for the bric-a-brac. Clearly, it was not a home meant for them.

"I know I must sound like a nag," Sandra would tell Ed after each of these visits, "but boys are so different from girls, and I haven't had any experience with them. They're just—well, careless, I guess."

Ed's stepdaughters complained to their mother when the boys used their bedrooms on visits. They claimed that the boys "messed them all up." His sons' visits became less frequent. It became a source of dissatisfaction between them. At present, the situation is not yet resolved, and the antagonism between Ed and Sandra is growing.

By contrast to his example, when a stepfamily starts over in a new house, neither family has prior claim on the territory. Agreements concerning who gets what rooms, how the house will be furnished, and other such things can be worked out by family council. Some of you may consider this a minor matter. I can assure you it is not minor, from a psychological point of view. The house is something that people live in every day of their lives. And if one part of the stepfamily feels deep down that "This is my house," and the other part of the stepfamily feels "This is not my house; I'm an outsider here," then the entire stepfamily is headed for trouble. If a stepfamily can begin life together in an entirely new house, a number of psychological problems can be avoided.

4. *What should my stepchild call me?*

To begin with, don't ask him to call you Father or Mother. He already has a father or mother and will resent you for trying to take his parent's place and his parent's name.

I think the safest thing in the beginning is to ask your stepchild to call you by your first name. This is a natural form of address and does not tread on any tender toes. Sometimes the child will devise a nickname for you. One patient of mine was courting a woman with two daughters, and the first time he sent her flowers he signed it "Your Secret Admirer." Somehow this appealed to the two little girls and they began calling him "S. A." And that's what they continued to call him affectionately after he and their mother were married.

If you start on a first-name or a nickname basis, and if all goes well with the stepchildren and no attempt is made to pressure them into it, they may end up calling you Daddy or Mommy. One of my patients with two daughters married a woman who also had two daughters. They all lived together. At first his own children continued to call him Daddy and his stepdaughters called him Jack. After a year and a half, one of his stepdaughters announced, "It isn't fair. They get to call you Daddy and we don't. From now on, we're *all* going to call you Daddy." My patient was very pleased and felt that they had decided to call him Daddy because he hadn't pressed the issue and asked them to call him that from the beginning.

5. Should I legally adopt my stepchild?

Only if the other parent has moved away or otherwise dropped out of the picture. If the other parent is still very much in the picture—visiting faithfully and maintaining regular contact with your stepchild—then I think it would be a psychological mistake for you to adopt the child. For one thing, it would wound the child. Down deep he still has a loyalty to his parent, and his sense of identity is still bound up with his original name. Furthermore, it would hurt the parent and perhaps cause him to psychologically move away from his child, even if the two of them have been reasonably close. If the parent drifts away, this, of course, would have a negative psychological effect on the child.

6. My folks refuse to accept my new stepdaughters as their grandchildren and it's causing a lot of bad feelings between the kids. What can I do about it?

Relatives, especially grandparents, can be a source of help or a source of friction. Blessed indeed are you stepparents whose new in-laws treat your children as if they have always been a part of their family. Loving grandparents can often serve as psychological buffers between antagonistic elements and bring stability to the whole family. If they have the respect of the different members of the family, they may even act as arbitrators in difficult matters.

If, however, either through intent or ignorance, the grandparents favor their natural grandchildren over the stepgrandchildren in an obvious way, you are in for problems. Hopefully they will listen to you and your spouse when you explain that their behavior is causing jealousy and friction among the children. (Use the mutual problem-solving technique, chap. 11.) If gifting is a problem, explain that your family harmony suffers when they give gifts only to their natural grandchildren. (Sometimes you may have to pay for additional gifts to get them to cooperate and do this.) If they take only their natural grandchildren on outings, explain what this is doing to the children and encourage them to take both groups of children on outings.

If you use the mutual-problem solving and feedback techniques and they still won't listen to you, you might try a few consultations with a professional counselor to see what suggestions he may have. Finally, if nothing else works, you may have to forbid them to see *any* of the grandchildren if they cannot treat both sets of grandchildren reasonably equally. This will usually bring them around. But if it doesn't it is better for them not to see their grandchildren than to make your entire family miserable with jealousy and conflict.

7. *What special discipline problems should I expect with my stepchildren?*

Discipline is often a problem for the stepparent. In some respects, the ways you discipline children in an intact family are the same in a stepfamily. All the methods of discipline discussed in the early chapters of this book are as applicable to the stepchild as to the biological child. But the stepfamily creates a different *setting* for discipline than the biological family does.

Some parents will effectively discipline their own children, but be weak or hesitant in disciplining their stepchildren. I think this is a mistake. You want to start out *slowly* in disciplining your stepchildren, but you are abdicating your position of authority in the home if you leave all of the disciplining to your spouse.

Remember what I stressed at the beginning of this book.

Emotional rapport is an absolute prerequisite to discipline.
Your first job as a stepparent is to build emotional rapport
with your stepchildren.

Remember also not to confuse *discipline* with *punishment.*
Most of the discipline techniques covered in the beginning of
this book are positive in nature. Your job in disciplining your
stepchildren is to reward positive behavior and use a variety
of techniques to discourage misbehavior.

At first stepparents usually feel somewhat hesitant in disciplining their stepchildren. But after they have established
good rapport with them, they should feel as relaxed in disciplining their stepchildren as they do when handling their own
children. Unfortunately, many stepparents don't. After two
years as a stepparent they may still feel that they are walking
on eggs with their stepchildren. As one stepparent put it, "I
don't shout at my stepchildren. I only shout at people I'm absolutely sure of."[20] If you have this problem, you can help
yourself by using the technique of negative thinking (chap.
15).

Some stepparents can be very lenient about their own
child's faults, but very strict when their stepchild does the
same thing. Family council is a good place to iron this out.

8. *Will it add to the tensions of our blended family if my
husband and I have a child of our own?*

My answer is yes. And no. In some stepfamilies where
children from both marriages are living in the same home, a
new child could become a psychological link between the two
families. Here a new child is a positive factor. But in the
other blended-family situations it can be a negative factor.
For example, if the family includes only one spouse's
children, who do not get along well with the stepparent, the
new infant may be looked upon as one more wedge to come
between them and their natural parent. And so the child may
be greatly resented. There are many variables that affect this
situation: the ages and sexes of the children, the tem-
peraments of both children and adults, the relationship between stepparent and stepchildren before the birth of the
baby, and more.

Don't decide whether or not to have a child by its possible
effect on the stepchildren, or by taking a poll of the stepchildren. Decide it the way you would if you were a husband and wife with no stepchildren to consider. That is, if

having a child is important to you and your marriage, then have it. If not, don't.

So far, I've been talking about live-in stepchildren. But there is another kind of stepchild: the stepchild who comes for a day, a weekend, or part or all of a vacation. The part-time stepchild is often difficult to handle because no matter how skillfully both sets of parents avoid bringing up comparisons between the two homes, the child is bound to make them. Children bring with them habits from their regular home and don't hesitate to complain when you're not doing things the way they are accustomed to having them done.

If you are a part-time stepparent, you know how difficult it can be. Here are some suggestions that may make your situation easier.

First, set up a regular schedule of visits and stick to it whenever possible. It creates a sense of stability for the child and helps make it easier for both households. If there are several children involved, you may like to have them all together, or you may find it easier to have them visit one at a time. Giving each of the children separate visits and then occasionally having them all together is often best. That way each child can have all of your attention on some of his visits, which can be very good for the relationship. And having all of the children together helps promote a feeling of being a family, even if it's a part-time family.

Second, it is important for you and your spouse to agree on ground rules that will apply to all the children concerned. The visiting children should be told what the rules are when they arrive. If they tell you they are allowed to act differently at home, you can reply, "This is how we do things in our house." This is a very effective answer, since you are not saying, "Your way is wrong and our way is right." You are simply saying what they already know, that different people have different lifestyles.

Third, it will help if you can provide a space for your occasional visitors to call their own and have it ready for them when they arrive. Most people are not wealthy enough to set aside a separate room for this purpose, but even if you only have a third shelf of the linen closet waiting for them, it will be important to them psychologically. It will be their "territory." You can keep some special toys and playthings in their special place. You will be surprised how important it is to their feelings to have this "place of their own" when visiting you.

Children who shuttle back and forth between parents often bring their uncertainties, tensions, and resentments with them. Sometimes this may take the form of playing on a seldom-seen parent's guilt and getting special gifts out of it. Sometimes these uncertainties masquerade as arrogance. Children want to be loved, but shuttle-children often need to test your love. They unconsciously think to themselves: "If I'm really ornery and he still loves me, that means he *really* loves me." This is a backward way of going about it, but it often happens.

I had a patient, Robert, whose seven-year-old son behaved fine on weekend visits until it was time for him to leave. Robert said, "As soon as I get Bobby in the car to go home, he starts finding some way to drive me absolutely batty. By the time I get him to his mother's house, I'm furious with him and he's in tears." Robert was quite distressed about the situation but could not seem to prevent its happening until he began to see Bobby's behavior as a plea for reassurance of love from his father. Once Robert realized this, instead of responding to the bait and becoming angry when Bobby misbehaved, he would hug his son and tell him that he loved him and would see him again soon. After a few times of getting this reassurance offered directly, Bobby no longer needed to make a shambles of the end of every visit.

These back-and-forth children are also weekly reminders of the old spouse. Some ex-husbands and wives are able to get along reasonably well together in making plans for their child's present and future. If you are married to a person who has this kind of an amiable relationship with an ex-spouse, it's natural to feel a little jealous. However, believe me when I say it is much easier to have an ex-spouse who is cooperative and friendly than it is to endure an ex-spouse who is vindictive and uses the children as pawns against you and your spouse.

My patient Marian told me this tale of woe about her stepson's recent visit.

"Tom got off the plane dressed in the cruddiest pair of jeans you can imagine, topped with a T-shirt that looked as if it had been used to wash the car and clean the valves. His bag was filled with dirty socks, one very gray towel, and a pair of rancid sneakers. I thought that maybe he'd packed it himself—he's almost eleven. But no, he hadn't. He said his mother did it.

"I was furious! Especially since she had asked for more money just so he'd have some clothes for this trip. And we sent it, like fools! I don't know what she did with it, but obviously she didn't spend it on him!"

"What did you do?" I asked.

"Well," she answered with a shrug, "my first impulse was to say something to him like, 'That's just what I'd expect from your mother.' But I didn't and I'm glad of it. It's not his fault that his mother is such a vindictive bitch. I just said something like, 'I guess you'll need some new clothes.' And the next day we went shopping for some. It sure hurt to have to swallow that crap from her, though."

Marian is a wise woman. She resisted the all-too-human temptation to point out the comparison between herself and the child's mother. This almost always backfires. No matter what a wretch his mother is, the child will usually defend her. After all, she is the parent he has to live with! Also, he loves her. A child may criticize his parent, but he will almost always resent anyone else's doing so. He may act out his resentment by withdrawal, by open hostility, or by unconsciously trying to pit one parent or stepparent against another. If Marian had vented her feelings about his mother, she would probably have succeeded only in making the child's visit with her and her spouse an unhappy one.

I have tried to give you an overall view of the world of stepparenting. You need to know what the territory is like in which you will be disciplining your children and stepchildren. I have especially tried to point out the booby traps and land mines that infest the territory so that you will know where they are and how to avoid stepping on them. In doing so, I hope I haven't given you too pessimistic a view of stepparenting so that by now you are throwing up your hands in despair and saying to yourself, "The situation is hopeless!"

I have tried to show you the reasons why stepparenting is much harder than parenting in an intact home. But I have not said that stepparenting is impossible! Let me use this analogy. It is much harder to learn to speak Japanese than to learn to speak Spanish or French. It is not *impossible* to learn Japanese; it is only *harder*. Learning to discipline children in a biological family is like learning Spanish or French. Learning to discipline children in a stepfamily is like learning

Japanese. I would be doing you a disservice if I told you that learning Japanese was as easy as learning Spanish or French. I would be doing you the same disservice if I told you that learning to discipline children in a stepfamily was as easy as learning to discipline children in a biological family.

Good luck!

20

HOW TO USE THE
REST OF THIS BOOK.

We have talked about twenty different discipline strategies and explained how each one can be used. Here they are:

1. Rapport, basic to all discipline because it builds a strong and enduring relationship between parent and child.

2. A positive reward system, the most powerful and efficient way for a parent to teach desirable behavior to a child.

3. Contracting, a way of negotiating an agreement between parent and child for positive behavior on the part of the child.

4. Detecting and eliminating the payoffs parents unwittingly give a child for undesirable behavior.

5. The Time Out, in which a child is given a five-minute Time Out in his room whenever his behavior is unacceptable.

6. The Reverse Time Out (for use with very young children), in which a parent locks herself in a room whenever her children are behaving badly.

7. Physical restraint of the very young child when he is misbehaving in a way that calls for immediate action.

8. Environmental control, in which the parent arranges the environment so that certain types of undesirable behavior cannot take place.

9. Natural consequences, in which a child experiences the educative effect of the natural consequences of bad behavior.

10. Spanking, its advantages and disadvantages as a method of discipline.

11. Establishing the authority of the parent, rather than falling into the permissiveness trap.

12. The feedback technique of showing a child you understand how he feels.

13. The mutual problem-solving technique for handling conflicts between parent and child.

14. The family council, a way of solving conflicts within the family and at the same time training children in the art of human relations.

15. How to teach ethics and morality to children as part of the total discipline process.

16. How to use "parental muscle" as a last-ditch discipline technique when it becomes necessary.

17. Negative thinking, a special technique for the parent to desensitize herself to annoying aspects of a child's behavior.

18. Discipline techniques for working mothers.

19. Discipline techniques in the special setting of a single-parent family.

20. Discipline techniques in the special setting of the step-parent and the blended family.

These discipline strategies were not picked at random from the research on child-raising. On the contrary, all these strategies fit together carefully. They have been designed to help you accomplish four fundamental goals in raising a child:

1. To build rapport and deepen the relationship between yourself and your child.

2. To provide payoffs for desirable behavior, so that it will be strengthened.

3. To withhold payoffs for misbehavior so that it will be weakened and eliminated.

4. To improve communication between yourself and your child.

Please do not think of these twenty discipline strategies as isolated gimmicks that you apply in an unrelated fashion to each discipline problem that comes up. All of the discipline strategies work together. And the purpose of each strategy is to help you accomplish one of the four basic discipline goals in raising your child. Ultimately those four goals fuse into one: to enable your child to mature so that at the end of adolescence he will no longer need your parental discipline, but will now be a self-disciplined adult. This is the bottom line of the whole child-raising process.

Now that you have an overview of the twenty discipline strategies, here is how I suggest you use the rest of this book.

First of all, it is very important for you to have a good grasp of the stage of development your child is in. Without an understanding of what children are typically like at each stage of development you will have a difficult time intelligently disciplining your youngster. Disciplining sibling rivalry between a nine-year-old and an eleven-year old is vastly different from disciplining sibling rivalry between a two-year-old and a four-year-old. If you have several children, they may be in quite different stages of development, and it is very important for you to understand "where they are at."

For each stage of development that I describe in succeeding chapters of this book I will give you a brief overview of that stage. For more detailed coverage of each stage of development from infancy through adolescence, you can consult my books, *How to Parent and How to Father*, as well as the series of books by Arnold Gesell, Louise Ames, and Frances Ilg, *Infant and Child in the Culture of Today, The Child from Five to Ten*, and *Youth*.

Once you feel you have a good grasp on the specific stage of development each of your children is in, you can begin to really use this book. If you have a particular discipline problem with a child, look it up in the index, then turn to a discussion of that problem and the techniques suggested for handling it. If the book suggests that, in connection with this discipline problem, you go back and reread one of the chapters discussing a particular discipline strategy, do that.

Think of this book as if it were a handbook on how to play tennis, or how to play golf. You wouldn't expect to read the book once and thereby learn to be a good tennis player or golfer. You would expect to refer to it again and again. You would expect to absorb the books's overall message and philosophy slowly. Believe me, learning to raise a child successfully from birth through adolescence is a much more complex task than learning to play golf or tennis. The parent who gets the most out of this book will have a well-thumbed and well-marked-up copy.

21

INFANCY

Overview of the Stage

This stage, which lasts from birth until the child begins to crawl or walk (which will vary according to the child), covers approximately the first year of life. This is the most important period of your child's life, for in infancy he is forming his most fundamental attitudes toward himself and his world. The developmental task of infancy is that of *learning either a basic trust in himself* and his world, *or a basic distrust*, or something in between. If your baby is fed when he is hungry, given plenty of physical cuddling, and not ignored when he cries, he will feel good about himself and his world and will develop a basically optimistic viewpoint toward life.

Most parents do quite a good job with their children during the stage of infancy, and discipline problems do not ordinarily arise at this time. The Harvard Preschool Project studied mothers in interaction with their children in the home and found that they did pretty well handling their children in the infancy stage. It was not until the child began to crawl and walk in the stage of toddlerhood that mothers began to have difficulties.

So most of the problems mentioned in this chapter will not be of the same nature as the discipline problems discussed in later chapters. Nevertheless, the child-raising problems unique to the stage of infancy are important—particularly to the first-time parent. The means by which parents handle these problems will either strengthen or weaken the discipline process that begins at a later stage.

During this stage, it is important for you to remember two things.

First, remember the importance of rapport as the foundation of discipline. Rapport is what makes you a much-loved person in the eyes of your child and rapport is what makes her *want* to obey you. And you are lucky that you have a whole year in which to build rapport by feeding her, cuddling her, talking to her, singing to her, bathing her, changing her diapers, and attending to her other needs. In doing all of these things you are building a solid relationship between the two of you. It is this reservoir of rapport and trust that you will draw upon to handle the discipline problems of toddlerhood. So as far as discipline is concerned, infancy can be thought of as the stage of rapport-building.

Second, I have already mentioned that some children are easier to raise than others. Since each child embodies a different combination of genes, each and every child in the world has a unique biological temperament that begins to manifest itself at birth. Researchers have studied babies in their first week of life and found vast differences among them in such temperamental factors as how active or passive they are, their rate of crying, intensity of reactions, distractibility, approach or withdrawal in response to a new stimulus, degree of persistence in the face of obstacles, etc.

I can confirm these scientific findings through my experience with my own two sons. They were quite different from each other in many ways from the very first month of life. For example, there was great contrast between the way each woke up for his early morning bottle.

My first son, Randy, was the forceful, demanding type. The instant he woke up in the morning he let out a blood-curdling cry that could be heard for blocks, and he continued this cry until his bottle arrived.

Rusty, my younger son, was completely different. He reminded me of those alarm clocks that begin by gently purring and end up by roaring loudly when you don't respond to the first gentle calls. Rusty woke up around the same early hours as Randy, between 5:00 and 6:00 A.M. But he would not begin crying at first. He would move around in his bed and make gentle purring noises. Then you would know he was awake. My wife and I would not respond to his first noises, hoping he would go back to sleep. Then after fifteen or twenty minutes he would usually begin to cry, but in a gentle whimper. The cries would get more and more lusty, until after about half an hour we knew he really meant it and got up and gave him his bottle. But the whole process from first awakening to the time he got his bottle might take thirty to forty-five minutes.

I am stressing the fact that every child has a different biological temperament because I find it so underemphasized in books on child psychology and child-raising. Many parents seem to believe that the environment they provide for their child is the only factor determining how the child turns out later in life. This is simply not true. It is the *interaction* of the child's basic temperament with the parental environment that decides how the child will turn out. So parents are *not* 100 percent responsible for the kind of adults their children become.

My oldest child, my daughter, Robin, was very easy to raise. If all children were as easy to raise as Robin, I would have thought it was a snap being a parent. My two boys taught me that some children are not as easy to raise as others.

What is the practical value of this information for parents? It is simply this: If you have a child whose biological temperament makes him easy to raise, certain discipline methods may work effectively with him. The same discipline methods may work poorly or not at all with a child whose different temperament makes him hard to raise. You may have to use different discipline methods, exert much more parental power, and develop more gray hairs raising a hard-to-raise child. But if you do, don't compare yourself with a neighboring parent who has an easy-to-raise child. Don't berate yourself for doing a terrible job as a parent. Recognize the simple fact that some youngsters are harder to raise than others and take more out of you.

Now let's talk about the problems that can arise in the stage of infancy. I have divided them into two groups: problems within the baby, and problems within the mother.

Problems within the Baby

1. *My baby cries all the time, and I don't know how to handle it.*

Of one thing we can be sure: Every time a baby cries, there is a reason. But we may not always know the reason. Since a baby has no speech, crying is his only form of communication. Every time he cries he is trying to tell us something.

A baby's "normal" crying falls into two classes. First, when he has been sleeping for some time and wakes up hungry, he cries. By this crying he is saying to us, "I'm hungry; I want to be fed." Second, a baby may have short periods of "fretful" crying, especially when he is getting ready to fall asleep. The "crying before sleeping" is typical of many babies, and a parent can learn to spot the unique quality of this kind of crying. Fretful crying that is not a prelude to sleep may be due to fatigue, to the immaturity of the baby's nervous system, or the immaturity of his digestive system.

You may read in some books on child-raising that a baby's crying may be due to a wet diaper or a bowel movement. Don't you believe it. Babies can go for long, long periods of time (even through the night) with a wet or soiled diaper and be perfectly comfortable, as long as the diaper isn't cold.

Most parents have no great trouble coping with the "normal" crying of babies I have just described. It's the crying that goes on and on for no apparent reason that drives a parent up the wall. So let's talk about this type and what can be done about it.

Let's start by admitting that we don't know what causes really prolonged crying in a young infant. Often such crying is ascribed to "colic." But this is actually just a nice word we have invented because it seems to be more reassuring to say to a young mother, "Your baby has colic," than to say, "We don't really know why your baby cries as much as he does."

I think it is much better to acknowledge that we do not really know the reason or reasons behind the long-continued fretful crying of a baby. But we can try various things to relieve this type of crying. We may never know exactly why a particular technique worked, but if any of them work, great!

First, if your baby has been asleep even for as short a time as an hour or hour and a half and wakes up crying, feed him. Don't say to yourself, "Oh, he can't want to be fed; I fed him only a little while ago." How do you know what he feels like and wants inside? So offer him the breast or bottle. If he rejects feeding by pushing away the breast or bottle, or by spitting up, then obviously he does not want to be fed. If he continues to cry, it must mean something else.

Second, you can swaddle your baby. This is done by wrapping the baby snugly in a blanket. Swaddling, which is a common practice in Russia, lessens muscular activity, lowers heart and respiratory rates, and is very soothing to an infant.

Third, you can hold your baby tight to your body. This provides the same advantages of swaddling as well as giving the baby the warmth of your body.

Babies differ in what soothes them, so try different methods of quieting your baby. You can rock him or croon or cuddle him. You can hold him in close contact over your heart. Often the sound of a heartbeat soothes a baby because in the womb he became familiar with his mother's heartbeat. Babies often respond to music because the tempo of most music is usually between 50 and 150 beats per minute, which are roughly the parameters of the human heartbeat.

Fourth, you can use a pacifier. This often gives relief to the baby who is subject to long periods of irritable crying (and to his parents). If you use a pacifier, be sure not to make the mistake of using the pacifier to put the baby to sleep. You are really opening a can of worms if you do this. Typically, the baby who sleeps with a pacifier will wake up and cry if the pacifier falls out. And this can happen ten or twelve times a night, much to the parents' dismay!

Before you decide to use a pacifier, you should know that the prolonged fretful crying will usually vanish by the third or possibly fourth month. At that time you can gradually wean your baby from the pacifier in a week or two, in order for it not to become a long-lasting habit. Or at that time your baby himself may tell you he's ready to give up his pacifier by spitting it out soon after you put it in his mouth, or by seeming to be just as happy without it. If you don't get him off the pacifier when he's in his third or fourth month, he may not be willing to give it up for a year or two.

Fifth, if your infant persists in crying for no apparent reason, one other possibility should be investigated. Your baby may be sick. If in addition to his crying your baby looks different in his general demeanor and you sense that he "isn't himself," take his temperature and call your physician.

So there are a variety of methods you can use to try to comfort and quiet a fretful, crying baby. If any of them work for your baby, fine! Try them again the next time your baby gets into one of his long crying spells. However, be prepared to face this unpleasant fact: None of these methods may work. Your child may continue to cry for long periods of time for reasons you don't understand.

This situation is very hard to handle. The typical scenario runs something like this: The baby seems to be saying by his crying, "Do something to help me. Can't you see how unhappy I am?" The parent tries this and tries that to soothe the baby, but to no avail. The parent soon feels very inadequate. "What's the matter with me? I must be a lousy parent." From feeling inadequate, the parent's mood soon changes to one of anger. "Damn you, shut up that crying. I've had enough!"

At this point the parent may feel guilty about being angry at her little baby—after all, he can't help it. Or she may allow her angry feelings to come out in angry actions. This is the point where much child abuse begins. The excessive crying of the baby gets on the parent's nerves to such an extent that she loses control and begins to strike the baby. If a mother or father actually does lose control and begins to hit the baby, then the parent should seek help—either through professional counseling or Parents Anonymous (see chap. 22, question 17 for information about where to contact this organization) or both.

If you have a baby who cries for long periods of time in spite of everything you do to comfort him, it is reassuring to know that most babies grow out of this by their third or fourth month. (Our best explanation is that as the baby's nervous and digestive systems mature, the internal pains that are probably causing the crying gradually diminish.)

Meanwhile, how will you live through your child's first three or four months of constant crying? My main suggestion is that you arrange for a baby-sitter so you can get out of the house at least twice a week for three or four hours. Please try not to feel guilty about this, as if you are "abandoning" your baby. You *need* to be away from your baby for these periods, or you will quickly develop cabin fever and become less effective as a parent.

Also, both parents might try taking the baby to a drive-in movie. The motion of a moving car is often soothing to a baby, and he may be asleep by the time you get to the movie. Hopefully, if he doesn't wake up when you get there, mother and father can enjoy a movie together without the baby's crying as a background.

Finally, if you have tried all of these methods and found that none of them works, then I suggest you try to take the attitude: "I've done all I can for my baby, and he still cries. It's probably due to his immature nervous and digestive systems, and he will grow out of it in a few months. Nothing I can do will hurry the maturing of his nervous and digestive systems. I will just have to wait, put up with the crying in whatever way I can, and know that in a few months Mother Nature will solve the problem for me."

2. *My baby is almost a year old and I can't seen to get her toilet trained.*

No wonder you can't. It's much too early for toilet training at this age. For a child to be toilet trained she has to master a number of complex skills, including neuromuscular control over her sphincter muscles. This neuromusclar control is ordinarily not adequate for the task of toilet training until the child is approximately one and one-half to two years old. It is *possible* to toilet train a child younger than that age, but usually you are going to have to pay a psychological price for doing it too early. Personally I don't think the price is worth it. So wait until your child is one and one-half or two years old and then begin toilet training.

3. *My baby wakes up at night and then won't go back to sleep after her feeding.*

Let me tell you what *not* to do. Remember chapter 3 on the positive reward system? If you give in to her demand for a period of playtime after a middle-of-the-night feeding, you are giving her a payoff for wakefulness after the night feeding. Pretty soon you may be horrified to discover that she is now waking up not once but several times a night for her playtime. She needs her middle-of-the-night feeding or she wouldn't wake up for it, so give her the feeding. But she has no physiological or psychological need for a middle-of-the-night playtime, unless you, by mismanaging the situation, train her to demand such nighttime play periods.

So what should you do? Give her absolutely no middle-of-the-night payoffs. All playtime with baby is reserved for the daytime hours. After feeding her in the middle of the night, tuck her back in bed, perhaps with a favorite cuddly doll or animal, kiss her and pat her lovingly, and march out of the room. Do not under any circumstances go back into the room. If she is used to having you give in to her nighttime demands, she may cry bitterly, usually for decreasing amounts of time, for several days to a week. Then she will probably stop, for she will now be convinced that there will be no playtime payoffs after her night feeding. She will either go back to sleep, or amuse herself for a little while and then go back to sleep.

Problems within the Mother

4. *I don't seem to have any maternal instinct toward my month-old baby. What's the matter with me?*

Nothing is the matter with you except that you, like other mothers, have been taught to believe in the myth of a "maternal instinct." Before they become parents, most people have never actually seen a very young baby. The chubby, apple-cheeked babies they have seen in pictures and ads are usually about four months old. Many newborn babies would not exactly win first prize in a beauty contest. The proud mother and father are often shocked by what their newborn baby *actually* looks like, as compared with what they had unconsciously expected him to look like.

Furthermore, *all* babies are going to disrupt the parents' habits in ways they hadn't really counted on. Oh, sure, before they became parents they *heard* about things like 2:00 A.M. feedings and babies that cry a lot, but now it's actually happening to them! (It reminds me of the story of the soldier in his first experience with combat saying in panic to his buddy, as the bullets whistled around them, "Hey, they're *really* firing at us!")

You may be lucky and have one of those babies who sleeps through the night after the first month. Most of us aren't so lucky. None of my three children slept through the night until they were at least a year old. And then you may be one of those parents who wins Low-Ball on the Parents Sweepstakes, with a fussy, irritable, hard-to-manage baby.

What all of this adds up to is that the actual management of your baby, particularly in his first three or four months, may be no bed of roses. And, therefore, it is easy to understand why you don't feel kindly and loving and full of sweetness and light, as the myth of maternal instinct says you should.

So, Virginia, there is no Santa Claus and there is no maternal instinct. Apart from a small minority of parents who have very positive feelings toward their baby right from the start, most of us have to *learn* to love our babies. And in the process of learning to love the baby we may have to learn to take a lot of frustrations and inconveniences in stride, especially in the early months of the baby's life. So don't berate yourself for not having a maternal instinct. Take care of your baby: feed him, burp him, bathe him, change his diapers, talk to him, sing to him, and play with him. And warm, deep, loving feelings toward him will grow and develop, never fear.

5. *I feel very inadequate in taking care of my new baby.*

Welcome to the club! That's a perfectly normal reaction for a new parent to experience with a first baby. If you never had a golf lesson before, wouldn't you feel inadequate playing your first eighteen holes? The first time we attempt any complex task, we are probably going to feel inadequate and unsure of ourselves.

At first you may worry about anything your baby does that is even slightly out of the ordinary. If she coughs, you may immediately think she is developing pneumonia. And so on. One young mother with her first baby told me, "As soon as I got home from the hospital with my baby I just burst into tears and said to myself, 'How in the world can I ever take care of her?'"

But these feelings will pass sooner than you think. You will feel increasingly sure of yourself as you feed, bathe, diaper, and take care of your baby. She is your baby and you will feel adequate and competent to care for her.

If you want to hasten the process of feeling competent, you can use the negative thinking technique described in chapter 15. Go back and review that chapter to get a good idea of how the technique works. Then, using the technique, say things to yourself such as: "Peggy, take care of your baby properly. Here you are a college graduate, but you can't even change a diaper right! And how can you be so awkward when you feed her? Why don't you just give up the whole thing and turn the job over to your mother or somebody who knows how to do things properly?"

6. Before my baby was born, I had such wonderful fantasies about her. But the actual reality of taking care of my baby is so different from what I imagined it would be.

Once we take the trouble to look into this matter, it becomes very clear why the realities of taking care of a young baby come as such a shock to many young parents. The mother probably played with dolls a good bit as a girl, and does not realize how her doll play may have unconsciously shaped many of her expectations about her baby and what she will be like. In doll play a little girl experiences what Martin Buber calls an I-it relationship. That is, the little girl completely controls the doll and the play. The doll is an "it." The doll does whatever the girl tells her to do and says whatever the girl dreams up for her to say. The doll never comes back unexpectedly with a life of its own.

But in her relationship with her baby, the mother no longer experiences an I-it relationship. She may not be aware of it, but unconsciously she has been expecting to have an easy and tension-free relationship with her new baby because of her prior experience with dolls. Instead, she and her baby have an I-you relationship. She is aware from the first that her baby is a person in her own right, not a passive replica of a doll from childhood.

In addition to the subtle influences of childhood doll play, the new mother has had conscious and unconscious fantasies for nine months of what her baby will be like. She may have pictured herself in sheer bliss nursing her baby, and then discovered, to her shock and surprise, that she has a very colicky baby on her hands.

This situation is analogous to what happens during the courtship process, when a man and woman weave wonderful fantasies around each other. Then, after they marry and settle down to the reality of day-to-day existence, the courtship fantasies fade away and the couple come to know each other as they really are, psychological warts and all.

Some babies are closer to their parents' prebirth fantasies and some further away. But all parents have to make *some* adjustment to the fact that their actual baby is not the fantasy baby they thought about before she was born. But I'll tell you a secret. Chances are that your real-life baby will bring you much more happiness in the long run than any make-believe baby who existed only in your fantasies.

7. *I'm ashamed to admit this, but there are times when I actually hate my baby*.

Such feelings are normal and natural. The trouble is, nobody tells new parents ahead of time that they are going to feel this way. A parent thinks, "How in the world can I have such terrible feelings about my baby?" It's easy to answer that question with a little bit of psychological analysis. Anything or any person that frustrates us makes us feel angry. The greater the frustration, the greater the anger. And there are many, many ways in which a small baby can frustrate you and make you angry.

Consider just one example: Your baby may wake up in the middle of the night and start crying and crying. Nothing you do will quiet him. There he is, crying his little head off, and there the two of you are, groggy and desperate for sleep, not knowing what to do. At a time such as this you may find yourself getting furious at your baby, maybe even yelling at him, "Shut up! Don't you know I need to get back to sleep?"

Don't feel ashamed to admit that there are times when you hate your baby. That's normal. There are times when all parents hate their babies, when their babies frustrate them terribly. Or when negative feelings about the baby have been building up for weeks, and then something trivial happens that breaks the psychological dam, and the negative feelings come pouring out. Admit your feelings to yourself, and try not to feel guilty about them. As your baby grows, many of the frustrating situations that cause the angry feelings will disappear.

8. *What can I do about people like my mother and my in-laws who keep giving me unwanted advice on how to raise my baby?*

Unfortunately most first-time parents do nothing about this situation. They say nothing to their parents or in-laws about the unwanted advice. But their antagonistic feelings continue to build up and build up, finally resulting in an underground poisoning of the relationship. This is a mistake. It would be much wiser to face the situation head-on. You need to say something like, "Mother, I know you want the best for your grandson, and you have certain ideas about how he should be raised. You are certainly entitled to your ideas on that subject. But I would appreciate it if you would not be so critical about how we are handling things. Jonathan is our son and we have our own ideas about how it's best to raise him." Put it in your own words, but put it. Sometime like that needs to be said.

If you have trouble communicating this point to your parents or in-laws because you are afraid to face them, try the negative thinking method. Review chapter 15 and say something like this to yourself, "Ellen, you have no right at all to tell your mother you don't want her advice on how to raise Jonathan. After all, she is your MOTHER! And you are only her daughter, even if you are twenty-seven years old. To be a good and dutiful daughter you should not only listen to what she tells you about raising Jonathan, you should actually raise him by her directions! You have no right to any ideas of your own about raising your son. After all, you're only his mother!"

It may cause some temporary difficulty in the relationship with your parents or in-laws if you bring this problem out into the open. But you will have much more difficulty in your relationship with them in the long run if you do *not* bring it out into the open.

9. *Since the baby arrived, the relationships in the family seem be completely different. How do I handle this?*

Your family relationships not only *seem* to be different; they *are* different. This is another one of those important facts that nobody tells parents ahead of time. Whether a husband and wife have been married for two years or seven years, during the time that they have been married their role relationships have become relatively stabilized. Unconsciously, and without giving the matter any particular thought, they assume these same relationships will continue when the baby arrives. Not so. The relationships will definitely change and be modified by the presence of the baby. It's exactly the same as if you took an eight-year-old child or a nephew or cousin into your house and family on a permanent basis.

The roles of wife and mother, on the one hand, and husband and father on the other, do not necessarily fit together smoothly, with no rough edges. Each of you has to *learn* how to put together the role of spouse and parent in one reasonable well-fitting package. And it will take time for you to learn that. Allow for that time.

For instance, one pattern that often develops is for the husband to be jealous of all the attention his wife is giving to the baby. After all, he got all of his wife's attention before the baby was born. He may be relatively aware of this jealousy or completely unconscious of it.

Some husbands may react by suddenly staying away from home a lot. They may work overtime at the office. Or stop off to "have a few beers" with their work mates and come home smashed at one in the morning.

This is only one of many examples I could give of the kinds of things that may need attention in your relationships after the arrival of the baby. You may want to do some conscious restructuring rather than letting the chips fall where they may. And this restructuring within the family will have to take place with the birth of each new child. I suspect, however, that the restructuring of the family relationships with the first child may be the most difficult.

10. *Due to the baby, my husband and I are having problems in our sexual relationship. The doctor says to wait six weeks before resuming sexual intercourse, and my husband resents this.*

I'm afraid you are a victim of what has been called the great "myth of coitus," the myth that the only kind of sexual relationship possible between husband and wife is that of coitus or sexual intercourse. However, there are other types of satisfying sexual relationships available, such as oral sex or manual sex. Intercourse may be verboten during those six weeks, but making love to each other by hand or by mouth is certainly not. And if your love-making has always been confined to intercourse, you may be in for some delightful surprises as you experiment with oral or manual forms of making love!

Neither you nor your husband should blame your baby for any difficulties in your sexual relationship. Nobody is to blame. Your only problem is that you have limited your focus to sexual intercourse. Broaden your sexual outlets and the problem will disappear.

11. *I feel so terribly alone and trapped sometimes, just me and the baby in the house. I need someone I can talk to about my feelings.*

What you need is what every first-time mother needs: your own special "hot line" where you can phone someone and air your feelings. You can set up this kind of arrangement with a friend or neighbor, or even organize a "hot line" on a more structured basis with five or six mothers who also have young babies.

You may not know that the La Leche League, an organization for mothers who are breast-feeding their babies, has such a "hot line." In addition, you may not know that you do not have to be a breast-feeding mother or belong to the La Leche League to avail yourself of the services of their "hot line." So if there is a La Leche League in your community, this may be a good resource for you.

But however you do it, you need to find or organize a semistructured relationship where you can phone someone and talk over your feelings of being alone and trapped. You can also help yourself by helping some other mother ventilate her feelings to you. It works both ways.

12. *How can I handle the blue feelings I am experiencing now?*

You can do any one of five things.

First, endure them and wait for them to go away. Blue feelings are a mild form of depression, and mild depression, in time, will lift and disappear.

Second, talk them out with a friend or friends. Blue feelings are worst when endured alone. Talking them out with someone helps to loosen their hold on you.

Third, use the method of negative thinking described in chapter 15. Lay it on thick to yourself about how terrible life is. "Charlotte, life is hopeless. Here you are stuck at home with this baby that does nothing but demand, demand, demand. Life will never get any better. The years will drag on and on and you will still be trapped at home with this baby."

Fourth, when you find yourself feeling blue, don't just sit there and let the blue thoughts run through your mind. Take action. Do something different. Get a babysitter and give yourself some time away from the baby. Go to a movie. Go shopping. Visit a friend. Do anything that appeals to you, as long as it gets you out of your house or apartment and away from the baby for a while.

Fifth, if the blue feelings persist or become sufficiently severe, seek professional help. A few visits with a psychologist, psychiatrist, or psychiatric social worker may help immensely.

13. *My neighbor says we should have another child soon, so that the baby and the new child can be playmates. What do you think?*

You, as a new parent, will probably find yourself bombarded by tons of free advice from friends, neighbors, and relatives on how to raise your baby. The advice will probably be worth the same as free medical or legal advice. Nothing. I am constantly amazed to see intelligent parents accepting advice from friends or neighbors on the psychological aspects of child-raising when they would not dream of going to the same friends and neighbors for an authoritative diagnosis of skin cancer or brain damage.

The advice to have children close together "so they can be playmates" falls into this category. Children spaced closely together will be able to play together. But they will also spend an enormous part of their time for about fifteen years in bickering and fighting and driving you up the wall. Closely spaced children is an almost infallible recipe for Parental Cabin Fever. Don't do it.

I would recommend that you space your children at least three years apart (or four or five years, if you wish). With that spacing the older sibling's jealousy toward the younger one will not be as intense as it would be if they were closer in age. My three children were all spaced five years apart, and for us it worked out very well.

14. *How can I get my husband more involved with the baby?*

This is a very hard question to answer because my observations have convinced me that a very high proportion of American fathers do *not* get involved with their babies. The one great exception of this rule is fathers whose wives had their baby by the LaMaze method of husband-coached natural childbirth.

There will probably never be a truly satisfactory answer to this question until we begin to educate high school and college students in how to parent, with particular emphasis on the father's role in parenting. Fathers do not have a "father instinct" any more than mothers have a "mother instinct." If we do become intelligent enough in our country to educate for fatherhood, then a much higher proportion of fathers will become involved in raising their children.

If you have the unusual type of husband who regards the child as *our* baby, not *your* baby, count your blessings. He will be involved in helping you feed, bathe, diaper, and take care of the baby. He will cuddle the baby and play with her.

But if he is like the all-too-many husbands who do not do these things, how can you get him involved?

First of all, don't directly ask him to feed or bathe or diaper the baby. Say to him, "Don, can you give me a hand with the baby's bath?" Or, "Can you help me change his diaper?" You are more likely to get him involved that way.

Dr. Ira Gordon has a very good book called *Baby Learning Through Baby Play*. Buy it, and then enlist your husband to work with you doing the "baby play" exercises in the book.

See if the two of you can attend a parent education course in the evening. The Red Cross has an excellent course, Parenting from Birth to Six. Phone your local Red Cross office for details. There are also courses in parenting in adult education classes and at community colleges throughout the country. If you can get your husband to go with you to such a course, that would be terrific.

One final hint: Get a good paperback book on parenting and leave it near the toilet in the bathroom. Don't laugh. You'd be surprised what a man will read when there's nothing else available!

Summary

Well, there it is—infancy, the first stage in your child's development, and the first stage in your development as a parent. If this is your first child, it is natural for you to feel awkward and unsure of yourself at the beginning. But you will soon begin to develop self-confidence as you care for your baby.

There really are no discipline problems, in the strict sense of the word, that will arise during this stage. Most of the problems you will encounter will be feelings within yourself: feelings of inadequacy, irritation, fear, or depression. But most mothers cope with these feelings and handle this stage rather well.

The stage of infancy is basically a time for establishing the *foundation* for discipline. Infancy is your opportunity to build a deep emotional rapport with your baby so that he will love you and want to obey you and please you in succeeding stages. Every time you feed him, give him his bath, change him, cuddle him, talk to him, and sing to him you are building bonds of closeness between the two of you. These close emotional bonds should not only be enjoyed for their own sake, but valued for how much they will help you in teaching and disciplining your child in later stages of development. So play with your baby and enjoy him. Make as many deposits in your "emotional rapport bank" as you want, for you will be drawing on those deposits in later stages of his development.

22

TODDLERHOOD

Overview of the Stage

The stage of toddlerhood begins when your baby first learns to crawl and walk and lasts until approximately her second birthday. Toddlerhood can be summed up in one sentence: It is the stage of exploration. No scientist will explore the world more enthusiastically than your little tyke will research her home and backyard. Very quickly she will earn her Ph.D., with a dissertation on The Underside of Things.

During the course of all this exploration she will be working on the developmental task of this stage: *learning self-confidence* versus *learning self-doubt*. She needs to be free to explore and research her environment, to use both her large and small muscles, to walk and run and climb and jump, to play with dolls and stuffed animals, to play with cars and trucks, to play with sand and dirt and water, to play and socialize with her parents, to babble and try new sounds as her language develops, to play with books and have her parents read to her. If she is allowed and encouraged to do all these things freely, this stimulating environment will help her acquire feelings of self-confidence, which will become part of her self-concept throughout life.

But if your toddler is forced to adapt herself to an alien and purely adult environment, if she is surrounded by what seem to her to be a thousand no-no's and restrictions, then she will develop feelings of self-doubt. She will feel, "I want to touch and handle things, I want to do new things and explore my world, but my mother and father say no-no whenever I do. I guess these feelings and impulses in me must be bad and I must be bad for having them."

If you want your toddler to develop self-confidence rather than self-doubt, the answer is simple. Childproof your house in the thorough manner I suggest a few pages ahead, reduce the no-no's to a minimum, and give her the freedom to explore!

1. *My child won't eat.*

Sure he will. Provide him with nourishing meals and let him eat what he wants and leave what he wants. But don't give him anything between meals. You have a powerful natural ally on your side: your child's hunger. If you provide him with adequate meals *and leave him alone* he will eat. The trouble often starts when a parent gets upset because her child balks at a few meals. The child quickly learns that there is a payoff for not eating: It upsets Mother! So provide him with food, play it cool, and sooner or later he will be eating quite adequately.

2. *I know this is called the Age of Exploration and all that, but my little girl gets into everything and it's driving me bananas! I feel that I can't do anything around the house without keeping one eye on her.*

I'll bet you don't have these feelings when you take her to a playground and let her play. Why not? Because you know she is completely safe there and so you can relax. The secret is to get your house and fenced yard to resemble a safe playground. Childproof the house. Be sure that *everything* you don't want her to get into is kept in a locked cabinet. And provide her with playthings that will allow her to work off that enormous energy. You might consider, for example, an indoor climbing toy such as The Indoor Play House (Childcraft, 20 Kilmer Road, Edison, New Jersey 08817) and an outdoor climbing toy such as the Geodesic Dome Climber (F.A.O. Schwarz, Fifth Avenue at 58th Street, New York, N.Y. 10022). Provide her also with a special lower drawer all her own in your kitchen where she can keep her own collection of used and battered kitchen utensils to play with.

If you follow these principles of environmental control, there is no rational reason for you to worry about her or feel that you have to keep a special eye on her lest she get into something dangerous and hurt herself.

3. *I'm very embarrassed to say that my fourteen-month-old boy is starting to bite other children. What can I do?*

There are two ways you can handle this problem, one long and one short. Using the long way, each time he bites another child you grab him firmly by the arms and say emphatically, "No biting!" In about six months you will probably get him out of the habit.

The faster way to handle the problem is this: Every time he bites another child, you immediately bite him, *but in silence*. This should not be a love-bite, or he will think of it as a game. Your bite should hurt. As soon as he realizes that every time he bites, he gets bitten, it won't be very long before he gives up the biting habit.

4. *My fifteen-month-old girl has begun waking up in the middle of the night. She crawls out of her crib, comes into our bedroom and crawls in bed with us. When I put her back into her crib she cries bloody murder. What can I do?*

First of all, do not take the easy way out, as some parents do, and let her sleep in your bed. It will be extremely difficult to break her of that habit when she grows older.

What you want her to do is to stay in her own crib and go to sleep. The principle you need to use is that she must receive no payoffs for getting out of her crib. First, you'll need a little technological assistance from your hardware store. Buy yourself one of those plastic gadgets that fastens on the doorknob so that it will twirl around but the door will not open. Now you are ready. The next night she wakes you up, go to her room and put her back in her crib, giving her a few loving pats and telling her firmly to go back to sleep. Then go out of her room, shut the door, place the gadget on the knob, and wait on the other side. When she finds she cannot open the door she will probably start crying and screaming. Say to her firmly, "You need to go to bed." You want her to know you are outside her door so that her obstacle to getting out of her room is a *personal* rather than an *impersonal* one. Do not say, "You need to go to bed" more than two or three times. You do not want to reward her crying by giving it too much of your attention.

She may cry for a long time the first night, but eventually

she will give up and go to sleep, perhaps on the floor by the door. Don't worry about where she sleeps; all you want to do is make it crystal clear that she is not going to get out of that room. Keep up the same routine until she has stopped trying to get out. How long this will take will vary with the individual child. But sooner or later she will come to feel, "Nothing I can do will get me out of my room at night." At that point she will stop trying.

You will have to sacrifice some sleep by standing outside the door until she stops crying each night. But it will be worth it to nip this bad habit in the bud.

Please don't worry that you will cause your child to have some terrible trauma by using this method. She will not like it, but you will not be doing her any psychological harm.

5. My friend says my fourteen-month-old boy is old enough to start toilet training. What do you think?

Negative. As I mentioned in the previous chapter on infancy, a child's neuromuscular control over his sphincter muscles is ordinarily not mature enough for toilet training until eighteen months or two years. I would favor waiting until around two years to begin. Your child is much more mature then, his language and manipulation of verbal symbols is much better developed, and in general he is much more ready for toilet training at that age.

6. How should I handle my toddler's temper tantrums?

It is perfectly normal for a child to have tantrums at this age because his frustration tolerance and impulse control are in a very primitive stage of development. You should be aware that you cannot communicate with a child in the midst of a tantrum. So however you choose to deal with your child's tantrums, wait until a tantrum is over before trying to communicate.

If you are by temperament the kind of person who can do it, the best way to handle a temper tantrum is simply to ignore the tantrum until it has run its course. In this way, you are eliminating any payoffs. (See chap. 5, the section of eliminating payoffs for undesirable behavior.) If you continue to ignore your child's temper tantrums, they will eventually disappear.

If you find it gets on your nerves too much to just sit there while his tantrum runs its course, then send him to his room to have the tantrum. Tell him he can come out when he feels better. If he refuses to go to his room, you may have to escort him there and deposit him. When the trantrum is over, then you can communicate with him.

What you should *not* do when your toddler has a temper tantrum is to give him any payoff. If you do, that will strengthen the tantrum and make it more likely that he will have one again. And remember that scolding him, lecturing him, yelling at him, or spanking him are payoffs to him, so beware of them! (See the section on The Law of the Soggy Potato Chip in chap. 5.)

7. *My eighteen-month-old boy is always getting into my six-year-old's things in his room. This infuriates my six-year-old and then he beats up on the younger boy and I have a real problem on my hands.*

Use the method of environmental control. The present environment (an unlocked door, with playthings and other fascinating possessions inside the room) is an invitation to Sibling Disaster. By changing the environment you can eliminate the problem. Simply get a lock for the door and give your six-year-old a key. He will be pleased as punch at what you have done to protect him, and he will be proud to have a key to his room and his treasures. And your eighteen-month-old will no longer be able to get into the room.

8. *My toddler plays with his sex organs occasionally. What should I do about this?*

Well, if you want to make his sex organs a taboo (but fascinating) plaything and lay the foundation for sex hang-ups in the child's later life, you could do what many parents do. You could slap his hands, and say, "Dirty, nasty, don't touch yourself there again!" Or, on the milder side, you could say, "Please don't touch yourself down there, son." What you *should* do, of course, is what you do when he plays with his elbow or scratches his ear. Nothing. Your outward reaction to what he does with his sex organs should be no different than your reaction to what he does with any other part of his body.

I'm assuming your question pertains to your son's playing with his sex organs around the house. If he does it in public, that's a different story. That is a type of situation where I cannot provide the answer in a book. I would have to know about the parents' feelings about sexuality in order to suggest the best ways of handling this. So if your youngster is presenting you with this problem, I would suggest you have one professional consultation to guide you in coping with the situation.

Please do not misunderstand me. I am *not* suggesting professional help because I think this is a serious problem and your toddler is in danger of turning into a sex fiend at the age of nineteen months. I am merely saying that the best way for parents to handle the situation is a highly individualized matter—too much so to be dealt with adequately in a book. This type of question needs to be answered by a personal consultation.

9. *My sixteen-month-old throws food on the floor at meal time.*

That's normal for this state, and you would be engaged in a fruitless, exhausting, and losing contest to try to get him to stop it at this time. Believe it or not, throwing food on the floor is part of his exploration of the world! He is researching his own laws of physics to see what happens to an orange slice if he drops it off his tray. I suggest you get a painter's drop cloth at a hardware store and put it on the floor every time you feed your toddler. Just take it for granted that a certain portion of every meal will go on the floor.

Above all, please do not assign the wrong reasons to your child's throwing-food-on-the-floor behavior. Your toddler is NOT doing this in order to (1) get attention (unless you have violated The Law of the Soggy Potato Chip and give him attention for doing it), (2) defy you, or (3) be ornery. A child of this age normally does not do these kinds of things for hostile or defiant reasons. It is simply part of his exploratory behavior and one of the ways he find out what the world is like. Don't worry about it. Sooner than you think, this type of behavior will stop.

10. *How soon can we start getting a baby-sitter?*

If you haven't already started in infancy, you can certainly start now. As I said in the last chapter, I believe it is important for mother and baby or young child to be away from each other for brief periods. It's important for mother because it gives her relief from the pressure of *always* being with her child twenty-four hours a day. It's important for the child because if he is to grow up to be an independent adult, he needs to take a few steps away from parental apron strings by being away from his parents for brief periods of time. Also, as I have stressed, the parents need to take time off from their roles as father and mother and be alone together as husband and wife (for dinner and a movie and an evening out).

Your child's development from a situation of total dependence on you to independence and being with someone else should be gradual, not abrupt. For example, his father leaves him every day and yet he adjusts to this situation because father comes home at night. This is a routine he has gradually become accustomed to. But if daddy stayed away for several days, the child might become very upset.

It's good for your youngster to know other people besides his parents. And baby-sitters can be included among those other people. I would begin by arranging for an evening out for husband and wife or an afternoon off just for yourself. See how things go and then repeat the process in two weeks. If your child makes a satisfactory adjustment, arrange for a regular weekly morning or afternoon out. Each child will have his own individual reaction to being left with a baby-sitter. But as your youngster becomes more independent and able to tolerate your absence, you can make more use of a baby-sitter when you need to.

11. *How can I best choose a baby-sitter?*

It would be a rare high school girl who would be mature enough to cope with a very young baby should some real emergency arise. For young babies I'd suggest a college student or other adult. Depending on what kind of person the grandmother is, she might make an ideal baby-sitter. (Or, on the other hand, she might be the last person in the world you would choose!) With toddler-age children, a high school boy or girl could be quite adequate.

What you need in a baby-sitter is someone with enough intelligence and common sense to handle whatever situation might arise, particularly emergencies. You also need someone who is warm, flexible, and loving, and who genuinely likes babies and small children.

Don't choose a baby-sitter simply by talking to her. Tell her you'd like to be with her the first times she takes care of your child. Give yourself the chance to observe her in action.

It will certainly be worth the money to have her there for one afternoon taking care of the baby while you're catching up on other work of your own.

Be sure to choose four or five potential baby-sitters to draw upon. That way you have a backup in case your first choice is sick or unavailable.

And by the way, do not overlook boys as baby-sitters. Many people, following typical sexist stereotypes, select only girls. My wife and I made extensive use of high school and college boys, particularly as our kids grew older. We would phone the local high school and get them to recommend school leaders (who might never have thought of working as sitters). We woulld then phone the boys and ask them if they would be interested in baby-sitting. I remember one high school boy who was splendid with our two elementary-school-age boys. He was bright, an excellent student, vice-president of his class, and majoring in biology. His ambition was to become a herpetologist, and he went backpacking in the desert to collect his snakes and reptiles. He was a fascinating companion for our two admiring boys.

12. *How long a vacation can my husband and I take away from our toddler?*

Although I have recommended that you use baby-sitters and enjoy regular intervals away from your baby or young child, long vacations are in a different category. A mother once asked me what the psychological effect would be on her fifteen-month-old if she and her husband took a month's vacation in Europe. I told her I would not recommend that long a time away from such a young child. To a baby or young child time is relative. A week without his mother can seem like an eternity to a fifteen-month-old.

Assuming your child has adjusted comfortably to your being away once or twice a week, I would begin working up to vacations by trying a weekend away, with a very reliable sitter, probably an adult. If that goes reasonably well, wait a few weeks and try another weekend away. If the first weekend away is a disaster, however, then your child may not yet be ready for that long a separation.

If the vacation you are thinking of is the family's regular several-week vacation each year, why not take your toddler (and other children) with you? The reason most families don't do this is because they know so little about handling children that the children are as much of a burden on vacation as they are at home. But if you learn to handle children effectively (as I hope you will from reading this book) and plan ahead intelligently, there's no reason why you can't have a wonderful vacation with small children. When my younger son, Rusty, was eighteen months, our family took a three-week vacation on the Oregon coast. We rented a small cottage right on the beach and had a delightful time. And Rusty was no hindrance at all to the enjoyment of the rest of the family.

13. *My twenty-month-old and my four-year-old are in the same room and they're always bickering and fighting.*

Shared rooms for siblings are a recipe for disaster. This is an example of what we might call *reverse environmental control.* If a psychologist were to design an environment for children that would drive parents crazy, a shared room would be it. So if it is at all possible, try to provide a separate room for each child. Even if this means putting up a solid partition to make two rooms out of one. It may not be as aesthetic as the shared room, but it is psychologically much easier on the children (and the parents). If you simply cannot avoid the shared room, then use a locked cabinet in the room for the older child's toys, for which he has a key. Even so, you are bound to have trouble with such things as different bedtimes and individual possessions in the same room.

14. *My toddler leaves the house in a perpetual mess!*

Good! That's the way it should be with a toddler. Toddlers just aren't built to be psychologically healthy, on the one hand, and keep a neat and tidy house on the other. If you are allowing your toddler to express his healthy urge for exploration, the house will not be neat. But make it easy for yourself by tidying up the house only once, at the end of the day. If you make the mistake of tidying up the house at noon, it will be in a mess again by five o'clock.

15. *I can childproof my own home so that no-no's are kept to a minimum and my toddler has the freedom to explore, but what can I do about taking my child with me on visits to a friend's house, where the place is full of breakable adult objects?*

If you take your toddler with you when you visit a house

filled with breakable adult objects, you are putting yourself and your child in a no-win situation. If you let your child explore freely as he does at home, your hostess isn't going to appreciate it at all, particularly if one of her vases gets broken. And you can hardly ask her to redo her house for your child's visit! On the other hand, if you try to make your child conform to her adult house, this will be difficult for both him and you. My conclusion? When visiting a friend who has a house that is not childproofed, get a baby-sitter and leave your toddler at home.

16. *I have trouble establishing a regular bedtime for my toddler.*

Bedtime is troublesome for parents because bedtime is a psychologically difficult time for children. When a child goes to bed, she has to leave the interesting and exciting world of the family and TV and Things Going On and go to her Dull Old Bed and go to sleep. What fun is that? Unfortunately, children don't always know they are tired or that they need to go to sleep. You can't completely change this environmental situation, but you can exercise some degree of environmental control. Here's how you do it:

You want to create a bedtime ritual in such a way that Step One leads inevitably to Step Two, and so on finally to bed. Step One can ideally be your child's bath. Let her have as much time as she likes for her bath, playing with the water and bath toys to her heart's content. Let her tell you when she is ready to come out. This leads to Step Two, which is a story or short book read by either mother or father to the child in her bed. (At toddler stage your best choice will not be a regulation "story" book. Buy something where you look at pictures of things and name them, such as Richard Scarry's *Best Word Book Ever.*) This leads to Step Three, a glass of juice or little snack in bed. All of these experiences connect some positive associations (story and snack) with bed and bedtime, which previously had no such positive meanings for the child. All of these steps lead inexorably to tucking the child in, giving her a good-night kiss and hug, and Bedtime. This kind of routine won't take all of the sting out of bedtime, but it will help a great deal.

You can try to establish a more or less regular bedtime for your toddler, but you will probably need to be flexible about it, particularly if you have an especially energetic child.

Sometimes she will be full of beans and vitality and simply cannot go to sleep at the regular bedtime, any more than you could go to sleep if someone put you to bed at seven o'clock. Make allowance for those times and don't try to put her to bed at her usual time. A child's ability to go to bed at a consistent time is usually more irregular in the stages of toddlerhood and first adolescence than it is at later stages. Beginning with the preschool stage (age three), your child's bedtime can be pretty consistent.

17. *I can't seem to control my urge to hit my eighteen-month-old boy when he acts up, whines, cries, or gets into things. I hate to admit it, but I guess I'm what people would call a child abuser. What can I do?*

You can do one of two things, or a combination of both. First, you can join Parents Anonymous, a non-profit organization of parents who are struggling with the same problems you are facing and trying to help each other. If you live in a large city, there is probably a Parents Anonymous group you can join. You can find out by calling information or looking in the phone book. If there is no Parents Anonymous group in your area, you can write to the national headquarters, Parents Anonymous, 2810 Artesia Blvd., Redondo Beach, California 90278, for information on how to start a chapter in your area.

Whether or not you join Parents Anonymous, you might also want to seek the help of a professional counselor. If your family budget will not afford your seeing someone in private practice, you can find a low-cost clinic where fees are scaled according to your ability to pay. With one or both of these resources at your disposal, I am sure you will be able to overcome your problem on losing control with your child.

18. *What do I do when my eighteen-month-old girl runs out in the street?*

The simplest and easiest thing you can do is to use environmental control: Locked front and back doors or a fence secured with a locked gate and high enough that she cannot climb over it will effectively prevent her from running into the street.

If for some reason this is not practical (and I would find it hard to think of a reason why it would not be practical), you may need to grab her firmly by the arms and say, "Kathy, no running into the street!" If this is not effective, you may have to give her a whack or two to get your message across. At eighteen months she is far too young and immature to understand logical explanations of why she should not run into the street.

Summary

Personally I find toddlerhood a delightful stage, and one in which few discipline problems need arise. I think there are two main reasons why parents begin to have difficulties with their children at this time. First, they do not know "the nature of the beast," and second, they do not provide the proper environment for the "beast" to live in. The nature of the toddler is that he is a tireless explorer of everything that comes within his reach. If you expect him to be like a sedate little cat who will curl up quietly on the living room sofa, you are in for a rough jolt. The proper environment for a toddler is one that he can explore to his heart's content, without being chained down by thousands of no-no's.

So the basic secret of handling a toddler is the discipline method of environmental control. Give him an environment in which he is free to roam and explore—a childproof house and backyard—and you will find him to be a delightful little tyke. Present him with a house and backyard that are not suited to his needs, and you will find him difficult to manage. And remember that a toddler does not normally do things to be ornery and defy you (as a first adolescent does). If a toddler tears the pages out of a book or magazine, it is not because he is feeling hostile or defiant. He is merely exploring his environment.

23

FIRST ADOLESCENCE

Overview of the Stage

This stage generally runs from the second to the third birthday. It is widely known in preschool educational circles as the Terrible Twos. I think this is a bad title because it simply labels the typical behavior of this age as obnoxious without giving a parent any real insight into what is going on psychologically within his child at this time.

I label the stage first adolescence because of its clear similarity to the teenage years, which we might call second adolescence. Both are *transition stages*. Teenage is a transition from childhood to adulthood. First adolescence is a transition from babyhood to childhood. During both stages children exhibit forward movements toward independence coupled with backward movements toward dependence upon their parents. In both stages the development of a negative self-concept precedes the development of a positive self-concept. This means that your two-year-old will first begin to develop his self-concept by resisting everything you tell him to do. He is very negativistic, and his favorite word is "No!"

This is an age of extremism. It is difficult for the child to make a simple, clear-cut choice and stick with it. He will shuttle back and forth with his contrary feelings until the parent feels she will go out of her mind: "I want it," "I don't want it," "I will," "I won't." The child's ability to share, to wait, and to take turns is very limited. He makes strong demands on the patience of a parent.

Because of the annoying behavior of a child at this time, I

think it is very important for a parent to understand the positive aspects of this developmental era. Much of the behavior of a teenager is annoying to parents also, but underneath that annoying surface behavior is a youngster trying to find his own self-identity. Your two-year-old is trying to do the same thing underneath his annoying surface behavior. Your two-year-old's negativism and rebelliousness are actually indications of positive growth forces. Without them he would remain permanently stuck in the equilibrium of babyhood. And in spite of his negativism, at times he can be charming, with his exubuance, his naïveté, his sense of wonder at the new and unspoiled world, his imagination, his generosity, and his enthusiastic zest for life.

It is ironic that parents want their child to grow up to be an adult with a strong and dynamic personality. But they have trouble accepting these dynamic qualities when their child is a two-year-old. And a first adolescent is nothing if not dynamic! How could anyone miss his hearty, rollicking, sensuous enjoyment of life, his demands for instant gratification, his lusty protests against restraint, and his enthusiastic commitment to the world as he experiences it? All the activities that make him a unique and genuine personality have come about as a result of this dynamic life thrust. Without it he would not have learned to sit, crawl, walk, or learn a language. This dynamic quality of your child is a very important psychological resource. Don't make the mistake some parents do during this time. Don't try to bleach this dynamic life force out of your child. Instead, foster and channel the force.

The developmental task of this age is *learning self-identity* versus *social conformity*, a miniature version of the same developmental task your child will experience much later in his teenage years. This is the first stage in which your youngster acquires a real sense of his own unique selfhood. And in order for him to define who he is and what he wants to his own satisfaction, he has to go through a stage of negating and defying what his parents want him to do.

I have tried to give you a clear and reasonably complete sketch of the psychological characteristics of this stage of development. Without knowing these characteristics you would be at a loss to know how to discipline this age child. There are two main mistakes parents can make in discipline at this time. First, they can make far too many demands for control and conformity, and the child may become overcontrolled. Or life can become a daily series of battles between parent and child. Second, a parent may be afraid to exercise control, constantly giving in to the excessive demands of the child, producing the Spoiled Brat Syndrome.

In general, the discipline needed at this age calls for a firm hand at the parental helm, but at the same time considerable flexibility in rules and regulations. Absolute and rigid rules simply do not fit this stage of development because the child is so full of ambivalent feelings and urges.

The various methods of discipline I sketched in at the beginning of this book should work well for a child age three and older. But disciplining a child in first adolescence between two and three is a different story. Sometimes a method (such as a positive reward system) will work beautifully. At other times it will not work at all. I am emphasizing this because I don't want you to have any false or illusory ideas about the process of discipline going smoothly at this stage. It may go smoothly with some children; it may be very difficult with others. But if you try some particular discipline method at this stage and it doesn't work, don't draw the false conclusion that it will never work at later ages.

1. *My two-and-one-half-year-old son can never make up his mind and it really tries my patience. He asks for milk and I get him a glass of milk. Then he refuses the milk and wants juice. When I get him the juice, he wants milk again. How do I handle this?*

The problem you describe is typical of his age. Give him two alternatives and tell him that as soon as he decides which he wants to do, you will dance a jig or stand on your head or wiggle your ears or something equally silly. After he has decided and you have done your silly act as a reward, be sure that he does as he promised. If he simply cannot seem to make up his mind under any circumstances, then you decide for him according to what you think he really wants deep down, or what you think would be best for him. Be firm about the decision you have made for him.

2. *What can I do about temper tantrums with my two-year-old?*

See chapter 22, question 6.

3. *When my two-year-old throws a temper tantrum in public, I just want to curl up somewhere and hide. How can I handle him when he does this?*

The problem isn't handling him, but handling yourself. He does not own the problem. You do. There's nothing you can do to prevent him or any other child from throwing a temper tantrum. Therefore, what you have to do is learn how to handle yourself when he is throwing a tantrum *in public*. You are bothered by what you believe the bystanders at the store or the parking lot or the doctor's office are thinking. Your best bet is to use negative thinking to help desensitize yourself to this situation. (See chap. 15.) Deliberately exaggerate the nasty things you believe the bystanders are thinking about you: "What kind of a mother is she? Doesn't she know how to control a brat like that? I wouldn't let *my* child get away with that kind of behavior. She must be one of those permissive parents who are ruining our country!"

4. *My two-and-one-half-year-old has started scribbling on the walls of our house. What can I do?*

If he has a room of his own, I suggest you make all four walls of his room suitable for scribbling and then limit scribbling to his room. With blackboard paint you can easily transform the four walls into four giant blackboards. This application of environmental control will not only channel his scribbling to his room, it will give him the benefit of having four giant blackboards all through his preschool years. Remember that children need to learn to scribble before they can learn to print and write. The giant blackboards will be very helpful stimuli for his scribbling, printing, writing, and drawing for many years.

5. *Should I send my two-year-old to nursery school?*

Not unless it is absolutely necessary because you are working, and perhaps not even then. Ordinarily children are not ready to cut the maternal apron strings and go to nursery school until age three. Most children are not ready emotionally to separate from mother until then. Even if you are working and absolutely must have someone care for him during the day, I would not automatically decide on a nursery school or day-care center. I would first see how he would respond to an individual caretaker during the day. Some two-year-olds respond better to an individual caretaker (a paid helper or a grandmother, for example), and some respond better to a nursery school or day-care center.

6. *My two-and-one-half-year-old boy keeps hitting his baby sister. What should I do?*

Try the Time Out (chap. 5) and see how it works. With some youngsters in this stage, Time Out will work fine. With others it will fail miserably. If the Time Out does not work, stop him physically each time he hits his sister. Grab him forcefully by the hands and say, "YOU MUST NOT HIT YOUR SISTER!" You can do this on the days when you are feeling in good shape emotionally. On days when you are uptight and have had it up to the eyebrows with his behavior, you will probably give him a good whack or two.

7. *My two-year-old keeps getting into his six-year-old brother's toys in his brother's room. How can I handle this?*

Use environmental control. Get a lock for the room and give the six-year-old a key (with several other keys in reserve in case he loses his). This solves the problem in one fell swoop, because the two-year-old can no longer get into the room to disturb his brother's toys.

8. *How can I control my two-and-one-half-year-old when we are at other people's homes? At the end of a visit, my nerves are frazzled and it spoils the whole time.*

Use the method of environmental control. Get a baby-sitter and leave your two-and-one-half-year-old home. In general it is very difficult to take a child of this age on visits to the houses of friends or relatives. The easiest way to make sure you and your husband have a pleasant time is to leave him home with a baby-sitter.

9. *You wouldn't believe it, but my two-and-one-half-year-old is still biting other kids when he gets mad. What do I do?*

See chap. 22, question 3.

10. *My two-year-old continually bombards me with questions. It's why, why, why, all day long until I could scream. What can I do?*

His questions are important to him. They are part of his exploration of the world and should be taken seriously. So try to answer them as long as you can. But you are human too, and there are limits to how long you can function as a question-answering machine. When his questions begin to get on your nerves, simply call a halt. Say, "Mother will answer one more question for you and then that's all the questions for today." Then be firm and absolutely refuse to answer any more.

I am assuming that you are talking about legitimate questions your two-year-old really wants answered. On the other hand, he may be just trying to tease and bedevil you with a series of "why" questions piled one on top of the other. If that is the case, do not reinforce his game by answering. Just say, "I only answer questions when you really want to know the answers."

11. *How can I control myself from the urge to hit my two-and-one-half-year-old when he behaves so badly and gets on my nerves?"*

Welcome to the club! All parents of two- and two-and-one-half-year-olds have "hot flashes" of anger toward their children from time to time. It helps to go into your bedroom and lock the door. Then get a pillow and pound the bed with it, at the same time putting into words the angry feelings you feel toward your child. If he is not around to hear you, give full vent verbally to your angry feelings. If he is within the sound of your voice, then "mouth" your angry words, but do not say them out loud. You'll be surprised how much good it will do you to get your angry feelings out of your system this way. One thing is certain. You won't get the angry feelings out of your system by just thinking about them. But a direct, primitive method such as pounding a bed will really work wonders.

12. *How well do the different methods of discipline work with a child at this stage?*

They work differently with different children. Obviously, a child of this age is much too young for the mutual problem-solving technique or the family council. The main question is whether you are dealing with a hard-to-raise child, or an easy-to-raise one. With an easy-to-raise child, the positive reward system, contracting, and the feedback technique will work. With a hard-to-raise child none of the discipline methods may work *at this stage*. But don't be discouraged if you try them now and they don't work. They will work at later ages, usually from three on.

For example, my older son, who was a real pistola at this stage, changed about 180 degrees shortly after his third birthday. About a month after he had turned three, he came up to me one night and said, "Dad, may I watch TV?" I almost fell over from the shock, because he had never asked my permission to do anything before in his life! But at the age of three, he had entered a new stage of equilibrium where he took pleasure in being cooperative and asking permission to do things. Discipline measures that had not worked with him in the stage of first adolescence now began to work.

13. *I'm a single parent. When I leave the house for a date, I feel guilty because my two-and-one-half-year-old is crying bitterly as I leave him with a baby-sitter.*

Single parents, particularly those who are divorced, must often contend with a vast reservoir of both conscious and unconscious guilt feelings. When a mother in an intact family goes out with her husband for the evening, her two-and-one-half-year-old may cry bitterly and plead with her, "Mommy, don't leave me!" But somehow this does not affect her as it does if she is divorced and the same thing happens. The only difference between the two situations is that in her divorced state her child's actions trigger off guilt feelings, and in her married state they do not.

So this is the cause of your difficulty in leaving your young son to go out on a date. You are the victim of guilty voices which say to you, "You've hurt him by getting the divorce, and now you're hurting him more by leaving him to go out on a date. How can you be so cruel? You can hear him piteously imploring you not to leave him. Don't be so heartless!"

All of these, of course, are irrational feelings, but that doesn't make them any less powerful in their effect on you. I suggest you use negative thinking (chap. 15) to get rid of these guilt feelings. Don't try to put them out of your mind. Instead, deliberately exaggerate them. Find a time when your child is asleep, and you are alone in the house. Say such things to yourself as: "You are a cruel, heartless brute to subject your poor, innocent child to such mental anguish by deserting him, leaving him, crying and broken-hearted, while you go out for a date. You've already done enough harm to your child by getting the divorce. Now you're just carrying it one step further. Instead of having a social life and going out on dates, you should stay home each and every night and devote yourself to your child." And so on and so on.

Do this regularly once a day. Sooner or later a sensible little voice within you will start to protest the negative thinking. Then you will begin to feel: "This is absolutely ridiculous! Certainly my child doesn't like it when I leave him to go out on dates. But he doesn't like it when I put him to bed at night either, or when I don't buy him a bag of candy in the store, and lots of other things.

"If I let my life be governed by what he likes and dislikes, he would be the authority in the home instead of me. I'm very much aware that he needs a substitute for his father, but if I refuse to allow myself to go out on dates I'm certainly never going to meet a new husband for myself and a new father for him!" When that little voice of sanity begins to speak inside your mind, you know you have licked the guilt feelings and stripped them of their power to push you around.

14. *My two-year-old is crippled in his legs. What special discipline methods do I need to use in raising him?*

You need no special discipline methods. You should use the same discipline methods you would use with him if he were not crippled. Do not discipline him differently than you would a normal child without any physical handicaps. The tendency of many parents who have a child handicapped in any way—blind, deaf, crippled, cerebral palsied—is to be overprotective or overindulgent with him, because of his physical handicap. This is unfortunate, because the child then learns that he can manipulate his parents, simply by trading on his physical handicap. So treat him as you would treat any other child in the family with respect to discipline, and things should work out fine.

15. *Should I get my two-year-old a pet?*

Only if you understand that you will take care of it. Even so, I would not get a child of this age a pet such as a dog or cat, because they are often too rough and do not know how to exercise restraint in their play with an animal. A pet at later ages, such as three, is perfectly all right, as long as you are quite clear that you, the parent, will feed and take care of the animal. Children of all ages promise parents that they will take care of a pet if the parent will get it for them. The gullible parent believes the child and then becomes furious when the child does not carry out his promise.

The truth is that children, simply because they are children, probably will not take care of a pet any more than they will turn out the lights when they leave a room. So as long as you are aware that *you* are going to be responsible for the pet, and want to give one to your child on that basis, go right ahead. But don't try to extract any promises from your child that he can't keep.

16. *I'm a stepparent. I have a two-and-one-half-year-old boy from my previous marriage and my husband has a seven-year-old girl from his previous marriage. His girl is shy and docile and blends in with the woodwork, the sort of child who would never give anybody any trouble. My boy is what I would call a "normal obnoxious two-and-one-half-year-old." He is feisty and rambunctious and what the psychology books call just a typical child for his age. But my husband thinks he is just terrible. His favorite names for him are "the little monster" and "King Kong." He lands on him like a ton of bricks, and then when I stick up for my son, the argument starts. What can I do about this?*

From your description, it sounds as if your husband is unconsciously expecting your boy to be the same kind of docile, quiet child his daughter is. But merely knowing that doesn't solve your problem. I believe the two of you should seek the help of a professional counselor to straighten out your conflicting views on what kind of behavior you can reasonably expect of children at different ages.

17. *Should I try to teach my two-year-old to share?*

No. A two-year-old is too immature to learn such things as sharing and taking turns. In his play, a two-year-old is still at the stage of what we call *parallel play*. This means that he may be playing in the geographical vicinity of another child, but he is not yet actually playing *with* that other child. It is only around age three that he moves from the stage of parallel play to that of truly *co-operative* play. At that point you can begin to teach him to share.

18. *My two-year-old definitely wants to dress himself, even though he has trouble and makes such a mess of it. If I try to help him, he yells at me, "No, me do it!" What should I do?*

I know it is much easier and faster for you to dress him than to let him dress himself. He doesn't learn much if you dress him. But he learns a great deal about dressing if he does it himself, even though he does it in his own primitive way. So stand back and let him do it. Remember, we are not merely talking about his dressing himself but about his drive for independence in taking care of himself. This is a valuable drive throughout his whole life span, and we don't want to discourage its early manifestations now.

19. *I'm a divorced father without custody. My only child is two-and-one-half and I'm supposed to see him every other weekend. If he were older we could play ball or things like that, but frankly, at this age you can't carry on much of a conversation with him, and I don't know what to do with him. I'm beginning to dread our weekends simply because I don't know what the hell to do with him! What can I do?*

It sounds as if you don't know much about this age child. So I recommend you take a morning off from work and visit a good nursery school or day-care center that has two-year-olds attending. Observe carefully what activities the children enjoy and how the teachers handle them.

Armed with the information you gather from this source, you can plan out the weekend, in rough outline, instead of leaving the events of the weekend to chance. If you are visiting him in warm weather, he is sure to like activities involving water: a beach, a river, a lake, a swimming pool. He will like a playground in a park. He will like a picnic in a park or forest, particularly if there is a stream he can throw rocks in. He will like a drive-in movie if there is a lot of action in it. He will like the zoo. He will always like to eat, particularly if he can do something like use a coat hanger to cook his own hot dogs, or roast marshmallows.

He will like to build things with blocks, or play in a sandbox with plastic army men or cowboys and Indians. These are only a few of the things you and he can do together, and there are many more activities you can learn about by reading and studying. When you become familiar with the characteristics of two-year-olds you will be able to truly enjoy your visits with your son rather than think of them as a chore.

20. *My two-year-old has to go to the hospital for an operation. What can I do to make him psychologically comfortable about this?*

The most important thing you can do is to prevail upon the hospital to let you stay in your son's room until he is ready to be discharged. The hospital may give you a hard time about this, but there is absolutely no reason why you cannot sleep on a rollaway cot in his room. I did this when my older son had an operation at two years of age. Some hospitals will claim that it "upsets their routine" or "it's never been done before," or they will come up with some other equally meaningless reason. If one hospital won't allow it, find one that will. Or if you have only one hospital in your community, go to the administrative head of the hospital and raise enough commotion so that he will finally give in just to get rid of you.

As you may know, hospitals are not exactly famous for their understanding of the psychological feelings of children (or adults either, for that matter). But you *are* concerned about the feelings of your child, particularly at this tender age. He will be feeling very lonely and unhappy and afraid of an operation (which he doesn't understand at all except to feel that from what people say it must be Scary and Bad). Then after the operation, he will be experiencing the same feelings plus physical pain. It makes all the difference in the world whether he has to endure these feelings by himself or whether you are there to give him understanding and emotional support. So however you have to do it, arrange to be there in the hospital with him from the day he is admitted until the day he's discharged.

I'm assuming, of course, that you will arrange to take some breaks from this hospital vigil from time to time, to check in with your husband and the other children, and things of that nature. Otherwise you may end up with a bad case of cabin fever in the hospital, and that won't be good for either you or your child.

21. *I'm trying to toilet train my two-year-old and having a terrible time of it. He keeps having accidents. My neighbor says I should spank him every time he has an accident and that will speed up the process of toilet training.*

No, no, no, and no! You should no more spank your child for accidents in toilet training than a piano teacher should spank a child when she makes a mistake in playing. As mentioned earlier, when you are toilet training a child, you are teaching him something, and punishment should have no place in teaching. The basic discipline method you should use in toilet training is the positive reward system (chap. 3).

Summary

First adolescence is a difficult developmental stage for most parents to live through. Methods of discipline that work well in later stages, such as the Time Out, may not work well in this one at all. But don't make the mistake of concluding that the discipline technique is faulty just because it doesn't work successfully right now.

In coping with a first adolescent child, above all strive to be flexible. Rigidity in handling this age youngster is sure to result in disaster. And remember that underneath all the negative and obnoxious behavior so characteristic of this age is a dynamic life force. This dynamic personality thrust is one of his most important assets in life, not just in his childhood but throughout his adulthood as well.

24

THE PRESCHOOL PERIOD

Overview of the Stage

This stage extends from your child's third to his sixth birthday. Although three-year-olds, four-year-olds, and five-year-olds are quite different in many ways, all three are grouped together into this one stage because they all share nine developmental tasks during these three years. How your youngster meets and masters these tasks will basically determine his personality structure, which will assume its stable and continuing form by the time he is six years old.

Here are the developmental tasks of this stage:

1. To fulfill his biological needs for both large and small muscle development
2. To develop a control system for his impulses
3. To separate himself from his mother
4. To learn the give and take of relationships with his peers
5. To express or repress his feelings
6. To stablize his gender identity as male or female
7. To form his basic attitudes toward sexuality
8. To work his way through the resolution of the "family romance" (See chap. 18.)
9. To go through a period of development in which he is particularly responsive to intellectual stimulation

Some of these developmental tasks appear in partial form in earlier stages, but it is in this stage that they play a major part in your child's life.

After the stormy ups and downs of first adolescence, the three-year-old, who has entered a stage of equilibrium, is a delightful child to have around. Some of the discipline methods that failed abjectly in first adolescence will now begin to succeed almost as if by magic. The age of three, incidentally, is a good time to begin many of the discipline strategies discussed in the early chapters of this book.

The four-year-old may pose some discipline problems, with defiance and negativism that will remind you of the Terrible Twos.

But the fifth year is another year of equilibrium, and discipline usually goes smoothly at this age.

1. *Our four-and-one-half-year-old got a shot from our doctor last month. I had to take him for another shot last week and he made a scene in the doctor's office. How can I best handle this?*

Here is how *not* to handle it. Do not say, "All right, LeRoy, I know you're terribly upset. So we'll skip the shot." If you skip the shot you are giving your son a big payoff for crying and throwing a temper tantrum, thereby reinforcing such undesirable behavior. (Believe it or not, I know one mother who did just that. When her eighteen-month-old son went for a booster shot he cried and screamed so much she let him get away without having it. She has continued in that same overprotective way through the years, with the consequence that he is now eleven years old and afraid to climb trees or do other things normal boys of his age can do. He is even afraid to put a worm on a fishhook and has to get other boys to do it for him. He is the product of years of training in which his mother rewarded his fears instead of his courage.)

What is called for in this situation is a combination of firm action and the feedback technique.

You must be firm with your youngster and see that he gets his shot, even if you and the nurse and the doctor all have to hold him down. Then he is learning, "Mother means business when she says I have to get a shot because it's important to make me well. And there's absolutely nothing I can do to talk her out of it or change her mind."

But in addition to being firm about whatever actions are required of him, you need to give him full freedom to dislike it and express negative feelings. He is free to yell, "No, no don't do it! I'm scared! Please, no shots!" Then you can feed back his feelings to him (even while holding him down). "You're awfully scared of the shot the doctor is going to give you!" So he learns that he has to take the shot because he needs it for medical reasons. But he doesn't have to like it. And he is free to express just how much he doesn't like it.

There is another factor. Your question mentioned his making a scene in the doctor's office. I get the feeling you are concerned about what the other people think of your child's yelling and screaming, or what they think of you as a mother. It sounds as if you could use some negative thinking (chap. 15) to desensitize yourself to the fact that others will be critical of you as a parent, or critical of your child.

2. *I know it's wrong to expect too much of very young children, but don't you think my five-year-old is capable of making his bed and hanging up his clothes and cleaning up the toys in his room?*

Yes, I do. The best way to get your child to do these simple chores is to set up a positive reward system. You can do this very easily, using a checklist like this:

	M	T	W	T	F	S	S
Makes bed							
Hangs up clothes							
Picks up toys							

Be generous in deciding whether he has done what he is supposed to, particularly in the beginning. Require him to make a bed like a five-year-old typically makes a bed, not so perfect it would please an army drill sergeant. The same with hanging up his clothes and picking up his toys.

For each check on the chart, he should get a reward that evening. Let's say you decide to use money—pennies or nickels, depending on the state of your finances and our inflationary economy. If he has hung up his clothes and picked up his toys that day, he gets two nickels. But you must be willing to leave alone whatever he did not do. No nagging, no lectures.

He simply misses getting the third nickel if he didn't make his bed.

If you need an even stronger reward (which you may if your child has already learned that he can wrap you around his little finger), then you can have some special treat at the end of the week for a certain number of check marks on the chart.

I think that the preschool period (ages three, four, and five) is an ideal time to begin such a positive reward system for simple chores in connection with your child's room. If you set up the system now and have it going well, it will be much easier to get your youngster to do these things when he is in the next stage of development, middle childhood (ages six to ten). Children respond more easily and quickly if you begin this kind of reward system for chores in the preschool period than in middle childhood.

3. *My four-year-old plays with her food and dawdles through the entire meal. What can we do to make mealtimes more pleasant?*

Be sure she gets no snacks between meals. Then put wholesome food on the table (including some of her special favorites) and let her eat at whatever pace she chooses. I suspect from your question that she is somehow "getting to you" by her dawdling. If that is so, you are breaking The Law of the Soggy Potato Chip and rewarding her for her dawdling by giving her negative attention. Some use of negative thinking (chap. 15) to desensitize yourself to her dawdling should be of help here.

When you and the rest of the family are finished with a meal, declare that the meal is over and clear the table. If she protests that she is not finished, say, "I'm sorry you haven't finished, but mealtime is over." But no lectures or moralizing on dawdling!

When you set up this kind of a program, you are giving payoffs for not dawdling, but no payoffs for dawdling. I would predict that her dawdling will decline and finally disappear.

4. *My husband has a four-year-old son from a former marriage who will be spending the summer with us. I've never had children before and need to know how to make this first visit a pleasant one for all of us.*

Your first job is to learn all you can about four-year-old children. You could start by reading Dr. Louise Ames and Dr. Frances Ilg's excellent book, *Your Four Year Old*. You can read up on the four-year-old and the Preschool Stage in general in my book, *How to Parent*.

Then, with this "book larnin'" on the four-year-old under your belt, I suggest you visit some nursery schools or day-care centers until you find a really good teacher. Take some time to see how she handles children of this age. The opportunity to see a skilled teacher handle real live four-year-olds in action will be more valuable than any book you could possibly read.

Then you will need to really absorb the teaching or discipline methods that are found in this book.

Armed with the knowledge of what four-year-olds in general are like, and how to teach or discipline them, you have taken a Giant Step toward learning how to cope effectively with your summer visitor.

You also need to learn as much as you can about the unique stepparent and stepchild relationship. I suggest you pay careful attention to chapter 19, Stepparents and the Blended Family. Also read the book *Living in Step* by Ruth Roosevelt and Jeannette Lofas.

You will now know a great deal about children in general and stepchildren in general. Next, you need to know as much as you can about *this particular child*. Find out from your husband all that you can about him, his likes and dislikes, his hobbies, favorite foods, movies he likes, etc.

You may feel that this is going to a great deal of trouble getting ready for the visit of your stepchild. It is! As an alternative to this kind of careful preparation, you can rush in, fly by the seat of your pants, and botch up the relationship the way many stepparents do.

Remember that your most important job in the first two weeks or perhaps even the first month of the summer will be to establish rapport with the youngster. You accomplish that by doing things with him that he enjoys. Above all, you establish rapport by going about it s-l-o-w-l-y. The child already has a mother and will probably be suspicious that you are going to try to take her place.

You say you have never had children before. But I am sure you have had work experience, and probably at least one job interview. If you were wise you prepared carefully for a job interview and did not stumble into it haphazardly. Prepare for your meeting with the child as carefully as you would prepare for a job interview. It will pay off.

5. *Our three-year-old daughter seems to have trouble playing with other children because she won't share anything. What can we do?*

First, remember that as a rule children aren't ready even to *begin* to learn to share until they are three. Some children learn to share quickly, others much more slowly. Your daughter may be one of the slow learners. Many parents try to teach sharing in the wrong way. They rely merely on verbal commands without payoffs or rewards. "Now share your toy with Debbie, Marcia dear. I SAID SHARE YOUR TOY WITH DEBBIE!"

Avoid this method of teaching a child anything, including sharing. The formula for teaching a child to share is simple. Payoffs, payoffs, payoffs. Try to "catch your daughter in the act of sharing," and immediately reward her. Simply observe her at play and reward her each time you see her sharing. Say something like, "I'm so glad to see you sharing your doll with Debbie. Here are some candies for both of you." But never try to push or force her to share. Sooner or later she will learn, and the payoffs will help her learn faster than she would without them.

6. *When my husband's sister comes to visit, she brings her five- and seven-year-olds to play with our children, who are three and five. There's more fighting than playing, and it makes for some very tense visits. Someone is always hitting someone else. What can we do?*

You can do two things. First, you can give a Time Out whenever anyone hits. See chapter 6 for more details on this. Second, you can give payoffs to the children when they are not hitting. Once again, candies are very good because you can hand them out so conveniently whenever you see the children playing without hitting. Just say, "I'm glad to see you children playing without any hitting. Here are some candies for you." You could use peanuts just as well. Or a visit to the ice cream store. Every time a child gets a payoff for playing without fighting, a little computer inside his head lights up and says, "Hmmm. Candies for no fighting. I think I'll fight less so I can get more candies!"

You can also arrange activities for the children where they will be so engrossed in the activity (such as a drive-in movie, a visit to the zoo or amusement park) that the chances for fighting will be minimized. When they are engrossed in a high-interest activity you will have more opportunity to reward them for not fighting.

With the system of Time Out to take care of the actual hitting, and payoffs for no hitting or fighting, the behavior of the four children will gradually be nudged in the direction of less hitting and fighting. This will not happen immediately, of course, but over a period of time. If you begin to lose faith in the system, count the number of times hitting occurs in any given day and keep a record from day to day. I am sure you will then see the improvement when you keep such a record.

7. *I notice that very few children in school today seem to be readers. I am an avid reader and would like to share the joy of books with my two preschoolers. How do I go about it?*

You begin by reading to them while holding them on your lap. Read to one at a time. Being held on your lap acts as a payoff or reward for listening to the reading.

When you read to a preschooler, you are teaching him that you love books and that you love to read. Therefore you are teaching *him* to love books and to love learning to read. So in the preschool years you can lay a foundation for teaching your children to love to read.

When they actually begin learning to read in the first grade, you can set up a positive reward system with them. Each time one reads a book and can tell you the story of the book, she gets a quarter or fifty cents or some agreed upon reward. (For such an important skill as reading I would personally choose money as the reward.) Having your child tell you the story of the book not only ensures that she has read it but gives her valuable experience in organizing and summarizing the book. As your child grows older and is reading longer books, you can increase the size of the reward.

Finally, when you see that your child has truly developed a love of reading, you can begin to phase out the reward. She may being to read a great deal and not even come to you to summarize the book and get her payoff. Which means she is now learning to read for the sheer love of it. Or you can take the lead in phasing out the reward. You can say, "You're doing so well in your reading, I think I only need to give you a dollar for every *two* books you read now."

I think it is well worth the effort involved in setting up a reward system if you want your youngsters to turn out to be avid readers. There are two obstacles that stand in the way of a child's learning to love reading: TV and the school system. The way TV is used today (as opposed to the way it could be used) makes it basically antireading. And many schools systematically teach children to hate reading by forcing them to read books that are boring to them. Therefore, if our children are to grow up to be avid readers, we the parents must be the people who cause this to happen. We need to begin when they are preschoolers and read to them often. Then when they learn to read, we need to set up a positive reward system that will develop strong and well-entrenched habits of reading and enjoying it.

8. *Our four-year-old son says "no" when I tell him to pick up his toys, says "no" when I tell him to eat, says "no" when I tell him it's bedtime. What can I do?*

Your child sounds in many ways like a typical four-year-old, who has much of the same negativism as a two-year-old. But you have lumped together several "no's" which need to be dealt with separately. When he says "no" to eating, you can simply rely on the natural consequences of not eating (hunger) gradually to bring him into line. Just tell him lunch or dinner is ready and let him either eat or not eat. Just be sure he doesn't eat between meals.

For a "no" at bedtime I would rely on the bedtime ritual, as described in chapter 22, question 16. And if all else fails at bedtime, you can give a good whack and see that he gets in bed and stays there.

A "no" to your request that he pick up his toys can be solved by setting up a checklist with positive rewards for picking up his toys.

I also suspect that you may not be distinguishing between verbal negativism and negative actions. It doesn't really matter a tinker's dam if he says "no" to a request as long as he ultimately complies with the request. It's when he doesn't comply in his *actions* that you need to be concerned. If he's just giving you a string of verbal "no's," that's nothing to get alarmed about, particularly with a four-year-old.

9. *I'm one of those rare birds, a father who really loves his children. I'm divorced and my ex-wife has custody. I'm supposed to have "reasonable" visitation, but many times when we've made plans for me to take them for the weekend, I show up at her house at the planned time and nobody's there. Later I find out from the kids that she's taken them somewhere for the weekend. Or I show up to take them out and find they've suddenly become "sick." And she refuses to let me in the house to see the "sick" kids. What can I do?*

You are a divorced father who cares and you're the victim of a vindictive mother who has custody. What can you do? First of all, you can take your ex-wife to court to get the times of visitation spelled out. The very fact that we have such a legal concept as reasonable visitation shows the sex-biased nature of the courts. Have you ever heard of such a thing as "reasonable child support"? You bet your winter underwear you haven't! The Divorced Mothers of America would rise up en masse if anyone tried to palm off something so ridiculous on them. But somebody palmed off "reasonable visitation" on a lot of unsuspecting fathers. You see, if the mother with custody *is* reasonable, then you will have reasonable visitation. But if she is vindictive, as you describe your situation, then the father does *not* get reasonable visitation. You will have to go to court to have the times of visitation spelled out specifically.

Next, I would suggest you take along a witness each time you come to pick up your children. Otherwise it's strictly your word against hers in court. But a witness can testify that he went with you to pick up your children and nobody was home. Also keep a diary, listing the date of each time you are prevented from seeing your children. Judges are usually impressed by detailed factual accounts of this nature.

10. *What can I do with a four-year-old who uses bathroom language at the top of his lungs when we're in public?*

You can do two things. First, you can say nothing and ignore it. In this way you are not making the mistake of getting upset by his language and thereby reinforcing it. Second, reading between the lines, I gather that it is the public nature of his language that bothers you. So I suggest you use negative thinking (chap. 15) to desensitize yourself to what you imagine other people are thinking about him and about you when he spouts off in public. If you do these two things, then sooner or later your child will give up this particular kind of language behavior. Incidentally, four-year-olds typically begin to use four-letter words at this age as a part of their general increased sensitivity to language.

11. *Our three-year-old is very jealous of the new baby. What can we do about this?*

There are two things that an older child often wants to do when a new baby is born. First, she may want to regress. It's as if she is saying to herself, "What good does it do me being three years old and weaned and toilet trained and eating with a knife and fork and all that jazz, when this little baby can't do any of the things I can do and he gets all that attention? So I want to be a baby again." Your three-year-old may suddenly revert to wetting herself or wanting to drink from a bottle or eating with her fingers. Most parents make the mistake of not allowing this. They say, "Come on, you're a big girl now. Big girls don't eat with their fingers or drink from a bottle." Wrong. Let her regress in whatever way she wants to. If she wants to be held and drink from a bottle, hold her and let her drink from a bottle. Her regressive behavior is only temporary. After she has had enough of regression she will return to the behavior she used before the baby was born. As far as regressive toilet behavior is concerned, treat it matter-of-factly but make her clean up her mess and change her clothes.

The second type of feelings she may have is intense jealousy and hostility. Here again, most parents try to con the older child out of such feelings. They will say, "How can you feel that way? He's your sweet little brother and you ought to love him." Don't fall into this trap. Give your older child ample chance to vent her angry feelings. You can even help it along. Since the baby can't understand what you're saying, say such things to your three-year-old as, "Babies are such a nuisance, aren't they? Babies are a mess; I'm glad you're three years old." You can also say, "I'll bet it makes you mad when Grandma and Grandpa and other people make such a fuss over that messy old baby!" If you allow your three-year-old to freely express the hostility she feels toward the baby, you are helping her drain the hostility out of her system. It will never be completely eliminated because there will always continue to be hostile rivalry between siblings, but the main thrust of it should be gone if you handle it this way.

12. *Our three-and-one-half-year-old daughter is afraid of dogs, burglars, the dark—you name it, she's afraid of it. What can we do to help her overcome these fears?*

First of all you need to know what causes such fears in children. Most parents make the mistake of thinking that the fear is caused by something external that stirs the child up inside. They think she must have seen a scary dog and that's why she's afraid of dogs. Not so. It is what is happening *internally* in the child's brain and nervous system that causes the fear of things such as dogs or the dark. What is usually happening internally is that she has learned to be afraid of her own angry feelings. It makes her anxious if she becomes aware of her anger. So she does not want to become aware that she has any angry feelings. Instead, she does what many children do to cover up these feelings. She uses the defense mechanism of projection. This is the way it works. It's as if she is saying to herself, "I don't have any angry feelings. I'm projecting them out onto other things. It's those other things that are angry, not me. Dogs, burglars, the dark—they are angry and they want to hurt me. So I'm afraid of them."

Since this is the way most children's fears originate, what you need to do is to try to get the child over her fear of her own angry feelings. You can do this gradually over a period of time by telling her it's all right to be angry, and it's okay when she's mad to say so. Then you use the feedback technique to help her get the angry feelings out. If the fears are overwhelming and you are not able to get her over them yourself, then you should probably seek professional help for her so that she can accept the normality of angry feelings and get over her fears. Whichever way you do it—by yourself or with professional help—don't try directly to get rid of the fears themselves because the fears are merely symptoms of her inability to accept her angry feelings.

Here are two books you could read to your child to help her learn to express angry and fearful feelings: *Sometimes I Get Angry* and *Sometimes I'm Afraid*, both by Jane Watson (Western Publishing Co.).

13. *When my four-year-old boy shouts, "I hate you,*

Mommy!" It just tears me up inside. How can I stop him doing such things?

I suggest you not try to stop him, for he is doing a good thing, not a bad thing. He is expressing his negative feelings in words, not in actions. Now if he were expressing his negative feelings in actions, by hitting or kicking you, then you should stop him, for this is not good behavior. But it's good for him to express his hostility in words, as he is doing. This enables him to get the bad feelings out of his system so they can be replaced by warm and loving feelings.

What may be bothering you or tearing you up inside, as you put it, is that he says, "I hate you, Mommy!" You may be misunderstanding this. You may think he means, "I thoroughly despise you and everything about you." Not so. Children are not very talented in the nuances of language. They usually cannot say, as we adults can, "I'm annoyed with you," "I'm irritated with you," "I'm teed off at you," "I'm angry with you," "I hate you," "I'm enraged at you." When he says, "I hate you," that's his way of saying, "I'm angry with you." It sounds as if you are taking this as a total rejection, which it is not.

So what your son is doing is not what I would class as misbehavior. He is putting his angry feelings into words and expressing them. If you do *not* allow him to do this, you will cause him to drive his feelings underground. Then his hostile feelings will come out in all sorts of sneaky and devious actions.

I think you need to use the feedback technique to help him get his angry feelings out, but above all you need to use negative thinking (chap. 15) to desensitize yourself to the expression of his feelings.

14. *Our daughter used to have a night light. My husband turned it off recently because he says she's four years old now and too old to have a night light. But putting her to bed now is a real trauma every night because she cries for her light. I don't know what to do.*

I am always amazed at the number of parents (or grandparents, or neighbors) who say, "Your child is too old to . . . have a night light, still be on the bottle, keep a special old security blanket," etc.! How do *they* know the child is too old for this special thing? Can they crawl into the child's mind in some magical way and find out what this special comfort device means to him? Of course not. They are operating purely from their outside-of-the-child, adult frame of reference. It would be like my saying to a father, "You don't need to make $15,000 a year; $12,000 is plenty. Give $3,000 back to the company." Ridiculous? No more so than the ridiculous statements we make about what children need or don't need.

I have never yet met a teenager who was still on the bottle, still had a security blanket, or still used a night light. So since your child will ultimately give up her night light, and since it harms no one for her to have it on, what's the big rush? I would let her have the light again, which apparently provides her with the extra security she needs in order to go to sleep peacefully.

15. *It's hard to keep from slapping my defiant four-year-old in the mouth when he refuses to obey me. How can I make him mind?*

Forgive my saying so, but it sounds as if you have a very naïve picture of what four-year-olds are like and how you get them to mind. It sounds like you are thinking, "When I tell him what I want him to do, he immediately, without question, should do it." Children simply don't function that way, particularly four-year-olds. It's as if you owned a bicycle and expected it to function like a car. When it doesn't it makes you so mad you feel like hitting it.

The most effective way to get a four-year-old to do something is to set up a positive reward system (chap. 3) or negotiate a contract with the child (chap. 4). And the best way to get a four-year-old to stop doing something is to use the Time Out technique (chap. 6).

So give up your naïve expectations that all you have to do to get a four-year-old to mind is to tell him what to do or stop doing. That kind of thinking went out with the corset. Use the new techniques I have suggested. They have been developed out of thousands of experiments on how you can actually get young children to mind.

16. *Our four-year-old has been diagnosed as mentally retarded. Some people have suggested we put him in an institution, but we would never consider that. But he's disruptive to the three older children. What can we do?*

First, remember that a mentally retarded child is still a

child. Therefore, all of the discipline strategies I discussed in the early chapters of this book also apply to him (positive reward system, Time Out, feedback, etc.). So first I suggest you familiarize yourself with all of those discipline methods until you have them down pat in your mind. Then you need to adapt these strategies so that they are tailor-made to fit your mentally retarded child. This can best be done by consulting with a psychologist or psychiatrist or psychiatric social worker who specializes in work with mentally retarded children. Working together with him, you can devise a number of discipline strategies to stop your child from being disruptive in the home.

I would like to mention one other thing. Your child has been diagnosed as mentally retarded. This does not mean that he will not continue to grow and develop. Your task as a parent should be to see that he receives all of the love and opportunities for learning that you can provide for him. He will need to be taught in a different way from your other children—by special teachers or with special methods that you can learn. But with this help he may learn a great deal more than you now think he can or the "experts" think he can. Just remember that all living things constantly change and mature. Your child is no exception to this, even if his growth is slow and requires harder work from both you and him.

17. *Every day our five-year-old daughter insists on dressing herself for kindergarten. But she changes her mind so often and takes so long that we are worn to a frazzle by the time her car pool comes. What can we do?*

Natural consequences is the main discipline strategy to use here. Explain to her very firmly and clearly that when the car-pool lady honks, she is going into the car, ready or not. Have some extra clothes tucked away in a bag that you could stuff with her into the car in an emergency. (Warn the carpool drivers in advance what you are going to do and why.) Your little girl will learn that the natural consequences of not being dressed on time is that she has to take potluck on clothes, and wear whatever's in the bag.

It is important that when she changes her mind about what dress she is going to wear and dawdles around, you make absolutely no comment. In fact, try to be in another room when she is dressing.

18. *You have said that one of the basic developmental tasks for this stage is to give a child intellectual stimulation. How can we do this?*

In two ways. First, you can offer your child intellectual stimulation at home. Your basic "textbooks" for learning how to do this are the two chapters entitled "School Begins at Home," parts 1 and 2, in *How to Parent,* and two books, *Give Your Child a Superior Mind,* by Siegfried and Therese Engelmann, and *How to Raise a Brighter Child,* by Joan Beck. In these sources you will find many, many more suggestions than you will possibly have time to use. You will find ways of stimulating his vocabulary and language development, his reading, his mathematics, his logical thinking, and his overall intelligence. Choose the activities that appeal to you and do them with your child.

Second, if you can afford it, send your child to a good nursery school. You need to understand the difference between a nursery school and a day-care center for working mothers. A nursery school operates only on a half-day schedule. A day-care center operates on an all-day schedule that permits a mother to leave her child at 6:30 or 7:00 A.M. and pick him up at 5:00 or 6:00 P.M. I think an all-day schedule is much too long for a preschool child unless it is absolutely necessary, as in the case of a working mother.

You can start your child out two or three days a week at a nursery school and work him up to five days a week if your budget will stand it. A good nursery school can be of enormous help in furthering both his emotional and intellectual development. Not only will it afford valuable intellectual stimulation to your child, it will also give him excellent preparation for kindergarten or first grade.

I am always amazed at how little some people—even very intelligent people—know about what a good nursery school can do to stimulate a child intellectually. I remember one banker who said to me, "Isn't nursery school basically just a glorified baby-sitting service?" To me, this is like saying, "Isn't Harvard basically just a glorified baby-sitting service for late adolescents?"

It has always intrigued me that many people are quite ready to borrow money to send a child to a good college, but practically no one ever borrows money to send a child to a superior nursery school. And yet the nursery school years shape the very foundations of a child's intelligence and attitudes toward learning. Dr. Benjamin Bloom, of the University of Chicago, has done research showing that approximately 50 percent of a child's intelligence is acquired by age four, another 30 percent by age eight, and the final 20 percent by age seventeen. Remember those figures the next time someone tells you that the early years of a child's life are not particularly important!

19. *Our five-year-old often comes home from his friend's house with toys in his pocket. When I ask him about them, he either says he doesn't know how they got there, his friend gave them to him, or he found them on the way home. How can I make him realize stealing is wrong? I've tried spanking and it doesn't seem to help.*

The reason spanking doesn't seem to help is that it violates the Law of the Soggy Potato Chip (chap. 3).

When your son gives you these ingenious explanations for where he found the toys, simply say, "I don't believe you." Then take him back to his friend's house to see if the toys can be identified. If so, have him give them back. If his friend cannot identify the toys, then say, "I know these are not your toys, so I will have to keep them." Take the toys away from him and dispose of them later. If you stay with this routine long enough (and how long you need to do it depends on how tenacious and stubborn your child is), sooner or later he will give up the habit of taking toys.

Above all, avoid such foolish things as saying, "You're stealing, and that's awful." Or, "You're lying to me and I won't have it!" Your negative parental comments will reward the stealing and the lying and thus reinforce the very habits you are trying to break.

20. *How do you explain religious concepts such as God and prayer to a four-year-old?*

Unfortunately, there are very few good religious books written for very young children, such as preschoolers. One exception is the books of Mary Alice Jones. I would read her books to your child and use them as the basis for a discussion of religious concepts. However, many such concepts are simply over the head of a preschooler. If he says he still doesn't understand, you can only say something like, "When you are a little older you can understand it better. It's hard to understand when you are young."

21. *How much television should we allow our fiveyear-old to see?*

I don't think you can give any absolute answer to this question that makes sense. Certainly there are fine TV shows for children such as *Sesame Street* and *Mister Rogers*. Rather than set arbitrary hours for TV watching, I would suggest that you make many different kinds of play materials available in the house and backyard for your five-year-old. Let him invite friends over to play and sometimes spend the night. Visit a good nursery school or kindergarten and notice the different kinds of outdoor and indoor play equipment they have: a tree house, a dome climber, hollow wooden blocks, a sandbox, plastic cowboys and Indians, plastic army men, toy cars and trucks, dolls, Legos and other building materials, crayons, paint, paper, and so on. When such materials are available to your child, TV viewing will fall into its proper perspective without your having to set any arbitrary time limits each day.

Although much of TV is an "educational wasteland," it still is beneficial to your child's language and vocabulary development. When I think of the truth of this statement, in spite of how bad most TV shows are, I can only gasp to think what we *could* do with TV as an educational medium for preschoolers. We could teach children to read by TV; we could teach math and history and logical thinking, and so much more. With the right kind of creative programming we could produce an educational explosion and raise the general intelligence level of our nation's preschoolers!

22. *I'm seriously dating a women who is terrific, but her three-year-old daughter seems to have taken an instant dislike to me. I'd ask her to marry me except for the thought of having to live with that child.*

At least you are looking before you leap. Far too many people assume that "love conquers all" and that the three-year-old will surely come around. This question is hard to answer, however, because you don't state whether the father is in or out of the picture, and that makes a tremendous difference.

At any rate, you need to take time and patience to es-

tablish rapport with the little girl. If she actively expresses
negative feelings to you, you can use the feedback technique
(chap. 10) to handle them. Find out from her mother what
things she particularly likes. The judicious use of gifts will
help in establishing rapport. Set up a positive reward system
so that, in effect, she gets positive rewards when you are
around. Don't try to go too fast with her; she might feel you
are rushing her and trying to bribe her. Try to be aware of
your own feelings as you relate to her so that gradually the
rapport will be two-sided, and you can begin having genuine
fun with her.

In all probability, she has taken a dislike to you because
she resents being deprived of her father and resents anyone
who tries in any way to take his place. This is another reason
not to push her, but to let the relationship develop gradually
and naturally.

The best thing you have going for you is the age of the
child. If she were six or nine or eleven, it would be much
harder to win her over. But three is still a very malleable age.
The kind of program I have outlined should, in time, win her
over to thinking of you as a friend. If it does not, then I
would suggest that you and the mother have a few
consultations with a professional counselor to see what suggestions he will make for you.

Above all, don't marry the mother until you are on good
terms with the little girl. Otherwise you are going to have a
very difficult stepparent-stepchild situation to cope with. Once
you are on good terms with the little girl, your marriage will
be built on a much more solid foundation.

23. *When my child turns five, his birthday will just barely
make him eligible to enter kindergarten next fall. I'm
seriously thinking of holding him back, but all my neighbors
think that's crazy.*

The free advice of your neighbors is worth exactly that:
nothing. Your child will always be at somewhat of a disad-
vantage if he or she is at the smallest and youngest end of the
class. And I'm thinking now not only of kindergarten and
first grade, but looking ahead. The child who is at the older
end of the class is more mature and educationally more
capable.

As Dr. Louise Ames has pointed out in her excellent book
Stop School Failure, many of our school learning problems

would vanish if the parents and school had been intelligent enough to hold the child back a grade, particularly in the early years of school. A year's more maturity would do terrific things for many children who are struggling to keep up with their class.

In spite of all this evidence many people feel it is almost a "mark of shame" to be held back a grade, and they counsel against it. Don't you believe it. Start your youngster in kindergarten late instead of early. Give him a year's advantage in maturity over the other children. It's one of the best gifts you can give him. Keep him in nursery school for another year and then enter him in kindergarten. I'm sure you'll be glad you did.

24. *No matter how many times we scold him, our five-year-old is simply not careful about riding his bike in the street. When we take his bike away to impress him about safety, he just borrows a friend's and goes on doing the same thing. We're very concerned about his safety. What can we do?*

First, you can stop scolding him. This negative attention violates The Law of the Soggy Potato Chip (chap. 3) and unwittingly rewards him for riding in the street.

Second, you can speak to the parents of all his friends. Enlist their cooperation in preventing their children from lending him their bikes to ride.

Third, when he does ride his bike recklessly in the street, you can take it away from him for three days or a week, whichever seems more appropriate for his personality and temperament.

Fourth, you can design a positive reward program (chap. 3) to encourage him to ride carefully. Since this could turn out to be a life-or-death matter, you will want to have a really big reward for careful riding (such as a special TV set of his own). Then each day that he rides carefully, you put one dollar into a special strongbox. That way he has an immediate daily reward that he can see accumulating toward the long-term reward of the TV set. A TV set is only one of the many possible rewards you could use. The important thing is that the ultimate reward be big enough and important enough so that it will really motivate him to ride carefully.

Above all, do not try to explain to him on an abstract, intellectual level how dangerous it is to ride his bike restlessly, how he might be injured or killed. This kind of talk goes right over his head. But seeing a dollar bill being put into the strongbox and thinking of the TV set he is going to get is right down at his level. So the secret of getting him to ride his bike carefully is to learn how to *motivate* him to do it.

25. *How do you explain about death to a five-year-old? His grandfather has terminal cancer.*

Our culture makes it difficult for children to understand death. This is because we ourselves are afraid to face the subject openly and honestly. We do more to repress the idea of death than we do to repress sex. For instance, we do not say someone has *died;* we say he has "passed away." Both adults and children in our society avoid facing the fact of death. This is the main thing that makes it difficult to explain death to a child.

Yet children can understand the meaning of death. There is a classic statement by Dr. Jerome Bruner of Harvard, which has had quite an impact on American education. Dr. Bruner states that any subject can be explained adequately in an intellectually honest form to any child at any stage of development. This holds true for the subject of death, as well as any other subject.

Let's get back to your specific question about the grandfather who is ill with terminal cancer. I would say nothing about it to your five-year-old until the cancer begins to seriously impair grandfather's functioning. Then you might tell him that grandpa is very sick, and leave it at that. When he is so sick that his time to live is measured in months, you might tell your son that grandpa is so sick it looks as though he is going to die in six months or three months or whatever.

Research has shown that preschool children are not able to understand death as a final event. To them death is a kind of sleep. First you are dead, but then you come alive again, like when you wake up from sleep. For instance, when President John Kennedy's son, John-John, came back to visit the White House after the death of his father, he saw his father's secretary. He asked her, "When is my daddy coming back?" You may have to contend with this difficulty in explaining death to your five-year-old.

Explaining grandpa's death to your five-year-old is not a

one-time event. It is a *continuing process,* an ongoing dialogue you will have with the boy before grandpa dies, when he dies, and afterward.

Being truthful is probably the single most important guide you have. What really worries a child is when he gets the feeling that adults are being evasive and withholding information from him. If you are truthful with him, half of the battle is won.

Most adults believe either that death is the end of life or that it is the beginning of a new existence. Others take the position that they simply don't know. Whatever your own belief about death, communicate that simply and honestly to your child. If you have religious beliefs, try to communicate them clearly and on his level of understanding.

Whatever you do, do not give a child an explanation of death or a life hereafter that you yourself do not believe in. The child will sense that you are sending him a double message, and this will make him feel anxious and insecure.

Should your child go to his grandfather's funeral? Definitely. When the grandfather dies, the child cannot help but pick up messages from other members of the family that something unhappy has taken place. Sometimes parents feel that it is kinder to shield a child from death, and they leave him with a friend or baby-sitter during the funeral. I think this is a mistake.

The child may come to feel that his parents are trying to hide things from him. Even though a funeral is a sad occasion, it cannot possibly be as bad as all of the things the child's imagination can picture when he is kept away while he knows the funeral is going on. So let him share the solidarity of sadness within the family by being present with you at the funeral.

After grandpa's death, your child as well as you will need to go through a period of mourning and do your grief work. Children grieve a loss as well as adults, although many children keep this inside. You can help him mourn and do his grief work by doing your own. Let out your sad and unhappy feelings. Cry if you feel like it. And above all, don't prevent your child from crying with foolish admonitions to "be brave and stop crying."

I have spoken as if you can take the lead throughout the process of grandpa's fatal illness and death in interpreting what is going on to your child. It may not work out that way. For instance, when you first tell your son, "Grandpa is very sick," he may say, "Is he going to die?" You will need to be honest and say, "Yes, he probably will." So be prepared for your child's taking the lead at times in asking you what is going on with grandpa. And always remember, the truth is your greatest ally in interpreting death to a child. For further discussion of this subject I suggest you consult the book *Explaining Death to Children*, edited by Earl Grollman (Beacon Press).

If you should have to deal with the death of a brother or sister, the process is much the same as what I have indicated for handling the death of a grandparent or parent. With one added factor. There are always undercurrents of jealousy and hostility toward the dead sibling that must be faced in one way or another. Sometimes, at a young age, such as in the preschool period, the child, who is still in the stage of magical thinking, may believe that his angry feelings toward his sibling caused his brother or sister's death.

It is often wise for you to invest in one appointment with a professional counselor to help a child get his ambivalent feelings about the death of a sibling out into the open where he can deal with them.

Summary

The preschool period is one of the richest stages in the life of your child, both emotionally and intellectually. So many exciting things are going on within him! Things that will form a part of his basic personality structure for the rest of his life. His gender identity. His attitudes toward sexuality. How he handles and resolves the "family romance." How well he learns to express his feelings. How he learns to get along with his peers and acquires his first lessons in the art of human relations. How his intellectual curiosity develops. And many other things. In each of these psychological tasks you have an opportunity to influence him for the better.

After the difficult period of first adolescence, the preschool period comes as a decided relief to most parents. You will usually find that the discipline methods that did not work in first adolescence are now highly effective. In fact, the preschool period, beginning at age three, is the time to begin using most of the discipline techniques discussed in this book. The positive reward system, contracting, Time Outs, the feedback technique, the mutual problem-solving technique—all these strategies will usually work quite successfully now.

25

MIDDLE CHILDHOOD

Overview of the Stage

The closing of the preschool stage brings about a stable integration of your child's personality. This personality equilibrium lasts throughout middle childhood, from approximately his sixth to his eleventh birthdays.

Middle childhood covers a longer time span than any of the earlier stages. It is a relatively tranquil period, compared to the dramatic ups and downs of the preschool years, which lie behind, and the stormy turmoil of adolescence, which lies ahead.

It is in this stage that the family is no longer the center of your child's world. Now he lives in three worlds at once: the world of school, the world of the gang, and the world of the family. His developmental task of this period is *learning mastery* versus *inadequacy*.

His self-identity at this stage is based on how well he masters the specific skills and accomplishments that are demanded in school, by his peer group, and at home. A good self-identity depends on your child's feeling secure in the knowledge that he can do the things that are demanded of him. If he is not able to master the tasks and skills required by school and his contemporaries, he feels a sense of inadequacy and inferiority.

Do not be fooled by your child's absorbing interest in his peers during this time and think that the family is of no importance to him. Dr. Barbara Biber has summarized his relationship to his family in a single trenchant comment in *The New Encyclopedia of Child Care and Guidance* (Doubleday, 1968). She points out that your child is "looking for ways to belong to his family and feel free of them at the same time." This can be a delightful time for you as a parent if you take the trouble to find out what children are *really* like at this stage. This can be a needlessly difficult time for you if you expect your youngster to be an "adultized" small person instead of a child.

1. *My nine-year-old son's teacher keeps sending notes home and phoning me that he is disrupting the class and that I must do something about it. What should I do?*

My answer to this question usually does not make me very popular with schoolteachers. I think that you, like many American parents, have fallen into the Teacher Trap. I want to show you how absurd the Teacher Trap is by asking you a ridiculous question. What would happen if *you* phoned the teacher on a Saturday or Sunday and said, "My son is being disruptive at home on weekends. You've got to do something about it. What are you going to do?" The teacher, of course, would reply, "I certainly have no responsibility for your son's behavior on weekends. Why do you expect me to do something about it?"

I am fully sympathetic with the problems teachers face in their work because I have taught all the grades from kindergarten through high school in the course of my own career. However, I believe that if a student is disruptive in class it is the teacher's problem to handle it, not the parents'. If teachers are well trained in the discipline methods discussed in this book and in Dr. Thomas Gordon's book *Teacher Effectiveness Training,* they should be well equipped to handle all but the most extreme cases of disruptiveness. The unfortunate fact is that many teachers are not well trained in the use of these methods. Many rely only on punishment power. When this does not work and they have failed *at their job,* which is to control their classrooms, they may try to pass the buck to you. Don't let the teacher do it. Tell her, in effect, "The buck stops with you. I'm responsible for my child's behavior at home, but you're responsible for my child's behavior at school. I can't pass my responsibility for his home behavior on to you. And I will not let you pass your responsibility for his school behavior on to me."

There is one exception I would make to what I have just said. If the teacher says to you, in effect, "I have tried every method I know to control your child's disruptive behavior and nothing works. In my opinion you need professional help for him." I think the teacher has every right to make this statement to you, and, in fact, she is doing you a favor by calling your child's psychological need to your attention.

2. *I'm anti–Little League for three reasons:*
   1. *The most athletically able kids always get to play.*
   2. *Too many parents get too emotionally involved.*
   3. *I always have to drive them to the games and stay to watch, and the schedule ties us down as a family every weekend.*

However, my eight-year-old son is begging to try out. I hate to dampen his enthusiasm, but—help!

My answer will not win me any points with the Little League Association, but I too am anti-Little League, for somewhat different reasons.

First, there is the physical danger. Pediatricians are familiar with such injuries as "Little League elbow" and "Little League shoulder." The child's musculature is not yet strong enough to take some of this adult-oriented activity. I agree strongly with the American Academy of Pediatrics, which suggests that the beginning age for competitive sports should not be earlier than twelve.

Second, there is the psychological pressure. Young children experience far too much strain and pressure performing before a crowd of emotionally involved parents. When I played baseball as a child between the ages of six and twelve, I never once saw a boy cry over the game as they often do in Little League. The reason is that we did not have to deal with the emotional pressure of playing before a crowd of adults, or a coach who might chew us out if he didn't like our performance. We were just having fun playing baseball and nothing more.

Third, if you are a star athlete, you run only physical dangers in playing Little League baseball. Psychologically you will probably do fine because you will win the plaudits of the crowd and the players. But very few boys are star athletes. What if you are not especially good as a batter or pitcher, infielder or outfielder? Does playing Little League ball do anything positive for your self-esteem? The answer is no.

For these reasons I suggest you say "no" to your boy when he wants to try out for Little League. He may be full of enthusiasm, but he has no inkling of the physical or psychological dangers involved. Since you do, you are in a position to make a wiser decision than he can. Sometimes we have to say "no" to a child out of love for him.

3. *My wife and I have decided to get a divorce. How can we explain this to our six-year-old and nine-year-old?*

How you are able to explain the situation to the children depends a great deal on how effectively the two of you can disentangle your negative feelings about each other long enough to discuss it with the children. If your feelings about each other permit it, it is best if you can *both* tell the children at the same time. If you have agreed that the mother will have custody, you can explain it this way:

"Mother and Daddy are not happy living with each other anymore. We know you won't be happy to hear this, but the time has come to tell you about it. We are so unhappy living with each other that we have decided to get a divorce and live separately.

"Even though Mother and Daddy are not happy with each other, we are both very happy with you kids. There was nothing either of you kids did that caused us to get the divorce. The divorce is something just between the two of us.

"We have decided that you two kids will live with Mother, and Daddy will live somewhere else. But Daddy will come and see you kids regularly. We know you kids are probably not very happy with this news, but we think that in the long run it will be best for everybody.

"Now, are there any questions you kids want to ask about this?"

Chances are that the children will not ask questions at this time unless they are very outspoken. But at least give them the chance to ask questions if they are ready to do so.

If *both* parents tell the children at the same time and present it as a joint decision it is far better for them psychologically than if only one parent tells them. I have seen situations where the father simply moved out but said nothing about it to the children, and the mother had to tell them. This is not good. The children inevitably feel, "Why didn't Daddy tell me? Aren't I important enough to him to tell me the news, even if it is bad news?"

Even if one person wants the divorce and the other does not, I think it should be presented as a joint decision (which in one sense it is). If it is presented to the children as only one person's decision, then that person becomes the "bad guy" who broke up the family. And since children need to love and model themselves after *both* father and mother, it is not good for them to feel that one of their parents is the "bad guy." I know of divorce situations where the news has unfortunately been presented to the children in this light: "Your father has decided to move out and leave us." This makes it pretty difficult for the children to preserve good feelings about their father. He is cast in the role of the villain who is deserting Mother *and them.*

But suppose there is so much bitterness between the two of you that it is impossible to sit down with the children and tell them together. Then each of you will need to tell them separately, being careful not to bad-mouth the other. Bad-mouthing your about-to-be-divorced spouse is always harmful because the children need to continue a good relationship with both of you. Saying bad things about your spouse may actually weaken the children's relationship with *both* of you. For better or worse, each of you will continue to be a parent to your children as long as you live. So your children need to think of *both* of you in a positive light. *You can get a marital divorce but you can never get a parental divorce.*

I would suggest that you set up a regular schedule of visitation immediately. When the children know that every Wednesday night they have dinner with Dad or every other weekend they spend with Dad, this gives them an order and regularity in their disrupted lives that they can hang on to. And this is especially important in the early, unhappy months of the divorce. Of course if both parties are in agreement you can make allowance for other spontaneous visitations (if convenient) in addition to the regular schedule.

The more the two of you can work out together regarding child visitation, child support, spousal support, and the division of the property before lawyers enter the picture, the better off you will be psychologically. When the lawyers come in they are adversaries, and whether they are aware of it or not, they will incite the two of you to be adversaries. It is almost a psychological law that the hostility on both sides increases enormously when the lawyers enter.

There is a very helpful book you can buy for each of your

children. It is called *The Boys and Girls Book of Divorce* by Richard Gardner, in paperback. It is written for boys and girls, not for adults, and it covers just about anything your child may want to know about divorce. The book can also be the springboard for helpful discussions between you and your child about the divorce and his feelings about it.

4. *My ten-year-old has acquired two new friends I think are bad for him. They get in a lot of trouble at school and, all in all, they are not the kind of children I want my boy to associate with. How do I go about breaking up his friendship with them?*

Don't. I think you would be making a mistake to try to break up his friendship with them. If you did try, your son would feel hurt and angry and would merely continue to see them behind your back.

You are obviously concerned that these boys will exert a bad influence on your son. You are afraid that they will influence him to get in trouble at school and elsewhere. If this should actually happen, then you would have a valid reason for breaking up the friendship. You could say, "Philip, I know that Danny and Chuck influenced you to steal candy in the school cafeteria, and I don't think they are good friends for you to have." Philip might not like it, but he would have to inwardly acknowledge the truth of your comments.

But I gather that your son has not actually gotten in any trouble because of the influence of these friends. Therefore, you have no legitimate complaint that will hold up in "children's court." All you can say to him at this point is, "I don't want you to play with these two boys and have them as friends because I don't like them." And no child, unless he is a pretty spineless one, will accept that as a valid reason.

What I'm saying is that your child has the right to make friends with other kids that you personally don't like. Just because you *fear* they will get your son into trouble is not a valid reason for breaking up the friendship. Only when the other children have *in fact* gotten your child in trouble do you have reason to break up the friendship that will make sense to your child. And anyway you may be surprised. Your child may pal around with these rowdy kids and enjoy their company for a couple of years, yet never once get into trouble because of them!

5. *Should I give my six-year-old an allowance? If so, when?*

Yes, I think every child should have an allowance, and it can take one of two forms. First, the child can continue the financial positive reward system of the preschool years for household chores, only with larger amounts of money. He might get a potential allowance of fifty cents a week, broken down into five separate household tasks valued at ten cents each. Under such a system it is entirely up to him to earn his allowance.

The other way to do it is to give your child an allowance of, say, fifty cents per week simply because he is your child and you love him. Then if he wants to earn more money each week you can offer him various household tasks that he can do to earn money.

Personally, I prefer the second way of handling it, and this is what I have done with my three children.

I think that five years old is a good time to begin giving your child an allowance. Whether it is earned through work or unearned, it can be gradually increased as the child grows older. For example, it might stay the same from six to ten, and then be increased at eleven, and again at thirteen or fourteen.

6. *Our six-year-old daughter was born with a noticeable birth defect. One hand has no fingers. Things weren't so bad in kindergarten, but now that she's in first grade, the kids make fun of her. I hate to see her hurt, and I just don't know what to do.*

Your problem is basically the same as that of a parent whose child is teased by other children for any number of reasons. He's too fat, he's too skinny, he wears glasses, he can't stand up for himself. Teasing can be very hurtful to any child, and you can't prevent it from making your daughter feel bad. But there are some things you can do to help.

For one thing, teach her how to handle the teasing. There are two ways of doing this. If you know a foreign language, teach her three or four words of it until she has them down pat. Then instruct her as follows: "When other kids tease you, just look at them and say, 'He gay melaina.' Never explain to them what the words mean. Just say them automatically every time a child teases you. If a child says, 'What does that mean?' you say, 'Gee, you're dumb. I thought everybody knew what that meant.' If you keep this up long enough, the other kids will get tired of teasing you."

The other way to handle the situation is this. Teach your daughter to agree with everything the teasers say. Here is a sample dialogue:

"You've got a wimpy hand."

"You're absolutely right, I've got a wimpy hand."

"You must have left your fingers home today."

"You're right, I left my fingers home today."

"If somebody's fingers are missing, it's bound to affect their brain."

"You're right. If somebody's fingers are missing, it's bound to affect their brain."

If your daughter keeps this up long enough, it will wear down the opposition. The teasing kids will begin to feel as if they're putting on a show but the audience has left. Sooner or later this trick of agreeing with whatever they say will get on their nerves, and they will give up the teasing.

In addition, I think it would be a good idea to give your daughter karate lessons as soon as the local karate school thinks she is old enough. When she learns karate, she will know that she can physically handle a teasing child, even a much larger one, and knowing this will do great things for her self-confidence.

Incidentally, I recommend that *all* children learn karate, for a variety of reasons. It may help a child cope with a larger bully at school or in the neighborhood. Or later in life it may save her life at the hands of a rapist or mugger. I think it is particularly important for girls to learn karate, since they do not ordinarily acquire any formal or informal training in the use of their bodies in danger situations.

7. *I strongly suspect that my ten-year-old son is lying to me about various things, but I'm not positive. On the one hand, I hate to accuse him of being a liar, but, on the other, I want to get to the bottom of the matter. It happens often enough that I'm stymied. What can I do?*

First of all, do not play Perry Mason and try to wring the truth out of him. Children can be very persistent and continue barefaced lying in the face of accusations. On the other hand, it would be a mistake to ignore the whole thing. A parent rarely *suspects* his child is lying to him unless there

their feelings. "I know you don't want to see me today, but it's my turn to see you." Remember, the court can't stop your ex-wife from bad-mouthing you, but the court can force her to let you visit your children. In the early stages, take them to some special things you know they will like, such as a special movie or an amusement park.

Yours must be a long-range game. It will take time. But sooner or later, if you keep up your regular visitation, you will overcome your ex-wife's bad-mouthing. I was consulted in a case recently where the mother constantly talked against the father. She did everything she could to prevent his seeing or having contact with his two little girls. If he phoned to speak to them, she hung up. At one point he had to send telegrams to them at their school.

It was a hard and painful struggle for him, but it finally paid off. A few months ago his oldest daughter, now eighteen, ran away from her mother's house. She phoned her father and asked if she could come and live with him. He said, "Of course," and she is now living with him and his new wife. The daughter's language is unprintable when she describes her feelings about how her mother tried to prevent her from seeing her father all these years. So don't give up—as many fathers do—in such a frustrating situation. Continue to see your children in spite of your ex-wife, and in time your children will be old enough to see the situation clearly.

10. *What kinds of movies should I allow my nine-year-old to see?*

I think it is best to raise children without censorship in any form. I am not only against censorship of books, I am against censorship of movies or TV. I am quite aware that my point of view is distinctly a minority one compared with the way most people raise their children. But the way most people raise their children produces a high proportion of neurotics, psychotics, dope addicts, juvenile delinquents, alcoholics, and criminals. So you don't necessarily want to do what "most people" do.

My position is that you can take your child at any age to see any movie you think is really good. The *content* of the movie is irrelevant as far as I am concerned. I have taken my children to all kinds of movies. My only criterion has been the quality of the picture, not the subject matter, or a G, PG, or R rating. I think the rating scale for movies is foolish.

One magazine for parents does absolutely ridiculous movie reviews. For example, they will say of a movie, "Much cursing." When I read that I wonder to myself, "Has this reviewer spent any time recently on a school playground listening to sixth and seventh and eighth graders talk? Is he afraid that children who already know how to curse fluently are going to learn cursing from seeing a movie where the characters curse? Absurd!" Does he think children never cursed before movies and TV were invented?

Our family has gone to drive-in movies a great deal. I find this quite educational since the parents can comment on incidents in the movie or exchange information with their children. I remember one movie we saw when my daughter was ten, in which the word *prostitute* was used. She turned to me and asked, "Daddy, what's a prostitute?" I replied, "Robin, a prostitute is a woman who has sexual intercourse with men for money." "Oh," she said, and we went on watching the picture.

My kids have always felt free to ask questions about any book they read and any movie or TV show they see. If someone were to tell them that they were too young to see a certain movie, they would probably be bewildered and ask the person to tell them exactly why it would be bad for them.

I imagine that some people are afraid of their children's seeing certain movies for fear the movies will scare them. As I pointed out in the answer to question 12 of the last chapter, it is not the movie or TV show that scares the child, but the child's fear of his own angry feelings. I saw perfect proof of this psychological fact when my older son, Randy, was ten. I took him to see *In Cold Blood*, a movie some parents wouldn't have dreamed of taking a ten-year-old to see. That night he slept like a baby. No nightmares, no fears. But about four months later, Randy and I had been having a go-around with each other all day, expressing angry feelings to each other. That night he had a nightmare. Obviously he had not resolved his angry feelings toward me by bedtime, and that is what caused the nightmare.

Other parents believe that they shouldn't allow their children to see movies or TV shows with violence in them for fear their children might grow up to become violent people. I am well aware that the popular thing is to agree with this position. Blaming TV is a very popular solution to the problem of violence in America. And, in my opinion, a very wrong solution to a very real problem. The reason I do not go along with this point of view is because I do not know of any hard experimental evidence indicating that seeing violence on the screen caused children to become violent. Violent people are caused by poor parenting, not by what children see in movies or on TV. For a more extensive elaboration of my point of view on this important subject, I suggest you read the chapter entitled "Your Child and Violence" in *How to Parent*.

To those who firmly believe that TV shows cause violence, I ask a ridiculously simple question. What caused violence in America before TV existed? My answer is: The same thing that caused violence in America before TV came to this country is what causes violence now: poor parenting.

Since I wrote *How to Parent*, there has been one solid scientific experiment suggesting the exact reverse of what a lot of people think about the effect that viewing violence on TV has on children. This study, done by Drs. Jerome Singer and Seymour Fishback studied boys between the ages of eight and fourteen living in several boarding schools. The experimental group watched nothing but aggressive TV shows. The control group watched nothing but nonaggressive TV shows. Then the two groups were compared on their expressions of aggression toward their peers and teachers. Guess what the results were? The group that had seen nothing but aggressive TV shows were siginificantly *less* aggressive toward their peers and teachers than the control group! Drs. Singer and Fishback interpreted this to mean that the viewing of aggressive TV shows had a cathartic effect on the children, enabling them to get some of their aggressive and violent impulses out of their systems vicariously without having to indulge them in real life.

To me the scientific evidence is clear that violence on TV does not cause children to become violent children or to grow up to be violent adults. When children are exposed to poor parenting, which fills them with hatred and violent feelings, that is what causes them to become violent adults. But if a child is raised with good parenting, he is not going to be full of violent feelings and he will not grow up to be a violent adult.

My position is that we should not waste our efforts attacking a scapegoat, violence on TV. Instead, we should try to eradicate the root cause of violence in America, which is the poor parenting violent adults received as children. Let us, through courses and training of every description, attempt to improve the level of parenting in the United States. Only then will we lower the level of violence in our country.

This is my scientific analysis of the problem, and my suggested solution to it. But my experiences in conducting lectures and workshops all over the country have made me aware that a number of people do not agree with my point of view. Although my analysis of the problem makes sense to me, it does not make sense to them. Down deep in their hearts they feel very strongly that there *must* be something about violent or aggressive TV shows and movies that is not good for their children.

If this is your belief, then the answer is simple. Do not allow your children to see violent or aggressive TV shows or movies. Turn off the TV when such shows come on and furnish your child with wholesome and creative things to do. The fact that I think what you are doing is unnecessary is irrelevant. For your feelings are not my feelings. And if it makes you feel more comfortable *not* to allow your child to watch violent or aggressive shows on TV, then I suggest you handle things that way.

However, there is one question for which I have no simple answer. If one parents thinks violent shows are bad for kids and the other parent believes the opposite, you have a problem. The two of you will need to have a creative dialogue in which you try to negotiate your way to a position acceptable to both of you. Try the mutual problem-solving technique of chapter 11 as a means of accomplishing this task.

There is one exception I have made in allowing my children to see any movies they want to see. When my kids were in middle childhood, they often pestered me to see horror movies with titles such as *Gallons of Gore* or *Buckets of Blood*. I told them I thought these were poorly done movies and I didn't want to see them or take our family to see them. I said that if they wanted to see them, I would drop them off at the theater and pick them up, but I personally didn't think they were worth seeing. That seemed to take care of everybody's needs nicely! They ended up going to very few of them, though they did go to some.

11. *I used to think it was tough getting my four-year-old to go to sleep, but that was nothing compared to getting my nine-year-old bedded down. What can I do?*

I suggest a very simple remedy. Set a definite hour by which your youngster must be in bed, say eight thirty or nine o'clock. Then tell him that he can read in bed as long as he wants until he gets sleepy. This will usually work beautifully. The child will read until he gets sleepy and then put out his light and go to sleep. If you discover he is taking advantage of this rule and staying up until midnight or some such hour, then tell him he may read in bed, but not over an hour. This not only solves the problem of getting the child to bed but gives him extra practice in reading! WARNING: Do *not* let your child talk you into staying in bed and watching TV or listening to his radio. These activities are too stimulating and will tend to keep him up longer than you want. Only reading should be allowed.

12. *My ten-year-old is so secretive about everything these days. I can't find out anything about him anymore. If I ask him what happened in school today he answers, "Oh, nothing." If I ask him where he's going as he goes out the door he says, "Out." What can I do?*

You can learn to stop asking him questions and respect his right to keep things to himself. It is characteristic of middle childhood that a youngster wants to keep things from adults. That's why secret societies and clubs flourish as they do at this time. If he *wants* to tell you about something, he will. Otherwise, leave him alone and respect his privacy.

13. *What can I do about the constant bickering and fighting between my eight-year-old and my ten-year-old?*

I refer you to my answer to question 6, chapter 24. There I suggested you not reinforce the fighting by scolding or other punishment, since that approach violates The Law of the Soggy Potato Chip and actually reinforces the fighting. I also suggested you use a Time Out whenever fighting actually breaks out. In addition, I suggested you set up a positive reward system for nonfighting.

Now let's go a little deeper into the subject. First, it's important to understand the basic cause of sibling bickering and fighting. It is the jealousy each child feels because he has to share his mother and father with the other siblings. If it were up to him, each child would gladly flush the others down the drain and that, as far as he is concerned, would solve the problem. Obviously you cannot do that, yet you can do some things which at least partially gratify this desire of your child's.

You can give each child special time alone with you, on a one-to-one basis. This way the child is getting what he wants, at least for a while—a relationship with you that he does not have to share with anyone else. Giving each child regular time alone with you will help to take the edge off the sibling fighting.

Another thing you can do is to let each child take a friend along when the family goes on a weekend trip or vacation. Your child will often be so busy and occupied with his friend he will not have as much time for fighting or getting into mischief with his brother or sister.

A word of caution: If your children want to take friends, but one child's friend cannot go, it's better to take no friends at all. The child without a companion will feel left out. He may want to spend all his time hanging around you. Worse yet, he is likely to try to steal the attention of his sibling's friend, causing a lot of bickering and jealousy.

But remember, no matter how many discipline strategies you use for sibling bickering, you will never be able to completely eliminate it (unless one child manages to do the others in!). All you can hope to do is to reduce the intensity of the fighting to reasonable limits. If you succeed in accomplishing that, you have accomplished a great deal!

14. *What sorts of things can I do with a six-year-old and a ten-year-old to maintain the emotional rapport you say is so important as a foundation for discipline?*

It is easy to maintain rapport with your children when they are in the stage of middle childhood. There are a whole bunch of indoor games you can play, on either a one-to-one or a family basis: checkers, chess, Monopoly, and card games such as hearts, poker, or blackjack.

Many parents make a common mistake playing these games with, say, a nine-year-old. The father and daughter may be playing checkers or chess, for example. The parent plays at an adult level and keeps winning game after game. Pretty soon the child grows discouraged and doesn't want to play anymore.

Instead of this, let me suggest an alternative that can make the playing of the game quite stimulating and challenging for you as a parent. Try to make enough errors so that your child wins approximately 50 percent of the time. It is important not to give away to the child what you are doing. It is quite a challenge to a parent to lose about 50 percent of the time without the child's catching on. For example, while playing chess you manage not to see that your Queen is in danger, and when your daughter captures the Queen, you exclaim, "Holy smoke, how could I be so dumb as to get my Queen captured!"

Besides indoor games, there are many other things you and your child can enjoy toegther: going to the movies, watching sports events, playing horseshoes, playing miniature golf, playing croquet, going fishing, going camping—and many other things. In all these activities you are not requiring anything of your child. The two of you are simply enjoying some activity together. And this is building a solid and deep rapport between you.

15. *I've been thinking of offering my ten-year-old five dollars for every A he gets on his report card in order to stimulate him to work harder in school. What do you think?*

Don't. Many parents try something like this, offering money or presents if the child gets certain grades. It almost never works. Superficially this approach sounds like what I have called a positive reward system, but the structure of this one dooms it to failure. Here's why. First of all, the reward is too far away in the future to motivate the child day after day, in the here and now. A reward that doesn't take place until the end of the semester has little motivating power at the beginning and middle of the semester. Second, the reward is not for the child's working on school assignments but for getting a certain grade. Grades are chancy things, for a number of reasons. Some teachers take pride in not giving *any* A's. Or a teacher may be biased or prejudiced against your child and not grade him fairly. Your child may, in reality, not be as intelligent as you think he is and not actually capable of getting A's. In over twenty years of clinical practice I have never seen a system such as this one actually work.

If you do wish to start a positive reward system for your child's schoolwork, then let it be based on *effort* rather than grades. Set up a daily reward or a checklist for each hour spent on schoolwork each night. This is something your child can realistically do. It is not dependent on a number of chancy factors as grades are. And the reward is immediate each day, not far off in the future at the end of the semester.

16. *I'm a single mother with a six-year-old and an eight-year-old. My divorce was final just last week, and I feel absolutely overwhelmed in coping with my two children. What can I do?*

You sound as if what you need is an emotional support system. Here you are, a single parent, faced for the first time with 100 percent of the responsibility of handling two children. Married friends simply cannot understand what you are going through because they are in an entirely different psychological situation.

I think you need to find some new friends and make contact with other single mothers who are in your position. So the first problem you need to deal with is not with your children but with yourself. Your problem is basically that you are having to expend a lot of emotional output in working and coping with the children without enough emotional input from other people to meet your needs. Your input-output emotional ratio is out of balance. So your job is to find where you can get more input for yourself. No one else can do this for you. Only you can solve the problem of finding more emotional input.

Everybody has heard of marriage counseling. But I think we need more divorce counseling. Divorce is one of the most traumatic experiences that can happen to a person, and everyone who goes through a divorce would benefit from counseling during this upsetting process.

So if you can afford either individual or group counseling, I would certainly recommend it. This would be another way in which you could receive the understanding and emotional support to help you handle your life and your children successfully.

The trouble boils down to this: If you are sick with the flu and have a temperature of 103, you cannot cope with the children as adequately as when you are well. The psychological wounds of the divorce and their impact on you are as disabling as any illness, and you cannot cope with your children when you are in this condition. So first you have to find ways to "get well" and restore your own psychological equilibrium before you can handle your children successfully.

17. *My six-year-old son whines whenever he doesn't get his way·or when I have to say "no" to him. It's really getting on my nerves.*

Whining is easy to deal with. Give him a Time Out (chap. 6) each time he whines. If he wants to whine while he's in his own room during a Time Out, that's up to him. The consistent use of Time Outs is usually very effective in breaking a child of this habit.

18. *Do nine-year-old boys ever talk in a normal tone of voice?*

No. I'm assuming you mean "normal tone of voice" as far as adults are concerned. If you mean, "Do nine-year-old boys ever talk in a normal tone of voice for nine-year-old boys," the answer is "Always."

19. *My seven-year-old is a bed-wetter. What can I do about it?*

When a child is wetting the bed after the age of five, you should have your doctor check him to see if there is any physical reason for this. Ninety-nine times out of 100 there is no physical cause. This means that the reason is psychological. There are two ways to lick the problem.

Go to the toy store and pick out a supply of the kind of inexpensive toy trinkets beloved by young children. Put these in a strong, sturdy box with a lock on it. Then explain things to your child as follows: "Richard, I know that it bothers you when you wet your bed at night. I also know that it isn't your fault and no one should blame you, because you're asleep when you do it. So if you wake up and your bed is wet, all you have to do is change your sheets, and it's no big deal. But if you wake up dry in the morning, then you get one of these toys."

When you speak to your child in this way you are communicating directly with his subconscious mind and saying, "If you don't wet the bed, you'll get a toy." This solution is effective with many children over a couple of months.

If the first solution doesn't work, you can try the second. Buy a device in the Sears catalog which consists of two pads of metal foil with a fiberglass lining between them. With the first drop of urine, the dampness of the lining activates a buzzer. This device works strictly on conditioning principles. It does not shock or harm the child in any way. At first the child wets and the device wakes him up, but gradually the child is conditioned to wake up as he is *about to wet*. Then he can go to the bathroom and, *voilà!*—the bed-wetting problem is solved.

Be sure to explain to your child just how the "bedwetting alarm clock" works, and demonstrate its operation. You want him to feel that this is *his* device to cure *his* bed-wetting, not something that someone is forcing on him.

Sometimes medications prescribed by your physician will help either of these psychological methods to work.

20. *How can I raise my six-year-old boy and my nine-year-old girl in a nonsexist way?*

First we need to understand the psychological facts about boys and girls and then we must decide what we mean by sexism. The research that has been done on boys and girls (and it is considerable) suggests that the two are actually very different psychologically. For example, at the same age, girls are approximately two years more mature than boys, up to high-school age. Boys are more thing-oriented and girls are more people-oriented. But just because boys and girls are *different* psychologically doesn't mean that one sex should be favored over the other. *That* is sexism.

In practice, this means that women should be paid as much as men for the same job in industry. Women should not be excluded from any job because of their sex. Children's books should not depict men exclusively as doctors and women exclusively as nurses, men only as lawyers and women only as secretaries. It means that if it's good for a little boy to learn karate for self-defense, it's equally good for a little girl to learn karate. My slogan for a truly nonsexist society is, Different but equal. Different in psychological makeup but equal in opportunity to fulfill their individual potentials.

Now, how can you implement this nonsexist philosophy with your youngsters as they grow up?

First, you can make sexism and nonsexism a topic that you talk about from time to time at the dinner table. Just as you will discuss racism and help your child to be nonracist, you can talk about sexism and help your child to be nonsexist.

Second, you can encourage your children, particularly your little girl, to read nonsexist books. Admittedly, there are many children's books full of the old sexist stereotypes, but when she reads one of these, you can point out the stereotypes for her.

Third, you can discuss with your children what they want to be when they grow up, and help them to make this decision without limiting themselves in any sexist way. Of course you have to be realistic about this in terms of their intelligence levels. For example, if neither your boy nor your girl has a high enough intelligence level to become a doctor or a lawyer, then it would be foolish for you to encourage these vocations for them, regardless of any sexist stereotypes.

Fourth, you and your spouse can set a good example for your children by not making sexist discriminations any more than you would make racial discriminations.

21. *At what age should I begin preparing my child for puberty?*

I think age ten is an excellent one at which to begin preparing your child for puberty and providing the sexual knowledge he will need at adolescence. I choose ten for several reasons. For one thing, ten is an age of equilibrium, and at this age your child is more amenable to a heart-to-heart talk with you. At eleven or twelve you run into preadolescence, when your youngster becomes more abrasive and much more difficult to talk to. Also, youngsters usually begin masturbating at twelve, and sometimes at eleven, and you want your talk to precede this.

Here's how I would go about handling the situation. Fortunately, you have two excellent books to help you, both by the same author, Dr. Wardell Pomeroy. One is called *Boys and Sex*, and the other *Girls and Sex*. (Incidentally, I applaud Dr. Pomeroy's nonsexist wisdom in writing *separate* books for boys and girls, rather than trying to lump them together in one book called *Children and Sex*.) I suggest you give one of these books to your youngster at the tenth birthday, but take the child aside and give it to her or him privately.

Then you can say something like this, but in your own words, "Jimmy, do you know what *puberty* is? [Chances are 99 to 1 that he doesn't.] Well, let's put it this way, Do you know that you have different glands in your body, and what these glands do? [He probably doesn't know that either.] Well, you have a bunch of different glands and the purpose of these glands is to manufacture chemicals called hormones, which go into your bloodstream and help your body work right. For instance, your pituitary gland has a lot to do with how tall you are. If a person's pituitary gland is not manufacturing enough chemicals, he will be very small, maybe a dwarf. If your pituitary gland is making too many chemicals, then you might be seven feet tall or even a giant.

"All the glands in your body start functioning from the moment you are born, except one. That one is your sex gland. Your sex gland hasn't started to function yet. In a few years it will, and then it will be manufacturing hormones that will go into your bloodstream and make you think of sex and girls. It may give you feelings you've never had before. This can be scary. That's why I'm giving you this book, *Boys and Sex*, so that you can understand the new sexual things you will need to know when your sex gland starts working. After you read this book we can talk about it again if you like. We can discuss anything about sex that you would like to know."

Above all, be sure to tell your son or daughter that masturbation is a normal thing for teenagers to do, and that they do not need to feel bad or guilty about it. If your youngster seems embarrassed about discussing the subject of sex with you, don't push it, but be sure he has the book to read on his own.

22. *My ten-year-old child wanted to learn to play the trumpet, but now that he has started, he likes the lessons but he won't practice regularly. What can I do?*

This is a question I've heard from parents for over twenty years. From the parents' point of view, if they are going to buy an instrument and pay for lessons, then, by George, their youngster is going to practice! However, they find it very difficult to make him do it. They ask me to advise them what to do.

If your youngster seems to have real musical talent and is going to make his living as a musician, classical or popular, then I think it is worth it for a parent to go through the hassle of making the child practice. But in over twenty years I haven't run into a single case like this! All of the children I heard about were kids who were learning to play an instrument purely for recreation. In that case I don't think it is worth forcing the child to practice. If the purpose of learning to play an instrument is to have fun, what fun is there in being forced to practice? So you can let the child have the lessons and practice when he wants to (or perhaps devise a positive reward system for practicing). Or you can discontinue the lessons. Forcing a youngster to do something that is supposed to be fun just doesn't make sense to me.

Incidentally, if your child asks you what would be a good instrument for him to learn to play, I would advise the piano or the guitar, which are great for singing along with. A guitar also offers another social advantage to a teenager. When the crowd is at the beach or having a picnic or whatever, an adolescent who can play a guitar has a built-in social enhancer.

23. *Do you believe it is good for a child to go to summer camp? If so, at what age should I send him?*

Yes, I think that it is psychologically helpful to send a child to a good sleep-away summer camp. The YMCA and YWCA usually have excellent camps of this nature, and there are also a large number of independent summer camps. If at all possible you should drive up for a day and see the camp in action before sending your youngster. Use the same general standards I suggested in chapters 23 and 24 for picking a good nursery school. Observe the teachers and leaders in action. What "vibes" do you pick up from the session? Is the general atmosphere warm and friendly?

Before sending a child to a sleep-away camp it would be wise to send him to a good day camp for a week when he is about eight years old. Then, when he is nine, you could probably send him to day camp for two weeks. By the time he is ten I would feel he is old enough and has had enough experience with camping to go away for a week. By eleven you could increase his camping time to two weeks.

The main psychological advantage a child gets from summer camp is that he is learning to function without his parents and to adjust to a new and strange peer group all by himself. It is a maturing experience for him to learn how to do this.

24. *My child is nine and in the fourth grade and just beginning to have homework to do. What's the best way to handle this?*

First of all, let me say that the fourth grade is the proper time for your child to begin to have homework. In my opinion there is absolutely no reason for a child to have homework in the first three grades.

When homework first begins it is best for you to explain to your child that homework and school are his work, just as mother and father have their work. Tell him that if he needs help with his homework at any time, you will be willing to help him. But do not hover over him, asking him what homework he has to do tonight, making sure he has finished his homework, or checking his homework. In other words, leave it up to him to get his homework done.

This is the way I handled the matter of homework for all three of my children, and it worked out fine. But suppose it doesn't? Suppose the teacher reports to you that your child is not doing his homework consistently, and is falling behind in class?

In this case I suggest that you work out either a positive reward system (chap. 3) or a contracting system (chap. 4) that enables your youngster to get some reward each night for doing his homework. Be sure to avoid the kind of far-in-the-future motivation I described in question 15.

Summary

During the stage of middle childhood, parents often find a number of discipline problems arising in connection with the school, the peer group, or the home. Many of these parents use punishment power as their only method of dealing with problems. Schools also seem to be unaware that there are other ways to handle discipline difficulties. This is highly unfortunate. Punishment power violates The Law of the Soggy Potato Chip and usually only makes matters worse.

Armed with the information in this book, you will probably not make these mistakes with your youngster. You will have begun in the earlier preschool period using methods that do not involve punishment, such as the positive reward system, Time Outs, contracting, the feedback technique, and others. By the time your youngsters get to middle childhood, they will be accustomed to more reasonable and loving discipline methods, and more likely to obey you.

Your child's personality will be basically stabilized between the ages of six and ten, and if you continue to use the positive discipline methods you began in the preschool period, you should have no serious problems now.

26

PREADOLESCENCE

Overview of the Stage

I said in the previous chapter that your child's personality in middle childhood is reasonably stable from the years of six through ten. But the stability of middle childhood cannot go on permanently, or a child would never be able to grow up psychologically and become an adult.

Previous stages have each had *positive* developmental tasks for your child to master. This is the first stage in which the task is *disorganization*.

This is not a permanent disorganization of your child's personality, but the kind that makes room for the new constellation of psychological patterns that constitute adulthood. The old childhood patterns must be broken up so that a higher organization of his personality can take place. The first step in this breakup occurs in preadolescence.

Let me use this analogy. It's as if your child owns a lot on which he has built his "house of childhood." In order for him to build a "house of adulthood," he must first tear down his old house. This tearing-down process usually begins around his eleventh birthday, when the stage of preadolescence starts, and lasts until approximately his thirteenth birthday.

A parent can usually tell quite easily when his child has shifted from the stage of middle childhood to preadolescence because the child suddenly becomes obnoxious in almost every way you can think of. I remember vividly how my daughter, Robin, let us know that she had entered the new stage. One evening I asked her to take the trash out, as I had done many evenings for years. She had always done it, although sometimes she had grumbled a bit. But this time she let out a blast: "ALL RIGHT, IF THAT'S WHAT LIFE HAS TO BE LIKE IN THIS DICTATORIAL FAMILY IN WHICH CHILDREN HAVE NO RIGHTS. IF YOU WANT ME TO TAKE THE TRASH OUT AND WILL FORCE ME TO DO IT IF I REFUSE, THEN I WILL BE YOUR SLAVE AND TAKE THE TRASH OUT." "Holy smoke," I said to myself. "She's entered preadolescence!"

This stage usually hits parents with a wallop. Your stable, reasonable, and well-behaved child seems suddenly to have taken an overdose of Obnoxious Pills. Your most reasonable parental requests—that your child wear a sweater if it is cold, or that he go to bed at a decent hour—will be met with surly outbursts of irritation or snotty remarks. The parents of a preadolescent can usually be readily recognized by the harassed gray look they constantly wear.

Unbeknownst to them, the preadolescent has been engaged in a careful psychological study of his parents for many years. During preadolescence he will choose precisely those actions and attitudes that he knows will most irritate his parents. For example, if he knows that school grades are very important to them, his grades will suddenly turn downward. If he knows that foul language will shock them, his speech will soon begin to make a longshoreman blush. Wherever his parents are emotionally vulnerable, there he will stage his psychological commando raids.

This kind of behavior is so difficult for most of us parents to handle that it is hard for us to see how important and necessary it is for the child to behave this way. He has no room on his lot to build his new house of adulthood until he has demolished his house of childhood. It is important for us to realize that no matter how uncomfortable this process is for us, every preadolescent needs the chance to let out some type of wild behavior in one form or another. The preadolescent who never steps on adult corns, defies adult rules, or gets into trouble will have a great deal of difficulty making it successfully through adolescence into adulthood.

So no matter what specific discipline problems you may encounter with your child, you may as well reconcile yourself to the fact that preadolescence is a rough stage generally for parents to live through.

1. *Our twelve-year-old daughter is just plain boy crazy. There's no other word to describe it. Should we be concerned, and if so, what should we do about it?*

Being boy crazy is perfectly normal behavior at this age. And who's harmed by it? Besides, you couldn't do anything about it anyway. So let her be boy crazy and enjoy it. Believe me, there are lots of things she could be doing at this age that are much worse.

2. *What can I do about the constant barrage of caustic criticism I get from my eleven-year-old boy? According to him, whatever I'm doing is wrong, and he doesn't hesitate to tell me how wrong I am.*

Let me answer this question by describing a personal incident. When my older son was eleven, one of the things about me that he singled out for criticism was my driving. One afternoon he and I were driving somewhere and I was undergoing a constant barrage of criticism from him. "Dad, didn't anybody ever teach you how to come to a stop? You should ease up on the gas and then slowly apply the brake. You're not supposed to jam on the brake at the last minute. And by the way, are you English or something? I notice you tend to drive on the lefthand side of the road! Why don't you stay to the right of the yellow line the way you're supposed to? I don't mind you risking your own life, if you have some psychological compulsion to drive the way you do, but it's my life too, y'know." And so on and so on. Well, after about fifteen minutes it got to me. I turned to my son and said, through clenched teeth: "Randy, I'm sick and tired of your blankety-blank snotty comments about my driving. Now just keep your blankety-blank mouth shut until we get where we're going." He didn't say a word from then on. I cleaned up my language a little for this book, but I think you get the general idea. When you have had it up to your eyebrows with your child's typical preadolescent sarcastic remarks, let him know it in no uncertain terms.

3. *My eleven-year-old boy is starting to defy me. I don't mind letting him sound off and express his feelings, but he is going beyond that. He is refusing to comply with my requests. When I ask him to carry in the groceries he gives me a snotty look and says, "Do it yourself." Or if I ask him to*

clean up some milk he's spilled, he says, "I'm not your slave,"
and walks into the living room. How can I handle this?

You can use the *no-bank*. When you ask him to do something or stop doing something, and he refuses, say, "I asked you to clean up the milk and you refused, so I guess I'll have to make a deposit in the no-bank." Then take a small notebook (which you have bought for this purpose) and make a single short mark in it. He will wonder what you are doing and he may ask you about it. Say, "You'll probably find out some day." Keep making marks in the no-bank whenever he refuses to obey you.

Then sooner or later he will ask you for something. "Can I go with Tommy to the movies this Friday night?" Answer him, "I'll have to consult your no-bank and see if it's got any deposits in it." You see one mark in it. You run a pencil through the mark and say, "You want to go to the movies with Tommy Friday night. That cancels out one deposit in your no-bank." (In other words, he can't go.) He will get the idea very quickly. You may get an explosion from him, but stand fast. He will very soon realize that he is only penalizing himself when he refuses to obey you.

Kids are smart, and here's a warning about one trick he may try. He may suddenly ask you if he can do a whole bunch of things, solely for the purpose of canceling out deposits in his no-bank. If he tries this strategy, just say, "I see through what you're trying to do. You're asking me if you can do all of these things just to cancel out deposits in your no-bank. Sorry, but it won't work."

4. *The manager of our local grocery store caught my eleven-year-old girl stealing last week. He phoned me, and after I went down and talked with him, he said he wouldn't go to the police about it. What should I do to punish her?*

If you think she has been sufficiently chastened by the experience, you do not need to punish her. She has learned her lesson.

But if she has a defiant attitude and you think that the only lesson she has learned is the Eleventh Commandment, "Don't get caught," then you can do something like this. Let's suppose she stole some things worth approximately five dollars. Tell her: "Since the things you stole were worth about five dollars, I'm going to deduct half of your allowance each week until we have accumulated five dollars, and then we will give it to some worthwhile charity." (You should deduct half rather than all of her allowance because the psychological effect on her is greater.) If she should steal again, do the same thing. If she steals something worth a huge amount, say fifty dollars, then you could deduct money equalling half the value of what she stole. This technique will impress on her very forcefully that every time she steals something *she loses money*.

5. *Our son used to be home and part of the family. Now, at eleven, he's always at one friend's house or another. His friends' parents are much more lenient than we are, and I don't like these outside influences. How can we get him to stay home more or bring his friends here?*

You can't. What you are describing is the loss of the tight control over him that you formerly had when his world was pretty much circumscribed by your own family. Now he is branching out beyond your family, and he will be branching out still further when he gets into adolescence. What you describe is typical of the preadolescent child, and there is nothing you can do about it. Oh, you can issue rigid rules for him and try to get tough with him, but it will almost always backfire. If you try the "get-tough" policy, you may turn him against you and have some real trouble on your hands. I suggest you try to yield gracefully. Accept the fact that he's moving into ever-widening circles of life, and that you are inevitably losing the tight control over him you once had.

6. *Don't you think that an eleven-year-old girl is too old to still be sleeping with her teddy bear?*

Why not? No harm is being done by such an innocuous habit. Why make a fuss about it or let it upset you? Let's put it this way: I don't know of any grown women who still sleep with teddy bears. So somewhere between age eleven and adulthood, your daughter will voluntarily give up sleeping with her teddy bear. If her friends tease her about it, she'll give it up sooner, but why not leave it entirely up to her?

7. *I have heard that there are a lot of drugs around the junior high school my twelve-year-old attends. What should I do about it?*

First, let me tell you what *not* to do about it. Do not panic and start lecturing him about drugs and how he'd better not start fooling around with them, etc. This is what I call the "Don't put butter on the couch" mistake that many parents make. If you tell a four-year-old, as you are leaving him with a baby-sitter, "Now be sure and don't put butter on the couch!" you can bet your prize petunias that when you return you will find the couch well buttered. He didn't have the faintest idea of buttering the couch until you put the idea in his mind and gave him the challenge.

So don't make that mistake with your twelve-year-old. He is attending junior high school and you are aware that there are drugs at his school. But you have absolutely no evidence that he is involved in the drug scene. Until you have such evidence, say absolutely nothing to him about it. No lectures, no moralizing, no warnings. The first thing for you to do is to zip your lip.

Second, get some information about drugs. You may be surprised to learn that adolescents often have more accurate information about drugs than their parents do. Of course if this is true, it reduces the authority of the parents on the subject of drugs to practically zero. Here are some excellent books that will help you understand drugs and the drug scene: *A Parent's Guide to the Prevention and Control of Drug Abuse,* by Paul Goldhill; *Overcoming Drugs,* by Donald Louria; *You, Your Child and Drugs,* by the staff of the Child Study Association of America; *Marijuana, A Signal of Misunderstanding: The Official Report of The National Commission on Marijuana and Drug Abuse.* Most parents actually know very little about drugs and the drug scene. Don't make their mistake. Do your homework and know more about drugs than your twelve-year-old does.

Third, be honest with your child about drugs. If you are not, you will destroy your credibility with your child. For example, suppose your twelve-year-old says, "Smoking a joint of grass [marijuana] every once in a while actually does less harm to you than the pack a day of cigarettes that you two smoke." He's right, and you had better admit it honestly.

This doesn't mean, of course, that your smoking cigarettes should be an automatic license for him to smoke marijuana. You can say something like this. "Herb, you're right. And frankly I wish I had never started smoking cigarettes. They are easy to get addicted to and very hard to give up. But just because I'm hooked on cigarettes doesn't mean that it's good for you to smoke marijuana." Then you can tell him the specific reasons you think it is not good for him to smoke marijuana. (Incidentally, although marijuana is technically not a drug, I am classing it here as one, for convenience of discussion.)

Being honest with your child includes not using such false reasoning about drugs as one classic I have heard many parents use: "All heroin addicts first started on marijuana." This implies that smoking marijuana causes a person to become a heroin addict, which is not true. Let's say for argument's sake that all heroin addicts did start by smoking marijuana. But millions of kids have smoked marijuana and did not go on to heroin. Or, for that matter, all heroin addicts started on mother's milk or a bottle, but that doesn't prove that this is what led them to become heroin addicts.

So know your facts about drugs. And if your child points out inconsistencies in your reasoning, be honest enough to admit it if he's right and you're wrong.

Fourth, avoid prying and becoming a private detective instead of a parent to your child. You wouldn't believe the things some parents do when they get panicked by the thought that their child might be using drugs. They go through his room with a fine-tooth comb. They listen in on phone conversations. If your youngster has thought of trying drugs but hasn't yet done so, the private-detective approach will probably push him over the line.

You may be wondering, "How will I know if my child is using drugs?" Many articles in parents' magazines or books advise parents to watch for certain symptoms that supposedly indicate the use of drugs. The list of "symptoms" may include such things as redness of the eyes, a drastic increase or decrease in appetite, an excessive taste for sweets, anxiety, sloppy dress, and the like. I think this approach is all wrong for parents.

For example, suppose your twelve-year-old suddenly begins burning incense in his room. This may be on the list of symptoms, since many adolescents use incense to cover up the odor of marijuana. But on the other hand, your twelve-year-old may be burning incense because it is an "in" thing to do and denotes that he is in the "big-time" now. A list of symptoms may be very helpful to a professional, but it may only turn a parent into a worried conclusion-jumper.

Instead of a list of symptoms against which to measure

your child, I suggest only one commonsense measure which any parent can apply. Your child is twelve years old. You have known him for a good many years. You know what his basic personality structure is like. If this child, whom you have known so well, suddenly begins to act weird, if his behavior becomes strange and off-beat, then you may suspect he is using drugs. (Even if your child is not on drugs, it would be unnatural for a parent to ignore strange behavior on the part of his child.) So you can say to him something like this: "Bert, I'm concerned about you. You have been acting in ways that are strange and not like you. [Tell him specifically what these ways are.] Because of this strange behavior, I get the feeling you are using drugs. Is that true?"

If you discover he has been using drugs, avoid playing the heavy-handed parent, who thunders, "Well, I won't have it! You're going to give up drugs immediately or you're in big trouble!" If there is any approach calculated to make the situation worse, I don't know what it could be. Believe it or not, I know a psychiatrist who discovered his son was using drugs and bellowed at him, "What are you trying to do—ruin my reputation in the community? You're going to get off drugs immediately or so many bad things will happen to you you won't believe it!" This neither brought father and son closer together nor resolved the drug situation.

When you discover your youngster has been using drugs, you should have a heart-to-heart talk with him. You need to find out information from him. What caused him to get into drugs in the first place? What has he been using? How does he feel about the whole situation? You can obtain this information from him only by understanding him and using the feedback technique, not by berating and scolding him.

Once you have gotten the information you need, I suggest you use the mutual problem-solving technique (chap. 11) or contracting (chap. 4) in order to work out a solution to your child's problem.

In general, your chances of working out a solution at age twelve are pretty good because he has not yet entered the defiant stage of early or late adolescence. He may be defying you verbally, but underneath he is still a little boy looking up to you as an authority (something which he will not be doing in later adolescence).

If you and your child cannot work out a solution to the problem by yourselves, then I would strongly advise you to consult *together* a professional counselor or perhaps a pastor. Don't let the problem continue. Nip it in the bud in preadolescence or it will snowball in adolescence.

8. *Recently I found one of my bras and panties, along with a lipstick, hidden under some clothes in one of the drawers of my twelve-year-old's clothes cabinet. I guess I really didn't want to face what it might mean, because I did nothing about it. Then just yesterday I came home unexpectedly and found him parading around in his room dressed up in my bra and panties, wearing lipstick. What should I do?*

It is obvious that your son is having some sexual problems or problems in gender identity. These problems will not go away; they can only get worse. I suggest that he needs immediate professional help from a psychologist, psychiatrist, or psychiatric social worker. Simply tell him, "Steve, I think you have some sexual problems that you need help with. So I've made an appointment for the two of us to see Dr. Nelson." If he protests and says, "Oh, Ma, I was just fooling around. What harm is there in fooling around?" Simply say, "I know that you have some sex problems. I love you very much and I'm going to see that you get help."

It will be very helpful if you and your husband can work together on this. But he may be one of those fathers who thinks, "This psychology stuff is a lot of bunk." If this is his attitude, you will simply have to proceed without him.

9. *My eleven-year-old never comes to where I am—in the kitchen, for example—to make a request. Instead he stands in his room and bellows, "Mother! I need my jacket! Where is it?" This type of behavior is grating on my nerves more and more.*

This is easy to change. Have a talk with your son and explain that if he wants something from you, or if he wants you to do something for him, he is to come to wherever you are and tell you in a reasonable tone of voice. If he stand in another part of the house and bellows, a strange thing will happen to your ears. They will plug up and you will be unable to hear him.

I suggested this approach to one mother who had this problem. She followed my instructions. At first the boy continued his usual ways. But his mother did not respond at all. Finally in frustration he left his room and came to the kitchen. "Didn't you hear me calling you, Mom?" he demanded irately. "No, Harold," she said, "as I explained to you, from now on my ears will plug up whenever you yell from some other room of the house instead of coming to where I am and talking to me in a normal tone of voice." Harold tried his old strategies a few more times that week, and from then on he adopted the new method of coming to where his mother was and speaking to her in a reasonable tone.

10. *My eleven-year-old knows he's supposed to be home at six o'clock for dinner. But often he comes in at seven or seven thirty. I'm getting sick of this and sick of having to warm his dinner up for him.*

The use of natural consequences should work wonders here, expecially with eleven-year-olds, who are notoriously ravenous eating machines. Tell your son that dinner will begin at six and that when dinnertime is over there will be no more opportunity to eat. Stop heating dinners up for him, and let him suffer the natural consequences of getting home late for dinner.

If this should not work, you can still use the positive reward system, contracting, or the mutual problem-solving technique to solve this problem. For example, with the positive reward system, you can say, stating it in a positive form, "Jerry, every time you're on time for dinner at night, you can watch TV that night. If you're not on time for dinner, you miss your opportunity to watch TV." Always state the proposition in a positive form. Do *not* say, "If you're not on time for dinner, there's no TV that night for you, young man!"

11. *My twelve-year-old girl is driving me up the wall with what she does to her clothes. I'm not kidding when I say that she never hangs them up. She just drapes them on the floor in an interesting collage and leave them there. I tell her to pick them up and she says she will, but she never does. It makes me absolutely furious!*

I suggest you get a big cardboard box and label it "Goodwill" or "Salvation Army." Then tell your daughter that once a week (and she will not know just when) you will descend on her room with the Big Box. Every piece of clothing left on the floor will be put into the box and immediately taken to the Goodwill or Salvation Army. The visits of Big Box will continue once each week. Meanwhile you should buy her no new clothes until she learns to hang them up instead of dropping them on the floor.

Your daughter is faced with a no-win situation. Since you control the purse strings, she can't get any new clothes without your permission. And if she keep up her old habits, the clothes she now has will gradually disappear. What else can she do but change her behavior?

My experience has been that one or two visits by Big Box are usually sufficient to cause a child to change her clothes-dropping behavior. But if your child is especially stubborn, she may need to lose everything except one or two outfits before she decides to change her ways. Be patient, and I guarantee you her behavior will change.

When I explain this method to some mothers they say, "I'm certainly not going to give away clothes that I've paid good money for!" Then I say, "Fine! Then get over being exasperated when your daughter drops her clothes all over the floor, and your problem is solved!"

12. *How can I cope with an eleven-year-old son who hates being clean?*

You can get your son to take baths or showers by insisting on it, but you cannot get him to *want* to be clean. Being clean is not high on an eleven-year-old boy's list of priorities. It's just not in the nature of the species at this stage. A typical eleven-year-old believes that he should take a bath or shower at least once a year, whether he needs it or not.

Observe an eleven-year-old boy going away to camp. He is wearing a T-shirt, pants, and sneakers, and carrying a suitcase or duffel bag that has been lovingly packed by his mother with a change of clothes for each day he is away at camp. When he returns from camp he will be wearing the same T-shirt and pants he was wearing when he left, which can practically stand up by themselves now. He will be carrying his suitcase or duffel bag, which will contain virgin changes of clothing for each day in the week, completely untouched by human hands.

So insist on his taking a shower or bath whenever you feel he needs it. But don't expect any motivation on *his* part to get squeaky clean.

13. *When our twelve-year-old son's friends come over to play, our nine-year-old son hangs around and tries to get attention. Unfortunately, he makes a pest of himself, and they retaliate by some not-so-kind teasing. It's just not a good situation. Should I step in, and if so, how?*

Yes, I think you should step in, and the simplest way to handle the situation is to get your nine-year-old to leave the older boys alone. Encourage him to have a friend over, or go over to a friend's house to play, or to find something interesting to do by himself. But tell him to leave the older boys alone.

14. *Our two daughters, eleven and fourteen, have to share a bedroom. The younger one is neat. The older one is not only messy, but she "borrows" her younger sister's belongings whenever the mood strikes her. Their constant quarrels are having a bad effect on the whole family. What to do?*

I would start with a little carpentry and environmental control. Put a dividing wall down the center of the room and make it into two rooms. Then give each girl a lock and keys for her own room. This simple change of the environment will help a great deal to reduce the quarrels. With regard to the quarrels that still remain, consult chapter 24, question 6. You could use such methods as Time Outs, a positive reward system for not quarreling, and the mutual problem-solving technique to handle any problems that remain.

15. *You have said that preadolescence is a difficult stage for parents to live through. Do you have any general overall suggestions to help us survive this stage?*

First, try to keep rules to an absolute minimum during this stage. A preadolescent reacts to a rule like a bull does to a red flag.

Second, concentrate on making sure your child obeys the few rules that are important to you regarding his *actions.*

Third, try to ignore your child's verbal flak as much as possible. When it really begins to get to you I would tell him in no uncertain terms to knock it off.

Fourth, maximize opportunities for maintaining emotional rapport during this difficult stage. Take him to movies, sports events, camping trips, and whatever.

Fifth (and I mean this quite seriously), look in on your

child for a few minutes after he is asleep. Somehow a child who can get on your nerves just terribly when he is awake and being difficult can look so helpless and appealing when he is asleep! A few minutes spent watching him when he is asleep can give you renewed courage to face him the next day.

Sixth, remember that the obnoxious behavior of this stage is necessary, but above all that *it is temporary.* It is not going to last forever—at the most two years! I mean that to be a comforting thought!

Seventh, follow these three simple rules for coping with your child's behavior during this stage:

1. Roll with the punches!
2. Roll with the punches!
3. Roll with the punches!

Summary

There is just no way around it. Unless you are fortunate enough to have a very easy-to-raise child, preadolescence is a tough stage for the average parent to live through.

This has been true for the parents I have dealt with for over twenty years, and this has been my own experience as a parent. The reason it is so tough is due to the unique developmental task of preadolescence. The task of this stage is to tear down all the childhood patterns of behavior in order to make room for adolescence, and later adulthood. In practical terms what "tearing down all the childhood patterns of behavior" means is that your child is suddenly going to become negativistic, defiant, stubborn, sassy, and just plain obnoxious in many, many ways.

After having a child who is reasonable and not too difficult to get along with for the five years of middle childhood, it comes as a considerable shock to the parental system to discover you have a new (and usually unpleasant) child on your hands. In many ways, he will remind you of a two-year-old, except that he is older, bigger, and has many more sophisticated ways of expressing his newly found obnoxious personality.

I wish I could give you some magic new discipline methods you could use with a preadolescent. If I could, I would put them in a book, make my million dollars, and retire! Unfortunately, there are no magic methods for handling children in this difficult time. I can only offer you two bits of advice. First, try the discipline methods suggested in this book and hope for the best. Second, remember that this stage will be over in two years!

27

EARLY ADOLESCENCE

Overview of the Stage

The phenomenon of adolescence does not have firm and fixed time boundaries. However, we can arbitrarily define adolescence as that stage of development that takes place between puberty and the attainment of adulthood. Neither *puberty* nor *adulthood* can be defined precisely as to the time of their occurrence. But puberty usually takes place around twelve or thirteen. And we can arbitrarily define adulthood as beginning with the twenty-first birthday.

Making another arbitrary division, I will say that early adolescence encompasses ages thirteen, fourteen, and fifteen, while late adolescence spans the years from sixteen to twenty-one.

Both early and late adolescence share the same developmental task: *to form an ego identity that is different from one's parents.* In early adolescence the teenager is trying to answer the question "Who am I?" He does this pretty much within the framework of his family, although with considerable rebellion. In late adolescence he grapples with that question within the larger framework of society, where he must cope with the very real questions of occupational choice and sexual maturity.

An adolescent is a civil war within himself. Part of him wants to become emotionally independent of his parents and stand on his own two feet. But another part wants to remain a dependent child, with all the comfort and security associ-

293

ated with being emotionally dependent on his parents. Your teenager, particularly in early adolescence, will fluctuate back and forth between the wish for independence and the wish for dependence.

Early adolescence begins with puberty. At that time your child must cope with an entirely new phenomenon within himself: sexual urges. Not only does he need to adjust to these new and powerful impulses, he must also adjust to a new body, a body vastly different from the one he was accustomed to as a child.

In addition to adjusting to sexual changes and changes in his body and body image, the early adolescent now begins in earnest what he had been working toward tentatively in preadolescence: overcoming his emotional attachment to his parents and achieving emotional independence. The most typical way to break away from your parents is to revolt against them and find flaws in them. Only by becoming hostile and critical can the adolescent cut the emotional cords of childhood and launch out as a person in his own right.

But the early adolescent is still too shaky in his self-confidence to stand on his own emotionally. He needs his peer group. They give him the security he requires in order to cut the parental ties. The catchwords of adolescence are "Revolt!" and "Conform!" In order to be able to emotionally revolt against his parents he needs to slavishly conform to the mores and customs of his peer group.

The main mistake parents make when their adolescents revolt is to take it *personally*. They seem to believe that if they handle things right, their teenagers won't rebel against them. But realistically we don't have that choice. We only have a choice of whether our adolescents will go through a *normal* rebellion or an *abnormal* one, involving trouble with the law, drug abuse, or sexual difficulties. Unfortunately many parents do turn a basically normal rebellion into an abnormal one by the foolish and bungling way they handle it. So your task during this stage is to learn what to expect and how to deal with the reality of it, rather than focus on the emotional pain it may create in you. And don't blame yourself for the unsettled nature of the relationship. If you think back, perhaps you can remember your own adolescence, and the exasperation your parents felt toward you!

Now I need to say some important words about discipline methods. Many of the strategies I have talked about will work fine up to approximately age twelve. But when youngster becomes a teenager, many of them cease to w Let me tell you a story to show you what I mean.

One night my sixteen-year-old daughter was dressing for a date. She came into the living room looking really terrific. I made a fatal parental blunder. I said, "Robin, you look really great." She immediately turned on her heel and went back to her room. She came back ten minutes later dressed in her scroungiest shirt and her scruffiest pair of blue jeans, and that's what she wore on the date.

What had happened? Had I violated the law of the positive reward system? No, she had just shifted the need for rewards, as every teenager does, from her parents to her peer group. She did not want me, her parent, to praise her. So if I praised her for the way she looked, then she absolutely had to change her clothes. The positive reward system works fine with a girl of ten; it does not work so well with a girl of thirteen or sixteen.

Some of the discipline methods will continue to work effectively throughout the teenage years, since they are based upon relationships between equals rather than relationships between Big Parent and Little Child. The methods that will continue to work are the maintenance of emotional building of rapport, the feedback technique, the mutual problem-solving technique, the family council, and contracting.

1. *My thirteen-year-old son is constantly getting phone calls from girls. He never calls them, but they call him. Don't girls have any modesty nowadays?*

No. This is merely one of a thousand examples that could be cited to show how the customs and mores have changed from *your* teenage days to your son's teenage days. And one of the mistakes parents continually make is to expect today's teenagers to follow the social models left over from when the parents were teenagers. I would suggest that any parent caught in this "thirty years ago" trap use negative thinking (chap. 15) to get himself out of it.

2. *Since my father died of lung cancer four years ago, I've been very opposed to smoking. In fact, I'm downright intolerant of it. My fifteen-year-old daughter recently started to smoke in front of me. We've had many harsh words about this. Can't she prove her independence some other way?*

First of all, we don't really know why your daughter has started to smoke. There could be many reasons. You are jumping to the conclusion that she is smoking to prove her independence, which may or may not be true.

Regardless of why she is smoking, you are confronted with the fact that she is. What can you do about it? Unpleasant as it may be for you to accept, the answer is that you can do nothing about it. If you forbid her to smoke in your presence she will simply do it behind your back. I am assuming that she knows all the facts about lung cancer and heart attacks, particularly with the example of her grandfather's lung cancer before her.

She is doing something that is decidedly foolish, but there is absolutely nothing you can do about it. She has the right to do such foolish things as smoke. It does no good for you to assault her with emotional attacks and harsh words. They are not going to stop her from smoking. All they will do is to chip away at the emotional relationship between the two of you.

Instead I suggest you say something like this to her: "I've been thinking things over about your smoking, Melissa, and I've decided it was wrong of me to get on your back about it. I still think it's very foolish of you to smoke when you know it can hasten your death by lung cancer or a heart attack. But, after all, it's your life and not mine. So I'm going to try to respect your right to do things your own way, even though I may think some of them are very foolish."

That's one of the things that makes it difficult being the parent of a teenager. You can no longer force her to stop doing something you think is stupid (as long as it is within the law) as you could when she was a little girl.

3. *Short of using dynamite, is there any way I can dislodge my fourteen-year-old daughter from the telephone? (She doesn't have enough money for her own line and our tight budget won't allow for one either.)*

I would suggest you try working with her to find some way she can earn enough money to have her own telephone. Baby-sitting, yard work . . . there are all sorts of possibilities if the two of you put your creative imagination to work on it.

If she is able to get her own phone, leave her strictly alone to talk as long as she wants. Be sure that she keeps the door closed, so that it won't drive you crazy.

If you can't figure out a way for her to have her own phone, then try the use of some peaceful discipline method to solve this very common teenage problem. Try mutual problem-solving, contracting, or the family council.

If none of these methods work, then you may be forced to exert a little parental muscle. Set a rough time limit on how long she can be on the phone for one call. If she begins to overstep the agreed-upon time limit, tell her she must be off the phone in five minutes. If she still persists, hang up the phone.

4. *I'm divorced and have a demanding job. I need help around the apartment. How can I get my fourteen-year-old daughter to cooperate more? She won't even pick up her own things, let alone do anything else around the place.*

I suggest you begin by using the mutual problem-solving technique (chap. 11). Tell her how you see the problems of getting things done around the house, get her views, and then have a brainstorming session to see how the problems could be solved. Contracting (chap. 4) might also be used.

If your daughter is absolutely noncooperative and makes it plain that she has no intention whatsoever of helping you with the apartment, you can always, as a last resort, go on a parental strike. After all, you do control the parental purse strings. You can refuse to cook her meals, wash her clothes, buy new clothes for her, or give her an allowance. Use these drastic measures only if nothing else will work.

5. *My son and daughter, ages thirteen and fifteen, both hitchhike. They say it's safe and all the kids do it. I say it's dangerous, They say they're careful. I say even careful kids end up on the obituary page. What can I do to convince them it's dangerous and they should stop?*

This question reminds me of question 2 on smoking. Many times when teenagers are challenged about dangerous things such as smoking or hitchhiking, the catch is that they secretly think it can't happen to them. No one can reason with such illogical logic.

So I'm afraid all you can say to your teenagers is something like this: "We both know how dangerous hitchhiking is. You've seen stories in the papers and magazines about hitchhikers who were brutally murdered. I'm kind of fond of both of you kids and I'd hate to have to go down to the morgue some day to identify your bodies. It would spoil my lunch, it really would. So I'm going to suggest you drop the hitchhiking. But there's nothing I can do to prevent you from doing it behind my back. It's your life, not my life. I can only make suggestions, but the responsibility for your life and death rests with you."

You just might get through to them with this kind of message, which puts the responsibility for their lives where it belongs, in their own hands. On the other hand, you might *not* get through, and you'll have to live with their hitchhiking. It's certainly easier being the parent of a young child isn't it?

6. *At what age should girls and boys be told about birth control?*

As I indicated in chapter 25, ten is a good time to talk to children about sex, including birth control. If you didn't do it then, by all means do it now. I believe adolescents should know about all the different methods of birth control and how effective each one is. We read in many popular magazine articles that this is the age of the Pill and that many teenagers are on the Pill. Don't you believe it! Those of us who are therapists and hear the intimate details of adolescents' sexual lives know that only a small minority use it.

In my own experience, a large number of adolescents use coitus interruptus or "withdrawal," and haven't the faintest idea that they can get pregnant by this method. Very few adolescents use condoms. Do you know why? Because the boys are afraid to go up to the drugstore clerk and ask for them! Many adolescents use vaginal foam. Can you guess why? Because girls are *not* afraid to buy it in the drugstore (with a perfectly straight face a teenage girl will tell the clerk's she's buying it for her mother). And the adolescents who use vaginal foam have no idea how unreliable it is, or how many "vaginal foam babies" have been born in the United States.

I hope I have impressed upon you the importance of giving birth control information to early adolescents.

But some of you may be thinking, "If I give birth control information to my adolescent am I not condoning premarital sex relations?" Let me answer that question this way. Whether you approve or disapprove of premarital sex relations isn't going to change the fact that an increasingly large percentage of adolescents are doing it anyway. Fo⟨r⟩ solid information about this I suggest you go to the l⟨ibrary⟩ and take a look at *Adolescent Sexuality in Contempo⟨rary⟩ America,* by Robert Sorensen. In Dr. Sorensen's book y⟨ou⟩ will find such statistics as these: 52 percent of all thirteen- t⟨o⟩ nineteen-years-olds in the United States will have had sexual intercourse before they are twenty. Among nonvirgin adolescents, 71 percent of the boys and 45 percent of the girls have had sexual intercourse by the age of fifteen. Only 5 percent of the nonvirgin boys and 17 percent of the nonvirgin girls waited until they were eighteen or nineteen to have intercourse for the first time.

What does this mean to you as a parent? It means that if you do not give birth control information to your adolescent, you only increase the probabilities that your daughter will have an unwanted pregnancy, or your son will cause an unwanted pregnancy. But if you do provide birth control information, you will decrease your adolescent's chances of getting into this kind of trouble.

7. *I'm a widow with a fifteen-year-old daughter. Recently I started dating a man in whom I am seriously interested. Whenever he's around, my daughter flirts with him outrageously. Maybe if I understood why she's doing this it would be easier for me to handle the situation. Right now I'm at a loss.*

As I have indicated in my book *How to Father,* little girls go through a stage I call the family romance from roughly three to six, when they fall romantically in love with their fathers. The purpose of this psychological process is to give them a model in their minds of the man they will ultimately marry. (The same thing happens with little boys and their mothers.) Then the family romance fades, only to start up again in the teenage years. But this time sexuality is added to it.

Your daughter has been deprived of her father by death, so she is using your new boyfriend as a substitute for her father in working her way through the process of the family romance. I would explain this situation to your friend and I'd advise both of you to ignore your daughter's flirting as much as you possibly can. She can't help the way she's feeling, and she's doing no real harm by flirting, so I certainly would not upbraid her for it. Sooner or later it will pass.

8. *My fifteen-year-old daughter is pregnant—for the second time. The first time, we helped her get an abortion and introduced her to birth control pills. This time she refuses to get an abortion and says she is going to have—and keep— the baby. How can we cope with such lunacy?*

You'r right; this situation cries out for professional help. The ideal solution would be for parents and daughter to see a therapist. But your daughter may refuse to go. If so, there is no point trying to force her. Then the therapist must deal with you and your husband, and counsel you on how to handle your daughter so that she can make a sensible decision.

Agreed, your daughter's behavior has been foolish. Nevertheless, there are reasons why she has acted and is acting this way. I could not possibly know those reasons from long range, and that's why the situation needs to be handled by a professional person on the scene.

9. *My mother-in-law always complains about how unkempt our fourteen-year-old son looks. It's true. He does look like a slob, but he's a nice kid otherwise. So we're pretty tolerant about this. He's starting to resent her comments. How can we get her off his back—and ours?*

The problem is definitely your mother-in-law's. Nobody gave her a license to go around criticizing other people's appearance. So I suggest that you use the mutual problem-solving technique with her. You can say something like this: "Helen, we have a problem I need to talk to you about. Both of us know that Freddie goes around looking like a slob. We figure it's part of a stage he's going through and we say nothing about it. But you make remarks to him about how he looks, and he resents it. And that creates a problem. I would like us to be able to find a solution to this problem so that you and he are able to get along better. So can we talk about it?"

If your mother-in-law is flexible and amenable, you should be able to work out a solution via this technique.

But if she is touchy or neurotic or inflexible, then you may simply have to lay it on the line with her. "I don't want you to make any more derogatory comments about Freddie's appearance. He is my child and I want you to leave him alone."

If she responds, "Well, he's my grandson, and I'll say any damn thing to him I want!" then you have no alternative but to say, "If you take that attitude you leave me no choice but to keep you and him away from each other until you change your attitude."

I know of one interfering mother-in-law who had to be confronted in that manner before she changed her behavior. The mother and father said to her, "Now, Margaret, things have gone far enough, and we are simply not going to tolerate any more criticism of Herb." She responded, "Well, as far as I'm concerned he's a no-good hippie type and he *needs* somebody to set him straight, and I seem to be the only person willing and able to do it."

As it turned out, the next time the family saw the mother-in-law it was Thanksgiving, and she let Herb have it, right at the dinner table. The father said, "Mother, we've spoken to you nicely about this, and you have paid absolutely no attention. C'mon kids, we're leaving."

And they walked out right in the middle of Thanksgiving dinner! They went to a restaurant and had their own Thanksgiving dinner. The mother-in-law moped and fumed for about three weeks, and then she decided it would be wise to change her ways. She phoned and invited them over for Christmas and promised that there would be no more criticism of Herb. And there wasn't!

10. *My fifteen-year-old son says he's a Communist and believes in free love. It upsets me a great deal to hear things like this. What can I do to straighten him out?*

Adolescents are absolute masters of a marvelous psychological stratagem that I call "baiting the hook." They throw out certain statements to their parents that they know will send them up on the ceiling. The parents take the bait, and the next thing they know they are hooked and dangling from the ceiling! It sounds as if your son is doing this. I don't mean that he's doing it as a deliberately plotted conscious strategy; it is usually unconscious.

When my son Randy was fourteen he pulled one of these unconscious stratagems. He said to me, "Dad, did you know that a man in England was taken up into the astral plane before three hundred witnesses?" I replied, "Now, Randy, what scientific evidence was there for this?" "I knew you'd say that!" he said. "Scientific evidence! Scientific evidence! That's all you know. Well, Dad, there are more things to life than your old science!" As soon as he said this, I realized I had taken the bait. If your father is a scientist, in this case a psychologist, what better way is there to get his goat than to present something occult and unscientific to him? Randy was into the occult for about a year, but I managed not to rise to the bait again. He would say things like, "Dad, did you know there is definite evidence of cases of demonic possession in France today?" I would reply, "That's interesting, Randy. Tell me more about it."

So don't worry about your son's "scare" terms. He probably knows as much about communism as he knows about astrophysics, and probably thinks free love is when a prostitute decides not to charge her customers on Valentine's Day. So listen respectfully to the "scary" statements he makes about himself, but don't take him seriously and rise to the bait.

11. *I have only one child, a thirteen-year-old boy. I've had a lot of small change missing from my purse lately. When I asked my son if he was taking the money, he denied it. I asked if his allowance is enough and he said it is. But the money still continues to disappear and there's no one else who could be taking it. How can I handle this situation?*

The simplest and easiest way you can handle this situation is through environmental control. Get a lock for a dresser drawer and always keep your purse in that drawer. In one fell swoop you have solved the problem of the disappearing money!

12. *Why would a fourteen-year-old boy hang a Nazi flag in his bedroom?*

See the answer to question 10. This is part of the teenage rebellion, ingeniously designed to get a rise out of his parents. I would simply ignore it, along with any other signs, slogans, or whatever else he might use to decorate his bedroom.

13. *We hear a lot about "being an individual" and "doing your own thing" from our fourteen-year-old daughter. If she's so fired up about being an individual, how come she has to dress just like everybody else she knows?*

Your logic is correct, but you'd be foolish to try to convince your daughter of her inconsistency. Parents all over the United States spend countless hours trying to point out to their teenagers that they are being illogical and inconsistent.

And all of it is wasted time. Believe me, you are never going to change your daughter's behavior by convincing her that she is illogical or inconsistent, so why try? It just makes for needless hassles between the two of you. Being inconsistent doesn't harm anybody, so just let her be. (And incidentally, there have been actual recorded cases where adults have been illogical and inconsistent too!)

14. *I'm worried about our fifteen-year-old son. He seems totally uninterested in girls and that doesn't seem normal. What can I do?*

Some boys are slow in developing an interest in the opposite sex. Your son may be one of them. I can think of a number of boys I knew who were totally uninterested in girls at fifteen, but were dating normally at eighteen or nineteen.

I wouldn't try to do anything about it now. Just let him develop an interest in girls in his own good time.

However, if he hasn't done this by eighteen or nineteen, then I would suspect that something is wrong, and I would have a consultation with a professional counselor.

15. *My fourteen-year-old son doesn't seem to want to do anything with me now, although he and I used to play baseball and football a lot. What can I do with him at this age to keep our rapport and our relationship going?*

You can take him to movies he's interested in, particularly R movies, which he can't get into by himself. You can take him to various sports events. You can take him fishing, if that's something he enjoys. You can take him camping or backpacking, if the two of you are into that. His peer group will look down on him if he does certain things with his father. But other things are okay to do, and the activities I have suggested are in the "okay" category.

16. *My fourteen-year-old son spends a lot of his time doing what he calls "hanging around" with his friends. A sixteen-year-old friend of his has a car and they spend an evening just cruising around, apparently doing nothing, with the exception of trying to pick up girls. Why can't he do something constructive?*

Because he's a teenager. "Doing something constructive" is something your *parents* want you to do. This is why a teenager avoids it like the plague. If a youth leader or a Sierra

Club leader or a scoutmaster or a minister has a job for a group that is "constructive," that may be entirely different. Since your parents didn't think of it, it's all right to do it.

But apart from those "constructive" activities organized by leaders respected by the adolescent group, teenagers of your son's age spend a lot of time just "messing around" with their friends. They feel accepted and reassured just being with their friends, and they don't have to be doing anything in particular. This is normal behavior for a teenager, and since he isn't getting into trouble, I would just leave him alone.

17. *Whatever has happened to old-fashioned respect for parents among the teenagers of today?*

It's out the window. And if you mean by *respect* what many parents mean by that term, out the window is a good place for it, in my opinion. What many parents seem to mean by respect is that when their teenager is feeling angry toward them he should keep his angry feelings to himself and not express them out loud. As I pointed out in chapter 10 on the feedback technique, I think it's a psychological mistake not to allow children and teenagers to express their feelings, including their angry ones, in words. If an adolescent is forced to keep his angry feelings to himself, they will come out in the form of sneaky and negative actions, and that's not good. Far better to have them come out in the form of words rather than actions.

So if by respect you mean "keeping angry feelings to yourself and not expressing them openly to your parents," that's not what I mean by respect. I think that my three children respect me. This means they perceive me as knowing a lot more about the world than they do, and as capable of being able to do things they are not yet able to do. That's the only kind of genuine respect I believe in between children and parents. Because my children feel quite free to tell me off or express angry feelings to me in words if they don't like something I've said or done.

18. *My fourteen-year-old son and another boy have been stealing hubcaps and selling them through a contact. Last week my son was caught by the police. They talked to him, and they talked to us. Since this was his first offense, the police decided not to bring him to court, but, to use their ter-*

minology, he was "counseled and released to his parents." I'm
worried sick and I don't know what to do.

If he seems sufficiently impressed by what has happened,
then I don't think he needs any further punishment. You
need to be emotionally supportive, using the feedback technique. Don't put the third degree on him, like, "Now why did
you steal those hubcaps?" He doesn't know why he stole the
hubcaps. Probably so other guys would think he is a big
wheel.

Let him know you are very glad that because it was a first
offense the police didn't take him to court, but released him
in your care. Point out (but don't lecture) that if it happens
again they will not be so lenient.

That's how you can handle it if your son is impressed with
the seriousness of the situation. But if he's not, you need to
handle it differently. If he merely put on an act of being
courteous and subservient with the police, but as soon as he
got home he said, "Oh, those stinking pigs! All I did was lift
a couple of lousy hub caps and they give me all that crap for
it!"—if that's the attitude he takes, then I think you need to
take him and yourselves to a professional counselor so that
you can prevent further trouble with the law. Only a
professional can find out what is going on inside your son
that is causing him to be so belligerent and hostile and engage in actions that break the law. And you want to find out
what to do about it *now*, rather than wait for a couple of
years when he might get in really serious trouble.

Summary

The stage of early adolescence brings with it vastly new
and different problems of discipline. Probably the most significant feeling parents of teenagers experience is that they
are losing control over their child. And if they have
mainly relied on punishment power up to now, they are all
too keenly aware that it no longer works. As one father la-
mented to me, "Now that he's gotten too big to spank, how
can I handle him?"

So the first psychological fact for parents of adolescents to
face is that they have lost much of the control over their
child that they once had. This does not mean they have lost
all control. But it does mean that more and more of the responsibility for their child's life has passed from the parents

to the adolescent himself. Try not to fight against this psychological fact. Accept it.

Many of the positive nonpunishment methods that worked fine in the earlier stages of development simply don't work now, in the more sophisticated stage of adolescence. This includes such methods as the positive reward system, the use of charts for good behavior, the use of Time Outs, etc. So give them up.

However, discipline methods that rely on mutual respect, rather than on the sheer authority of the parent, will continue to work with your teenager. Work on maintaining your emotional rapport, and use the feedback technique, the mutual problem-solving technique, contracting, and the family council. You can use these methods and use them successfully.

Above all, remember that your adolescent is no longer a child. He is now a half-adult and deserves to be treated as one.

28

LATE ADOLESCENCE

Overview of the Stage

As I pointed out in the last chapter, in early adolescence your teenager is struggling between the conflicting urges forward toward independence and backward toward dependence on his parents. The early adolescent, feeling the need to prove his independence, often rebels against *all* parental restrictions, even the most reasonable ones, as if they were the arbitrary rules of a sadistic despot.

In late adolescence, which occupies the years between sixteen and twenty-one, your teenager begins to realize he has "made it" with respect to the issue of independence, and during that time his self-concept changes to that of a half-adult. In early adolescence your teenager is trying to answer the question "Who am I?" pretty much within the framework of his family. In late adolescence he is struggling to resolve the central developmental task of adolescence—*establishing his ego identity*—within the larger framework of society. The late adolescent must (1) decide upon and prepare for a vocation, (2) work out a satisfactory relationship with the opposite sex and establish stable patterns of a heterosexual love life, and (3) complete his emancipation from parents and family.

Late adolescence may be a particularly hard time for many parents to handle because it often coincides with a very difficult time in their own life span, middle age, with its attendant middle-age crisis. Russell Baker has coined the term *middlescence* for this time in a parent's life. And when late adolescence and middlescence come together, that may be an explosive mixture! I think that all middle-aged parents of adolescents should read *The Middle Aged Crisis*, by Barbara Fried (Harper and Row). I'm sure you will find it helpful.

Even though adolescents may legally be adults at age eighteen, I consider the stage of late adolescence to span the years between sixteen and twenty-one. I do this because I think in one way or another the gradually maturing young person is still fighting his parents emotionally during those years. And as long as that emotional battle is still taking place he is an adolescent, not an adult.

Hopefully, when your adolescent reaches the age of twenty-two or twenty-three, he will no longer be rebelling against you either openly or subtly. Instead, for the first time in your lives, you and he will have a new and delightful relationship, that of older adult to younger adult.

1. *Our sixteen-year-old son rebels when we tell him we want to know where he is and have him come home at a specific time. He says that's "kid's stuff." Are we being reasonable or unreasonable?*

You are being reasonable on one thing, unreasonable on the other. You are reasonable to have a specific time when he is supposed to be home from a movie, a date, a party, or whatever. What that time should be is up to the two of you, using the methods of the mutual problem-solving technique. It's natural for him to protest any time restrictions, but it is perfectly reasonable for you to have a specific time established when he is to be home from a particular event.

But keeping tabs on his whereabouts is a different matter. When he was a young child, it was wise for you to know where he was going when he left the house. And when he said, "I'm going down to Andy's to play," that's usually where he was. But the teenage society just doesn't operate that way, particularly the late teens. The kids may start off at Barbara's, mosey down to Ritchie's, and then decide on the spur of the moment to drive over to the Wich Stand for hamburgers. Remember, teenagers are mobile (particularly with a car) in ways that young children are not. This makes it inappropriate for you to assume that your son will stay in any one place all evening. And besides, it sounds to him as if you're treating him like a little kid when you say, "I want to know where you are." So I suggest you give up that request, but stand firm on a definite time for him to return home.

And by the way, you would be naive to expect that he will always be in by the agreed-upon time! If the two of you agree on 1:00, he will probably be in by 1:15 or 1:30. But you would be wise to let it go. Only if he is supposed to be in by 1:00 and doesn't come in until 4:30 or so would I raise a ruckus.

2. *The only time our college-age daughter writes to us is when she needs money. But she complains bitterly when we don't write to her. I used to think this was amusing when I read about it in jokes, but now that it's happening to us, it's not so funny.*

I'm afraid you have run up against one of the facts of late adolescence that is difficult to adjust to. The relationship between parents and a late adolescent is almost always a one-way street. Your daughter expects you to do things for her, but she doesn't reciprocate. As you say, although she doesn't write to you, she expects you to write to her! I'm afraid this behavior is pretty typical of the animal. There's nothing I know to do but put up with it until she is capable of more adult reciprocal relationships.

But if the one-way street becomes too much for you to take, don't hesitate to tell her your feelings. For example, if she completely ignores your birthday, write her and tell her that she hurt your feelings.

3. *My father pushed me into going into his business, and I hated it and got out. So I don't want to do that to my boy. But is there anything I can do to help him choose a vocation without pushing him?*

Indeed there is. You can give him something that very few parents know exists: vocational testing and guidance. This should not be done until an adolescent is fifteen because one of the main tests used is not valid until he is that old. There are two main places you can get vocational testing: from a psychologist in private practice or at a college or university. In general, I think a psychologist in private practice provides better service because he tends to be more experienced and is inclined to take more of a personal interst in your teenager. However, testing at a school will probably cost you less.

The results of the battery of tests will tell your adolescent his areas of greatest strength, where he will be most likely to succeed in his vocation. Personally when I do vocational testing and guidance I like to tie it in to helping the teenager choose a college or trade school.

Tell your son about vocational testing, explain to him how it works, and ask him if he would like to give it a try. If he balks, don't push him into it. But if he agrees, this is one of the most helpful things you could ever do for him. For example, if I had had vocational testing when I was in high school I probably would have gone directly into psychology, rather than gone into another profession first and shifted over into psychology at age twenty-seven.

4. *I found a love letter to my nineteen-year-old son—from another man. When I confronted him with this, he admitted he was a homosexual. I can't cope with this. What can I do?*

You can take him to see a professional counselor, and one of two things will happen. Your son may decide he wants professional help to get over his sexual problems and become a heterosexual. Or he may decide he wants to stay a homosexual and does not need help. In that case you are going to have to learn to live with the situation. And it will probably take a lot out of you and your husband to learn to do that. I have two friends to whom this happened. Believe me, it wasn't easy for them to adjust.

There is absolutely no way you can force your son to undergo treatment so that he can become heterosexual. And I want to tell you my own clinical experience in this area. In over twenty years of clinical practice, I have treated a number of homosexuals, both male and female. Only two of them wanted help to change their sexual orientation. The rest wanted me to treat their anxieties, their depressions, their phobias, or their difficulties with other people, but *not* their homosexuality. They wanted to continue being homosexual but get rid of their anxieties, phobias, etc. So it may very well be that your son will choose not to seek treatment for his homosexuality.

It is strictly up to your son. If he *wants* to be cured of his homosexuality he can be cured, through treatment with a competent professional. If he doesn't want to change, then you will have to adjust to his homosexuality and live with it.

5. *How can we help our child choose a college?*

One of the best ways is to arrange to visit several colleges well ahead of decision time, during a vacation when your son is out of school but colleges are in session. If your adolescent drives, he can do this by himself or with friends, or the whole family can go. It's important that he be able to sit in on classes, talk with students, and generally get the feel of the place. Most high school students haven't the faintest idea of what any particular college is *really* like. So actual visitation will help your teenager replace fantasy with reality.

Often an adolescent is going to rebel against the colleges his parents recommend. I suggest you find someone at your adolescent's high school—a teacher, counselor, or whatever—your teenager trusts. Then work through this person to help your youngster make a wise choice of college.

Of course if your teenager actually asks you for help in choosing a college, after you have recovered from the shock, then you can discuss the pros and cons of such issues as: big university or smaller college, near a big city or in a small town, how competitive academically versus how relaxed, what majors, and so forth. But I emphasize again, even a practical discussion like this is taking place in the world of fantasy. Until a teenager has actually seen a college, sat in on classes, and talked with students, he is dealing with a fantasy college and not a reality college.

6. *Our sixteen-year-old son got his first job a few months ago. He spends his paycheck as fast as he earns it. How can we help him learn the value of saving?*

You can't, not while he's still living at home and getting free room and board. Life itself will have to teach him the value of saving money. If you try to give him little lectures on why he should save part of his money, it will only provoke hassles between the two of you and do no good at all. I am sure he feels that since he earned it it's his money and he has a right to spend it however he wants.

Too many parents are under the illusion that they can teach something to their teenagers by talking to them. But the fact is that a teenager can only learn experientially, by what actually happens to him in life. So don't try to teach him about the value of saving through verbal methods. Let life teach him about saving through the method of experience.

7. *Our eighteen-year-old son was caught with another boy breaking into a stereo and TV store, and his case comes up in*

a few weeks. I'm absolutely dumfounded that he would do such a thing. What can we do?

First, get a good lawyer. Since your son is eighteen he is now out of juvenile jurisdiction and into adult jurisdiction, which is an entirely different ball game. Because this is his first offense, chances are that he will end up on probation and will have to work with his probation officer and report to him regularly.

Second, use the mutual problem-solving technique and the feedback technique to find out what has been going on within him that led him to try to break into a shop to steal.

Also, you need to make sure he understands what can happen to him if he does this a second time. Breaking and entering is a felony, and if it happens a second time he can go to county jail for perhaps six months, depending on the judge. And your eighteen-year-old may not realize what county jail is like. In jail, he could be killed by a shiv or any other weapon made by a prisoner. He could be subject to a homosexual gang rape. A gang in jail could beat him up. Make sure he understands that jail is very real and it could actually happen to him on a second offense.

But do not lecture him or lay a heavy psychological trip on him, for that will backfire and defeat its purpose. You are just giving him information about what jail is like. But it is his life, and if he ends up in jail, that's his responsibility, not yours.

If you feel you are not succeeding in getting through to him, then I would get professional help.

8. *My son wants to take a year out between high school and college to travel. I can see some advantages in it, but I'm afraid he might not get back into the school track again and go to college. What do you think?*

I am all for adolescents taking a year out between high school and college. I think it's a maturing experience. Going right from high school to college still keeps them in the ivory-tower world of school. A year out gets them in touch with the real world in one form or another.

I would suggest that your teenager make the usual applications for college. When he is accepted, he can write the college and request a delayed acceptance, which means he will enter one year later. More and more colleges are doing this. It's much easier for him to actually get accepted while he is still in high school than if he takes a year out and then applies for acceptance. Once he has a delayed acceptance, he'll have an opportunity to spend fourteen months exploring the real world before entering college.

There are an infinite variety of choices open to him for those fourteen months. He could get a job abroad and live and work in one place for the entire time. There are several good books on how to obtain a job abroad that he can find in the library or a bookstore. Or he could work in several different countries during that time. He could work in an English-speaking country such as Great Britain, Australia, or New Zealand. Or if he has command of a foreign language, he could work in a non-English-speaking country. If he does not speak a foreign language, he could take an intensive two-week crash course at Berlitz or some similar language school.

He could spend part of his fourteen months in a foreign country under the sponsorship of the Experiment for International Living. This is a first-rate outfit, and I endorse their program wholeheartedly. My daughter went to Italy when she was sixteen under sponsorship of the Experiment. You can write to them for information: Experiment for International Living, Putney, Vermont. Or he might want to do something such as hitchhike through Europe or Asia. (Contrary to the situation in the United States, where it is unsafe, it is pretty safe hitchhiking in Europe or Asia, except for a few places such as Afghanistan and eastern Turkey.)

Your adolescent might also choose to live and work in an entirely new and different part of the United States. Or he could travel all around the United States by car or bus. *Not hitchhiking!*

Personally I think an adolescent would gain the most by living and working in only one or two different cultures for those fourteen months, as opposed to the more shallow experience of just traveling around. But in the final analysis, he is the one who must decide what experiences will best meet his needs.

Almost any of the things I have mentioned will probably give him more maturity than he can get in any college or university in the United States for a year. He can enter college the following year a much more mature person, able to get more out of his college experience for having taken the year out.

9. *My son is sixteen and he just despises the academic aspects of school (and 90 percent of it is academic). The only things he likes are wood shop, metal shop, auto mechanics, and PE. He does poorly in all of his academic subjects. But he is very good with his hands. He loves to take his car apart and work on it, and he's terrific when it comes to fixing our TV set or tinkering with radios or CBs. But college is coming up soon, and I don't know what to do.*

It is a crying shame that junior highs and high schools are not at all designed for people like your son. Unfortunately they are structured as if all the students were going on to an academic college. And they're not. Some of them are not at all academically inclined, and your son is one of them. From your description of him he seems ideally fitted for one of the skilled trades. That is the direction in which I would nudge him. Find a community college or a trade school nearby. Get its catalog and show him the different skilled trades in which he can get training.

Some parents have a snobbish resistance to the idea of their son or daughter learning a skilled trade instead of going to an academic college. I think this is a mistake. Better a good auto mechanic, happy at his job, than an unhappy and inept teacher or insurance salesman.

10. *My son is seventeen and a senior in high school. Do you think he should live at home and go to college, or go away to college? It certainly would be cheaper to have him live at home while he's in college.*

You're absolutely right. The financial cost would be less for him to live at home and go to college. But what about the psychological cost?

First, the cost to him. He will mature far less if he lives at home than if he goes away to college and lives in a dorm or an apartment with several other students. His psychological horizons will remain cramped if he continues to live at home.

Second, consider the psychological cost to you, his parents. During four years of college, he will go through drastic changes in his thinking and his life-style. Unless you and he are a remarkable exception to the rule, you are going to spend much of those four years at loggerheads. So in many ways a youth between the ages of eighteen and twenty-two who is going to college at home is a psychological recipe for disaster. For both his sake and your sake, if you can possibly afford it, send him away to college.

11. *We went away for a weekend, and decided to trust our seventeen-year-old son to stay by himself in the house, on the condition that there be no parties. He agreed. When we got home, we found a garbage can full of beer cans and the house reeked of stale cigarette smoke. We've since heard from a neighbor that the police were called because the party was so noisy. I think he betrayed our trust. What kind of punishment should we mete out, or should we just give him a good talking to?*

You're right. He did betray your trust. I would start with the mutual problem-solving technique and see how that goes. If it is productive, fine. If not, I think I would ground him with his car—take away his wheels—for two weeks. (Grounding a teenager for a month, as I have seen some parents do, is too long a time. The teenager comes to feel: "This punishment is so long I might just as well act up again.")

Giving him a good talking to, which is a fancy way to describe a scolding, is productive of nothing. He's not really inconvenienced by it. He doesn't have to engage in a meaningful dialogue with you, as he does when you use the mutual problem-solving technique. All he has to do is shut up while you scold him for a while and then he can resume his normal activities. Big deal!

12. *My husband is a salesman and maybe that's why he does what he does with our two teenage boys, sixteen and eighteen. He is constantly lecturing them. About keeping their grades up to get into a good college. About taking care of their cars. About relationships with girls. About saving part of the money they earn on their part-time jobs. And so on. Of course he doesn't call it "lecturing." They do. He says, "I'm trying to help them by giving good advice." The trouble is that they don't want to hear what he has to say. And he is really hurt and puzzled by their attitude. What can I do about the situation?*

The last thing a teenager wants is good advice from a parent, no matter how correct the advice is. A teenager will accept good advice from a peer in a minute. From a parent, never! Your husband apparently is unaware of this psychological law. I presume you have already talked to your husband about this and been unable to get through to him.

So you might try this little experiment. For a day, two days, or a week, lecture to your husband and give him good advice. On keeping physically fit. On jogging. On getting yearly physical checkups. On reading a book a week on salesmanship. Whatever. But plan your lectures out ahead of time and see to it that they last at least fifteen minutes each. See how he responds.

If he starts to get disgruntled about being lectured to, smile sweetly and say, "I'm only doing this for your own good, to help you. Why do you take that attitude?" When you sense that he has had the lecturing up to his eyebrows, you can tell him the purpose of the little experiment—so that he can understand how the two boys feel when they have to listen to unasked-for lectures.

13. *My eighteen-year-old daughter is painfully shy. Although she is physically attractive, she has never had a date. She has only one girl-friend, and otherwise she keeps pretty much to herself. She never goes on outings or parties with the other kids in school. What can I do?*

Only one thing can deal adequately with this problem: professional help.

Most people find a therapist through a recommendation from one person—a family doctor, a minister, or perhaps a friend. Then they dutifully go see that recommended therapist. I think there is a better way. I suggest you get *three* recommendations and that you spend an hour's appointment, at his usual rates, talking with each one. Do this by yourself; do not take your daughter with you. Then, on the basis of the "vibes" you get from the three talks, select the one you think is the best. If you can't get personal recommendations, you could call the city or county medical association or psychological association.

Armed with this information, go to your daughter. Tell her you are concerned about her because she is so shy and has trouble making both girl friends and boyfriends. Tell her you feel that the only thing that can help her is to have professional counseling. Explore with her what this would mean, and see if she would be willing to give it a try. If she agrees to try it, tell her you will find a good therapist for her. A few days later, tell her you have made an appointment for her with Dr. So and So. After that, it's up to her and the therapist.

If she refuses to seek help, respect her right to refuse. Say, "I'm sorry you don't want to go, but you have a perfect right to refuse. If you change your mind at any later date, I will be glad to make arrangements for you to see someone."

14. *My nineteen-year-old daughter tells me she plans on getting married. She's known the guy for only three months, and I think he's strictly for the birds. He works at a menial job and seems to have no ambition in life. My vision of a marriage to this guy is that it will last one or two years and then fall apart. But what can I, as her father, do about it?*

You may be able to do much more than you think. I encountered a very similar situation with a forty-two-year-old patient of mine some years ago. His twenty-year-old daughter told him she planned to marry a particular fellow. Privately he felt the marriage would be a disaster. But when she told him about it, he gave her a hug and said, "Darling, I hope you'll be very happy." I asked him why he acted that way when his real feelings were quite the opposite. "Well, it wouldn't do any good for me to tell her my real feelings," he said. "How do you know it wouldn't?" I replied.

I encouraged him to see his daughter alone and tell her how he really felt. To his amazement, she shared some of his misgivings about marrying this particular man. She told him she appreciated his leveling with her. And about four months later, she told him she had changed her plans about getting married.

I would encourage you to try the same approach. Tell your daughter your feelings about the situation, but don't tell her what she ought to do. Leave that up to her. Just tell her you feel that he isn't up to her standard and that you don't feel the marriage would last more than a couple of years. Then leave the decision strictly up to her—which it is.

15. *My twenty-year-old daughter has dropped out of college. For the past six months she has just been moping around the house or spending time with friends. She has made a few half-hearted attempts to find a job but nothing has turned up. How should I handle this situation?*

More late adolescents are in this kind of a situation than you would believe. I suggest you take the following action.

Set aside some time to have a private talk with your daughter. Tell her that if she decides to go back to college you and your husband will pay her way through. But if she doesn't want to go to school, then she will need to get a job, move out of the house, and find her own apartment. (Some parents let their late adolescents live at home and pay for room and board. I think this is a mistake because it keeps the young person dependent and in the parental nest.)

See what her response to this approach is. If she makes a decision either for college or work, and follows through on it, fine. But if she continues living in the house as she has been, with no real attempt to find a job and move out, then I would give her a time limit. "Joan, you still haven't done anything about either college or work, as we had discussed. I'm certainly not going to keep you in the nest like a child when you're twenty years old. So you have two months from today to find a job and get moved out."

If that works, fine. But if worst comes to worst, and she still hasn't done anything two months later, I would move her out and let her fend for herself. Then she would *have* to get a job and find a place to live. She would do it because she would have no other choice. (She might be able to bum lodging and meals off friends for a while, but that doesn't last very long.)

Some people might think that this is a cruel thing to do to a daughter. I don't. I think the really cruel thing is to reward a twenty-year-old's infantilization by giving her free room and board.

16. *My son made adequate grades as a college freshman. Now he's a sophomore and we just got a note from the dean that he is flunking out of college. We have had absolutely no indication of this from his letters. What shall I do?*

Get to his college as fast as you can and find out what's wrong. Don't phone; get there in person. Something drastic must be going on inside him if he is flunking out, and you need to find out what it is. Then, if your son is agreeable, see that he gets help from the counseling center at college. If he refuses to go, go yourself for advice on how to handle the situation.

17. *My twenty-one-year-old boy knows so little about the financial aspects of the real world, it's pitiful. He doesn't*

know how to shop and save money, how to establish a credit rating, how to borrow money wisely, what kind of insurance to buy and not to buy. He doesn't even know how to balance a checkbook! They ought to teach these things in high school and college, but they don't. What can I do to help him?

Give him a present of *Sylvia Porter's Money Book* (Avon Books). It's available in paperback and it contains exactly the kind of information your son will need as he makes his way out of college and into the real world of money and finance. It's a book he can use now, and a book he can keep for a life-time reference on almost anything pertaining to the financial aspects of living.

18. *My twenty-year-old is a sophomore at college. I got a letter from him this week saying that when he gets home for summer vacation, he wants to have a "gut-level" talk with me and get a lot of things off his chest he's been keeping inside for a long time. Help! How do I handle this?*

The main thing to do is to avoid being defensive. If you can stick to the feedback technique and let him spill out his feelings, it sounds as if it could do a great deal of good for your relationship. Obviously these are feelings he has been afraid to tell you about and he has finally found the courage to spill them. Whether these feelings are rational or irrational, let him get them out. Don't interrupt him with, "Yes, but . . ." He doesn't want to hear any "yes, but's" or "on the other hand's." He wants to spill out his feelings.

So give him the opportunity. Some of the things he has to say may give you a view of yourself that you've never had the opportunity to see before, which could be food for thought. At any rate, after he has unloaded these feelings, chances are that your relationshp will be on a much better footing.

Try not to feel that this meeting is going to be a disastrous encounter. Instead, think of it as a necessary step for a much deeper and sounder emotional relationship between the two of you. And don't think of it as a one-way encounter. You and he may be able to begin a dialogue that will enrich both your lives over the years.

Summary

In late adolescence your task as a parent is almost, but not quite, done. Your late adolescent is just a short step from adulthood and full psychological independence from you. But he is not quite there yet. He still has work to do to get closure on his self-identity as an adult and cut the last ties that hold him to the parental nest.

During these late adolescent years, he is still economically and, to a certain extent, psychologically dependent on you. Because of this, some discipline problems may still arise. But these problems should be handled on the level of one adult to another who is nearly adult, rather than on the Big Parent–Little Child level. In this spirit, the maintenance of rapport, the feedback technique, the mutual problem-solving technique, contracting, and the family council can be used as methods for the delineation and solution of any discipline problems that may arise.

Hopefully, by the time your child has reached twenty-two or twenty-three, he will have outgrown the parent-child relationship and reached a new and delightful stage of young adulthood. In this new stage, he can relate to you as a younger adult to an older adult. When that happens, it is truly a wonderful experience for a parent!

29

EPILOGUE: MORE JOY IN PARENTING!

One of the things that has made me sad as I have observed parents in action for many years is the lack of joy that parenting seems to bring to so many people. The parents are engaged in activities with their children that should be pleasurable: picnics in the park, camping trips, vacations of various sorts, playtimes on the beach, and the like. But so many parents seem unhappy and harassed, unable to cope effectively with the behavior of their children.

I hope this book will help change such a situation and bring joy and satisfaction back into the lives of many parents. This book is based upon a very simple premise: *The more you know about how to raise children the more you will be able to enjoy them.*

Being a parent has been one of the most rewarding and delightful aspects of my life. I wish all parents could feel that way. And I am convinced that a knowledge of how to teach your child to behave in a desirable manner will go a long way to make your parenting a richly rewarding experience rather than something to suffer through.

As a knowledgeable parent, you can enjoy the delights of re-experiencing childhood through your own parenting. You can have warmth and closeness and endless adventures in

321

serendipity and rollicking good times with your children that will remain fondly stored in your memories forever. I hope you do.

I wish there were some incredible invention that would enable me to talk with each one of you individually about your children. But, unfortunately, a book can only be a one-way conversation. I have to imagine your situation as a parent, and try to answer the questions I think you want answered. But I may have left out some important aspects of child-raising you are concerned about. Or you may disagree with some of the things I have said. So if you want to write to me for any reason, I would be happy to hear from you. You can write to me in care of my original publisher, Rawson Associates, 630 Third Avenue, New York, New York 10017.

NOTES

Chapter 4:
I wish to express my deep gratitude to Dr. Sharon Deacon for her help in writing of the chapter.

Chapter 18:
1. Lynn Caine, *Widow* (New York: William Morrow Co., 1974).
2. Karol Hope and Nancy Young (Eds.), *Momma: The Sourcebook for Single Mothers* (New York: New American Library, 1976).
3. Marie Edwards and Eleanor Hoover, *The Challenge of Being Single* (Los Angeles: J. P. Tarcher Co., 1974).
4. Caine, *Widow.*
5. *Ibid.*
6. *Ibid.*
7. Mel Krantzler, *Creative Divorce* (New York: M. Evans Co., 1973).
8. *Ibid.*
9. *Ibid.*
10. Caine, *Widow.*
11. *Ibid.*
12. Krantzler, *Creative Divorce.*
13. Edwards and Hoover, *The Challenge of Being Single.*
14. *Ibid.*
15. Krantzler, *Creative Divorce.*
16. *Ibid.*

Chapter 19:
1. Ruth Roosevelt and Jeannette Lofas, *Living in Step* (New York: Stein & Day, 1976).
2. *Ibid.*

3. *Ibid.*
4. *Ibid.*
5. *Ibid.*
6. *Ibid.*
7. *Ibid.*
8. *Ibid.*
9. *Ibid.*
10. Brenda Maddox, *The Half-Parent* (New York: M. Evans Co., 1975).
11. Roosevelt and Lofas, *Living in Step.*
12. *Ibid.*
13. *Ibid.*
14. *Ibid.*
15. Maddox, *The Half-Parent.*
16. Roosevelt and Lofas, *Living in Step.*
17. *Ibid.*
18. *Ibid.*
19. *Ibid.*
20. Maddox, *The Half-Parent.*

APPENDIX

A Parent's Guide to Books on Discipline

This annotated list of books is designed to help you find more good books on discipline which will aid you in raising your family. Some of the books listed here are for all parents, because they deal with universal aspects of discipline. Others will apply only to parents in special situations, such as single parents or stepparents.

I enthusiastically recommend every book on this list. This does not mean I agree 100 percent with everything in the book, but that on the whole I think that the book is a wise and helpful discussion of some aspect of discipline. I refer to the hardcover edition of each book, unless I specifically mention that it is available in paperback also.

Books Covering the Psychological Stages of Development in Children

1. *How to Parent*, Fitzhugh Dodson, New American Library, Signet paperback. I consider this book to be the single most complete guide for parents to the psychological development of a child from birth to age six. But I could be biased. The two chapters on discipline apply not only to the preschool child but to the school-age child as well.

2. *How to Father*, Fitzhugh Dodson, New American Library, Signet paperback. Don't be fooled by the title; this

book is for mothers too. Whereas *How to Parent* concentrated on the stages of development from birth to six years, this book covers the developmental stages from birth to twenty-one.

3. *Childhood and Adolescence: A Psychology of the Growing Person*, Joseph Stone and Joseph Church, Random House. A college-level textbook covering birth through adolescence. It is scientific and comprehensive. And it is also *readable*, which makes it one of the most unusual college texts ever written. You may want to skip over some of the early sections that are filled with psychological detail which has little practical value to a parent. Once past those sections, the rest of the book is useful reading.

4. *Infant and Child in the Culture of Today*, Arnold Gesell, Frances Ilg, and Louise Ames, Harper and Row. This book covers the development of the child from birth to five years. The most typical traits and growth trends of each age are summarized in a behavior profile and a behavior day. The behavior profile is a thumbnail sketch of the behavior and growth patterns of a child of that age. The behavior day describes a "typical" day in the life of a youngster of that age, using such categories as sleeping, eating, self-activity, sociality, play and pastimes, etc.

5. *The Child from Five to Ten*, Arnold Gesell, Frances Ilg, Louise Ames, Harper and Row.

6. *Youth: The Years from Ten to Sixteen*, Arnold Gesell, Frances Ilg, and Louise Ames, Harper and Row.

These books, along with *Infant and Child in the Culture of Today*, do not tell you how to discipline your child. But they do tell you what to expect from your child at different stages of development.

7. *Your Two-Year-Old*, Louise Ames and Frances Ilg, Delacorte.

8. *Your Three-Year-Old*, Louise Ames and Frances Ilg, Delacorte.

9. *Your Four-Year-Old*, Louise Ames and Frances Ilg, Delacorte.

These three books should be in every parent's library. Basically they are updated versions of the Gesell studies. Each book gives valuable background information about each particular age group—information a parent needs in order to intelligently discipline a two-, three- or four-year old.

10. *The Magic Years*, Selma Fraiberg, Scribners, paperback.

A psychoanalytic view of the first five years of life, written with keen insight into the minds of young children.

Books on Discipline

1. *Parent Effectiveness Training: The Tested New Way to Raise Responsible Children*, Thomas Gordon, New American Library, Plume paperback. I recommend this highly! Dr. Gordon's book is particularly effective in dealing with the thorny problem of conflicts between parents and children.

2. *P.E.T. in Action*, Thomas Gordon, Wyden Books. This follow-up book by Dr. Gordon shows what happens when parents try to apply his techniques in the home, and how they may misunderstand and misapply them. Very worthwhile reading even if you have read his first book.

3. *Between Parent and Child*, Haim Ginnot, Avon, paperback. A true classic in the field. It is particularly effective in convincing parents that they need to learn how to interpret the "coded language" a child is speaking through his behavior as well as his words. However, Dr. Ginnot is not as clear as Dr. Gordon in explaining to parents how to use the "reflection of feelings" technique with their children. Parents should be aware that this book deals only with children between the ages of six and ten. A really splendid book.

4. *Between Parent and Teenager*, Haim Ginnot, Avon, paperback. In spite of its title, I do not think this book really comes to grips with today's teenage scene. However, I believe it is well worth reading. Think of it as an expansion of *Between Parent and Child*, and you will get a great deal out of it.

5. *New Ways in Discipline*, Dorothy W. Baruch, McGraw-Hill. The late Dorothy Baruch has been a most important influence on my own thinking about parenting. She has written many books for parents, and she has never written a poor one. This is one of her best.

6. *Improving Your Child's Behavior*, Madeline C. Hunter and Paul V. Carlson, Bowmar Books. This book packs into only 130 pages an immense amount of clear and practical ad-

vice on how to discipline a child and improve his behavior. You are not likely to find this book in your local bookstore, and probably the fastest way to acquire it is to order it by mail from the publisher—Bowmar Books, 4563 Colorado Blvd., Los Angeles, California 90039.

7. *Children: The Challenge,* Rudolph Dreikurs and Vicki Soltz, Hawthorn. This book is basically a revision of Dreikurs' earlier book, *The Challenge of Parenthood,* which is still a good book to read. *Children* is a really fine book on discipline, based on Adlerian psychology, and makes great use of the principle of natural consequences.

8. *The Practical Parent: The ABC's of Child Discipline,* Raymond J. Corsini and Genevieve Painter, Harper and Row. This book, by two disciples of Dreikurs, covers many down-to-earth problems in the home from bedtime to fighting. Well worth reading.

9. *Living with Children: New Methods for Parents and Teachers,* Gerald R. Patterson and M. Elizabeth Gullion, Research Press, paperback. This is a unique book. It is a programmed book, which means it is like a teaching machine in book form. This makes it particularly easy to read. It is based on the same principles of reinforcement that I discussed in the chapter on The Positive Reward System.

10. *Child Psychology: A Behavioral Approach to Everyday Problems,* Roger McIntire, Behaviordelia Books. There are a number of books on child discipline based on what is known to psychologists as "behavior modification." Most of them are dull. Here is one that is not. Using the principles of behavior modification in a very practical, down-to-earth manner, Dr. McIntire covers a great many common problems parents must deal with.

Books for Single Parents

1. *The World of the Formerly Married,* Morton M. Hunt, McGraw-Hill. A "must" for every divorced parent, though you will probably have to get it from the library. It is valuable in helping you understand your situation as a divorced person and a single parent.

2. *Creative Divorce,* Mel Krantzler, New American Library, Signet paperback. In my opinion, this is absolutely the best book ever written on the subject of divorce. Krantzler's insights into all of the psychological aspects of divorce are

impressive, and he writes with sparkle and clarity. A must for every divorced parent.

3. *Raising Your Child in a Fatherless Home*, Eve Jones, Free Press. A very wise and comprehensive book for the divorced or widowed mother. Covers all aspects of the subject in great detail. Marred somewhat by a curious strain of hidden Puritanism which creeps into the discussion of sex. Otherwise a very good book.

4. *Part-Time Father*, Edith Atkin and Estelle Rubin, New American Library, Signet paperback. An excellent book that really gets down to the nitty-gritty problems confronting the divorced father as a single parent without custody. It also covers what happens if he becomes a stepfather.

5. "Divorce and Remarriage and Blended Families," a chapter in *How to Father*, Fitzhugh Dodson, New American Library, Signet paperback. Covers many aspects of parenting your children if you are a divorced father.

6. *The Boys and Girls Book About Divorce*, Richard A. Gardner, Bantam paperback. This is a unique book. It is written for children themselves to read (or have read to them). Yet parents can also read it and get some insight into how children feel about divorce. I recommend it highly for any divorced family with children aged five or older.

Books for Stepparents

1. *Living in Step*, Ruth Roosevelt and Jeanette Lofas, Stein and Day. This is an absolute gem of a book, the first really top-notch book to be written about stepparenting. The authors write with keen psychological insight into all of the problems that must be surmounted in order to achieve a happy and successful stepfamily. The writing is alive and sparkling, and it is a joy to read. I think every stepparent in America should read this book.

Books on Adoption

1. *The Adoption Adviser*, Joan McNamara, Hawthorn Books. A very thorough and comprehensive book that will be helpful to any family planning to adopt a child. Written by an adoptive parent.

2. *If You Adopt a Child*, Carl and Helen Doss, Holt,

Rinehart, and Winston. The Dosses themselves are adoptive parents, and they cover just about everything a couple planning to adopt a child needs to know.

3. *The Adopted Family*, Florence Rondell and Ruth Michaels, Crown, revised edition. Contains two books: Book I, *You and Your Child, A Guide for Adoptive Parents*, gives excellent and specific advice concerning all phases of adoption and after. Book II, *The Family That Grew*, is a picture and story book to read to the adopted child and to use in explaining the situation to him. A very good two-part package for all adoptive parents.

Books on Raising Black Children

For many years there were *no* books on parenting or child discipline for black parents. It was tacitly assumed that the problems of raising a black child in the United States were the same as those of raising a white child, although they obviously are not. Now, at long last, here are two excellent guides for black parents to use in raising their children.

1. *Black Child Care*, James P. Comer and Alvin F. Poussaint, Simon and Schuster. A thorough and comprehensive book which takes a hypothetical black child through all the stages of his development from infancy through adolescence. A superb book.

2. *The Black Child: A Parent's Guide*, Phyllis Harrison-Ross and Barbara Wyden, Wyden Books. This is a unique book, which the authors state is intended for white parents as well as black parents. It deals with the special problems of the black parent, but it also offers specific guidance to help white parents raise children with a total awareness and acceptance of both racial differences and similarities. First-rate.

Index

Index

father surrogates in, 139
lying in, 262–63
mutual problem-solving in,
    79–80
nonsexism in, 274–75
peer-group importance in,
    255–56, 260
privacy in, 269
puberty preparation in, 275–
    76
school problems in, 356–57,
    263, 271–72, 277–78
sibling rivalry in, 269–70
summary, 278
summer camps in, 277
whining in, 273
Mister Rogers, 248
morality, teaching of. *See* ethics
    and morality.
mother(s). *See* divorced moth-
    er; parent listings; single
    parents; widows; working
    mother
music lessons, 276–77
mutual problem-solving tech-
    niques, 72–81, 135, 182,
    189
    with adolescents, 77–78, 80,
        81, 124
    advantages of, 80
    in early adolescence, 297, 306
    examples, 76–80
    in late adolescence, 311–12
    in middle childhood, 80
    in preadolescence, 79–80, 81,
        290–91
    with preschoolers, 253
    procedure, 75–76
    situations needing, 73–75
    with younger children, 78–80
    See also family council

National Singles Register, 145
natural consequences, as disci-
    pline technique, 44–45, 188
    with preschoolers, 243–44
Naval Academy, cheating at, 86
negative thinking, 54, 97–105,
    189
    compared to positive think-
        ing, 98, 100–1

examples, 99, 101–3
in first adolescence, 226–27
for new mothers, 199, 202,
    204
for stepparents, 103–4, 105
for widows, 138
negativism, in preschoolers, 239,
    244
no-bank, as discipline technique,
    282
nursery schools, 112, 116–17,
    223–24, 246. *See also* baby-
    sitters and caretakers; day-
    care centers; play groups

Osborn, Alex, 76

pacifiers, 195
parent(s):
    as child psychologists and
        teachers, 53
    classes for, 53
    difference between, 56–57
    fulfillment of, 114–15
    in 1900s, 51–52, 106
    in 1940s, 113
parental authority, 49–55, 95–
    96, 189
    decline of, 49
    in 1900s, 51–52, 106
    reasonableness of, 50, 95. *See
        also* permissiveness
Parental Cabin Fever, 205
"parental muscle," 92–96, 189
    in adolescence, 92–96, 109
    as last resort, 92
    with young children, 93, 95
parental rights, 106–112. *See
    also* Bill of Rights for Par-
    ents; parental authority
parental strike, 93, 297
Parenting from Birth to Five
    (course), 53
Parents Anonymous, 196, 218
Parents Without Partners, 132,
    138, 144
payoffs, 189
    in contracting, 25
    effect on parent, 14
    eliminated for undesirable be-